FURTHER KEY ISSUES IN TAX REFORM

Other Books by FISCAL PUBLICATIONS

Administrative and Compliance Costs of Taxation, 1989

Practical Tax Administration, 1993

Successful Tax Reform: Lessons from an Analysis of Tax Reform in Six Countries, 1993

Key Issues in Tax Reform, 1993

Tax Compliance Costs: Measurement and Policy, 1995

More Key Issues in Tax Reform, 1995

FURTHER
KEY ISSUES IN TAX REFORM

Cedric Sandford (Editor)

Richard Bird
Roger Bowles
Donal de Buitleir
Andrew Dilnot
Elizabeth Filkin
Geoffrey Howe
Sean Moriarty
Leif Mutén
John O'Hagan
Stephen Smith

FISCAL PUBLICATIONS
1998

Copyright 1998, Cedric Sandford

All Rights Reserved. No part of this publication may be reproduced, stored in a retrieval system or transmitted in any form or by any means: electronic, electrostatic, magnetic tape, mechanical photocopying, recording or otherwise, without permission in writing from the publishers.

British Library Cataloguing-in-Publication Data

A catalogue record for this book is available from the British Library.

ISBN 0 9515157 6 4 Hardback

Printed in Great Britain by
Redwood Books
Trowbridge, Wiltshire

Published by Fiscal Publications,
Old Coach House, Fersfield, Perrymead,
BATH BA2 5AR
United Kingdom

CONTENTS

The Contributors vii

Introduction 1

PART I

TAX REFORM – STRUCTURE

1 **The Taxation of Savings** 7
   Andrew Dilnot

2 **The Taxation of Tobacco** 27
   John O'Hagan

3 **The Carbon Tax: A Tax Whose Time Has Come?** 44
   Stephen Smith

PART II

TAX REFORM – ADMINISTRATION

4 **Minimising Corruption in Tax Affairs** 65
   Roger Bowles

5 **Tax Law Simplification in the United Kingdom** 87
   Geoffrey Howe

6	**Dealing with Complaints – the Adjudicator: A United Kingdom Experiment** Elizabeth Filkin	110
7	**Tax Compliance – Managing the Landscape of Relationships with the Taxpayer** Sean Moriarty	132

PART III

TAX REFORM – SOME WIDER ISSUES

8	**The Role of Tax Incentives: The Irish Experience** Donal de Buitleir	155
9	**Minimising the Tax Effects of Inflation** Leif Mutén	169
10	**Administrative Constraints on Tax Policy** Richard M. Bird	183
11	**Tax Reform of the 'Eighties in Retrospect What Can We Learn?** Cedric Sandford	200

THE CONTRIBUTORS

RICHARD BIRD is Professor of Economics and Director of the International Centre for Tax Studies at the University of Toronto. Before coming to Toronto, he taught at Harvard University for several years. In addition to his academic posts, Bird has been an advisor to the Government of Colombia, Chief of the Tax Policy Division of the Fiscal Affairs Department of the International Monetary Fund, and Director of the Institute of Policy Analysis at the University of Toronto as well as a frequent consultant to the World Bank and other national and international organisations.

ROGER BOWLES is Reader in Economics and Director of the Centre for Fiscal Studies at the University of Bath. He was educated at the Universities of Bath and York and has held research or teaching positions at the Universities of Oxford and Nottingham. During the year 1994-95 he was a Visiting Scholar at the Centre for Advanced Study in Oslo, Norway. He is an Associate Advisor on Fiscal Studies to the British Council and was for ten years responsible for Bath's Masters programme in fiscal studies. During this latter period he travelled widely in Africa and Asia, visiting tax administrations and ministries of finance in many countries.

DONAL de BUITLEIR is a General Manager with Allied Irish Banks. He was formerly Secretary to the Irish Commission on Taxation and Assistant Secretary in the Irish Revenue Commissioners. He was a member of the Ruding Committee on EU Corporate Tax Harmonisation. He was a member of the Irish Working Group on Integrating Tax and Welfare.

ANDREW DILNOT is Director of the Institute for Fiscal Studies, a post he has held since February 1991. His main research interests lie in taxation and social security and government economic policy, and he has published widely in these areas. He has taught at LSE, Oxford and UCL, as well as overseas. He is a member of the Social Security Advisory Committee, of the Council of Queen Mary and Westfield College, and of the Council of the Royal Economic Society. He is a regular contributor to the printed and broadcast media.

ELIZABETH FILKIN has been the Adjudicator for the Inland Revenue since 1993. In 1995 she also began to investigate complaints about Customs and Excise and the Contributions Agency of the Department of Social Security. She was previously Chief Executive of the National Association of Citizen's Advice Bureaux and Director of Community Services (later Assistant Chief Executive) at London Docklands Development Corporation. Elizabeth Filkin is a non-executive Director of Britannia Building Society and Logica plc, a Member of Council of Royal Holloway College, University of London, Chairman of the Advisory Council Socio Legal Centre, Wolfson College, Oxford University, and a member of the ESRC Appointments Committee.

LORD HOWE of ABERAVON, lawyer, politician, Welshman, Wykehamist: Geoffrey Howe was born at Port Talbot in 1926, joined Edward Heath's government as Solicitor General in 1970, and served in Margaret Thatcher's as Chancellor of the Exchequer (1979-83), Foreign Secretary (1983-89), and Deputy Prime Minister (1989-90). He served as Chairman of the Interim Committee of the International Monetary Fund (1982-83) and was appointed a life peer in 1992. President of the Tax Law Review Committee of the Institute for Fiscal Studies, he was appointed Chairman of the high level steering committee of the Inland Revenue's Tax Law Rewrite Project in 1997 and lives in London and the Cotswolds with his wife, Elspeth, and their dog, Summit.

SEAN MORIARTY is an Assistant Secretary with the Irish Revenue Commissioners. He has had responsibility for national programmes in tax audit and compliance, for technical support services and, more recently, for human resources. He has been both a member and Chairman of the Tax Administration Liaison Committee and Chairman of the Black Economy Monitoring Group. He is a member of the Steering Group on Taxation of the OECD Centre for Cooperation with Economies in Transition. He has provided technical assistance under OECD and EU programmes in Romania, the Slovak Republic, Poland and Russia, covering tax compliance management, the structuring of tax administrations and agricultural tax policy.

LEIF MUTEN gained his doctorate in tax law at Uppsala University in 1959 and served as a Professor of Tax Law there until joining the International Monetary Fund as a senior adviser in 1968. Since 1991 he has been Professor of International Tax Law at the Stockholm School of

Economics. He has been a consultant for the OECD and has published widely on taxation.

JOHN O'HAGAN is Associate Professor of Economics at Trinity College, Dublin. He is the author/editor of several books, including *The Economy of Ireland: Policy and Performance of a Small European Country* (Macmillan 1995), and numerous articles on taxation and, more recently, the economics of the arts. He has been a visiting academic at the Universities of Bath, Cologne, Copenhagen, Witten/Herdecke and York.

CEDRIC SANDFORD is Emeritus Professor of Political Economy at the University of Bath and formerly Director of the Bath University Centre for Fiscal Studies. His specialist research areas are the compliance costs of taxation, wealth taxes and tax policy-making, on all of which he has published widely. In recent years he has undertaken consultancies for the International Monetary Fund, World Bank, United Nations and OECD as well as national governments and the United Kingdom National Audit Office. He is currently a consultant to the United Kingdom Inland Revenue.

STEPHEN SMITH is Professor of Economics at University College London. His main research and teaching interests lie in the fields of public finance and environmental economics. He began his career as an economist in the Government Economic Service, in the Department of Trade and Industry. In 1985 he joined the staff of the Institute for Fiscal Studies, an independent research institute specialising in the economic analysis of taxation and public finance, where he established a research group covering European fiscal policy, environmental taxation and local government finance. In 1990, he was appointed Deputy Director of IFS, and joined the Economics Department at UCL part-time, as a Senior Lecturer in European Economics and Integration. In 1997 he moved to UCL full-time, although he remains actively involved with IFS as a Research Fellow.

INTRODUCTION

Further Key Issues in Tax Reform is the final volume of a trilogy about significant areas which may need to be tackled in reforming a tax system.

This book and its two predecessor volumes, *Key Issues in Tax Reform* and *More Key Issues in Tax Reform*, taken together, cover a large proportion of the many issues which arise in updating and reforming taxes and tax administrations.

Like its predecessors, *Further Key Issues in Tax Reform* is intended to be helpful to policy-makers and administrators, whether in developed economies, in developing economies or in economies in transition. It should also assist serious students of taxation, wherever they may be found, to a fuller understanding of taxation matters.

Many of the authors in this volume have been at the cutting edge of tax reform as politicians, administrators or consultants. Lord Howe, as Sir Geoffrey Howe, was Chancellor of the Exchequer in the United Kingdom 1979-83; Donal de Buitleir was Secretary to the Irish Commission on Taxation. Nearly all our authors have wide consultancy experience in developed and developing or transitional economies and often all three; but perhaps especial mention might be made of Leif Mutén of Sweden, who led innumerable technical assistance missions for the IMF and Richard Bird of Canada, whose consultancy work has ranged across many types of economy and many countries. Another author deserving special mention is Elizabeth Filkin, who occupies a unique position as Revenue Adjudicator.

Like its predecessor volumes, *Further Key Issues in Tax Reform* is divided into three parts. The first part covers issues of tax structure. In the first chapter Andrew Dilnot, the Director of the Institute for Fiscal Studies, examines the taxation of savings and what changes are needed in the modern world. He poses the questions: should we favour some forms of saving over others? Can taxation affect the level as well as the composition of saving? Can we tax pensions more heavily? These are pressing issues as governments seek to shift responsibilities to the private sector and as taxpayers become more affluent and financially sophisticated.

The effects of tobacco and the various measures used by governments, including taxation, to influence them, have been very much in the news in 1997. Landmark court cases against tobacco companies, more restrictions on advertising and the effect of high taxes on the size of the illicit trade in tobacco have all gained much publicity. Chapter 2, by John O'Hagan, looks at the rationale for state intervention, especially through the use of taxation, in the tobacco market, the effects of such taxes, and the issue of harmonsation of tobacco taxes in the EU.

No less topical than tobacco taxes is the big environmental question: how can we achieve the large reductions in carbon dioxide emissions from energy use by households and industry which will be needed to avert the risk of major global climate change? Stephen Smith describes how some countries have introduced a 'carbon tax' on energy as part of their 'climate change' policies. He discusses how, like other environmental tax measures, a carbon tax may offer cost savings compared with conventional regulatory approaches to environmental protection; it could also raise substantial revenues, giving scope for major fiscal reform. But would it harm industrial competitiveness and place a heavy tax burden on the poor?

Part II, on Administration, begins with a chapter by Roger Bowles, the Director of the Centre for Fiscal Studies of Bath University on the minimisation of corruption in tax affairs. Tax evasion and the corruption of tax administration between them account for a severe loss of revenue in many countries. These twin barriers to the funding of public expenditure have often been tackled but rarely conquered. This chapter sets out a framework for thinking about corruption and explores some of the anti-corruption policies proposed and used in recent years.

Many countries found that the tax reforms of the 1980s failed to achieve the simplification that was often one of the declared objectives. In Chapter 5, Lord Howe outlines work taking place in various countries on tax law simplification and gives a detailed account of the objectives, methods and organisation of the Tax Law Rewrite Project of the United Kingdom Inland Revenue.

The provision of an impartial judge to whom taxpayers can appeal against bad administration is a way of seeing that justice is done and creating the confidence in the tax system which promotes voluntary compliance. In Chapter 7, Elizabeth Filkin, the Adjudicator for the United Kingdom Inland Revenue, Customs and Excise and the Contributions Agency (concerned with national insurance) looks at the background to the creation of the post and describes her experience as a method which other countries might wish to emulate.

The final chapter in this Part of the book is also about tax compliance. Sean Moriarty, drawing on his experience in the Irish revenue service and as an advisor to some of the newly independent states of the former Soviet Union, looks at the possibilities for developing a more consensual approach to tax compliance through a different landscape of relationships between modern tax administrations and taxpayers. The chapter examines the perspective of the taxpayer, looks at a different approach to finding centres of influence and channels of communication with taxpayers and considers the implications for organisation and strategy within tax administrations.

Part III of the book examines some wider issues. In Chapter 8, Donal de Buitleir considers the role of tax incentives. Based on the Irish experience he concludes that 'tax incentives are no substitute for good policy in other areas. Tax incentives should be well designed, carefully targeted and reserved for key priority areas. In general, tax bases should be widened as far as possible to keep tax rates low. Incentives should be avoided in cases in which the value of the incentive is likely to be capitalised in asset prices. If it is desired to remove an incentive which is already in place, the Irish experience suggests that this is more likely to be successful if the removal is phased in over a period of years.'

In the following chapter, Leif Mutén examines an issue of particular importance to developing countries – how to minimise the tax effects of inflation. Chapter 10 is also of particular relevance to developing countries and economies in transition. As Richard Bird points out, the importance of good tax administration in developing countries is as obvious as its absence. After discussing some of the key problems arising from administrative constraints this chapter reviews various solutions that have been proposed and concludes that the best approach is to design tax policy taking into account the limitations imposed by administrative realities.

The book and the trilogy closes with a look back at the tax reform of the 1980s running into the early '90s. The tax reform movement was remarkable for its worldwide scope, common features and common objectives. The chapter examines how far the tax reformers were successful at the time and how far their reforms have been sustained. Lessons are drawn from the experience of tax reform in this period which could prove of immense value to future tax reforming countries.

FURTHER KEY ISSUES IN TAX REFORM

PART I
TAX REFORM – STRUCTURE

CHAPTER 1

THE TAXATION OF SAVINGS

Andrew Dilnot*

Introduction

As individuals live longer, as the general standard of living rises, as governments are less inclined to promise what is seen to be adequate state provision of pensions or healthcare, or finance for higher education, as uncertainty is perceived to grow, the demand for saving seems likely to rise. The demand by individuals may often be matched by a desire on the part of governments to see more saving, both because of concerns at the macroeconomic level, and because higher personal saving is in some ways a pre-requisite of reduced state involvement.

The market for saving is one where the tax system has a crucial role to play, and can have very substantial effects on how people save, and even on whether and how much they save. In this chapter we set out a framework for describing the taxation of savings in section 2, and then discuss appropriate objectives for the system in section 3. Section 4 takes one particularly important part of the savings market, pensions, examines the current pattern of taxation in a range of countries, and considers the scope for raising more revenue. Section 5 concludes.

Taxing Savings

Saving is complicated. Individuals save for many different reasons, and in many different ways, from holding short term cash balances in a bank to contributing to a pension from which they will receive no return for several decades. This complexity often causes problems in both the discussion and implementation of tax policy with respect to savings. In

---

*Director of the Institute for Fiscal Studies.
The work embodied in this chapter was supported by the Economic and Social Research Council Centre for the Micro-Economic Analysis of Fiscal Policy at the Institute.

this section, we seek to set out a framework for describing and discussing savings taxation that is general enough to allow relatively straightforward comparisons between the taxation of different forms of saving. (This framework has been used in the past in the context of the taxation of pensions, see Dilnot (1996), Forman (1997)).

Any form of saving will typically have three components, or transactions, and it is these transactions that are the possible occasion for taxation

- initial payments into a savings vehicle;
- income earned on funds within the savings vehicle;
- withdrawal of funds from the savings vehicle.

There are examples within most countries of regimes that tax savings at many of the conceivable combinations of these points, and taking a number of countries together, almost every combination can be found. Despite this variety, we see some consistent patterns for some forms of saving, most notably short-term interest-bearing saving and funded pension provision. It is also important to note that certain patterns of taxation at these three possible points characterise alternative theoretical ideals for the tax system.

Table 1.1 illustrates four possible tax regimes, describing them in terms of whether tax is imposed at each of the three possible points. Thus the EET regime is exempt exempt taxed implying no tax on initial savings, no tax on fund income, and taxation on withdrawal. We assume for these examples that there is a single income tax rate of 25 per cent, that the rate of return that can be earned on savings is 10 per cent, and that we are considering a single contribution derived from earned income of 100, saved for one year and then withdrawn.

Regime A. Tax free saving and fund income, taxed withdrawal (EET)

This regime allows deductibility of saving from taxable income, allowing the whole of the 100 of earnings into the saving fund. No tax is charged on the investment income of the fund, but tax is charged in full on withdrawal. This type of tax treatment confers a post-tax rate of return on saving equal to the pre-tax rate of return. Faced with this regime an individual earning 100 can either choose to spend now, paying 25 of tax and consuming goods worth 75, or save now and consume goods one year later worth 82.50. The figure 82.50 is simply 75 x 1.1. It is easy to think of this regime as being a way of deferring tax liability until consumption occurs. This regime is commonly seen in the case of private pensions, as we discuss further in section 4.

Regime B. Taxed saving, tax free fund income and withdrawal (TEE)

This regime does not allow deductibility of saving, thus reducing the initial size of the fund from 100 to 75. As for regime A, investment income is free of tax. Withdrawal of funds attracts no tax. As for regime A, this type of tax treatment preserves the equality of pre- and post-tax rates of return. In the case of regime B it is easy to see the non-taxation of investment income which ensures this. The Personal Equity Plan (PEP) and Tax Exempt Special Saving Account (TESSA) in the United Kingdom are treated in this way (Banks and Tanner, 1996).

Table 1.1 Alternative Tax Regimes

Characteristic	A (EET)	B (TEE)	C (TTE)	D (ETT)
Earnings	100	100	100	100
Tax paid on entry	–	25	25	–
Pension fund	100	75	75	100
Net income earned	10	7.50	5.63	7.50
Fund on withdrawal	110	82.50	80.63	107.50
Tax on withdrawal	27.50	–	–	26.87
Benefit withdrawn	82.50	82.50	80.63	80.63

Regime C. Taxed saving, tax fund income, tax free withdrawal (TTE)

This regime is basically that applied to interest-bearing short-term saving in most OECD countries. There is no tax deductibility of contributions, investment income is taxed in full, and there is no tax on withdrawal of benefits, since there is no untaxed investment income. Unlike Regimes A and B, this tax treatment brings the post-tax rate of return below the pre-tax return. Here, the post-tax rate of return is 7.5 per cent (80.63 = 75 x 1.075)

Regime D. Tax free saving, taxed fund income, taxed withdrawal (ETT)

This regime produces the same outcome as C, and therefore the same post tax rate of return. Taxation of benefits and exemption of contributions is substituted for taxation of contributions and exemption of benefits.

Other combinations of taxing and relieving at each of the three points are possible, and indeed exist.

If taxing saving were as simple as implied by the above examples, much of the complexity of both legislation and of the saving industry itself would be unnecessary. We discuss in section 4 some of the problems associated with attempting to increase revenue in this area that are related specifically to the complexity of pension regimes in practice. We have, for example, assumed that contributions to savings funds can be identified. Non-contributory employer funded pension schemes make this quite difficult. We have assumed that funds exist, while there are many examples of unfunded pension schemes, and in some countries of effectively Pay-As-You-Go pension schemes. We have also ignored the problems of identifying investment income, in particular where the income is in the form of unrealised capital gains, and of allocating investment income to individuals in a saving fund held on behalf of individuals with varying marginal tax rates.

Finally, and perhaps most important, we have ignored inflation. For regimes A and B, which do not tax investment income, inflation causes no problem; for regimes C and D, where investment income is taxed, difficulties arise. If investment income is taxed ignoring inflation, the post-tax real return will fall still further below the pre-tax real return. Imagine that in our earlier examples 7.5 per cent of the 10 per cent interest rate simply reflects inflation. To maintain the real value of savings a 7.5 per cent post-tax rate of return is required. The outcome of regimes C and D was 80.63, which is precisely 75 x 1.075. So regimes C and D, if they ignore inflation, would in this case remove the whole of the real return. If the balance between inflation and real returns were to shift further towards inflation, regimes C and D would produce a negative post-tax rate of return. Regimes A and B retain their characteristic of equal pre-and post-tax real rates of return whatever the mix of inflation and real return in the nominal return. In the case of 7.5 per cent inflation the real return in regimes A and B is 2.32 per cent per year, equal to the pre-tax real return (1.075 x 1.0232 = 1.10).

Regimes of type A and B correspond to what has traditionally been called an Expenditure Tax while regimes C and D correspond to a Comprehensive Income Tax. The debate about which of these two types of system we should seek to implement has been one of the dominant strands in tax policy debate in the second half of the twentieth century. Early key works are Kaldor (1955), US Treasury (1977) and Meade (1978) on Expenditure Tax, and Carter Commission (1966) on Comprehensive Income Tax. Forming a view on what type of regime we should have demands a closer consideration of possible objectives for the tax system, and for the act of saving in itself. We turn to these issues in the next section.

Objectives for the Tax System

Many considerations seem to lie behind the attempts to review the tax treatment of savings so commonly seen at present. One is the concern for fiscal neutrality, the desire to achieve a tax structure that as far as possible avoids discrimination between different kinds of activity and that leaves choices unaffected by tax considerations. A second is a desire to raise revenue by eliminating tax subsidies to particular activities. A third is concern about the aggregate level of saving.

There is no feasible tax regime that both raises revenue and is fiscally neutral in all aspects. Taxes inevitably distort economic behaviour, so that the best we can do is to remove unnecessary deviations from neutrality and choose those which are least damaging in their overall economic effect. Two kinds of incentive are particularly important in considering the tax treatment of saving. One is the incentive to save, rather than to consume. The second is the choice of the form in which to save. We consider each kind of incentive in turn.

There are two ways of interpreting fiscal neutrality in relation to the decision to save. We might seek to be neutral between consumption and savings, or we might seek to be neutral between present and future consumption. Neutrality between consumption and savings is achieved by a Comprehensive Income Tax on real income of all types. Whatever the source of income, whether it be from work or from savings, and whether it is consumed or saved, it is taxed in the same way and at the same rate. It is worth noting that there are peculiarities associated with this approach. With a Comprehensive Income Tax (TTE in our earlier discussion), savings are treated as if they are simply another commodity, akin to consumption. But people do not, in the main, save for saving's own sake; savings are not a commodity in themselves, but a means to future consumption. This seems a strong argument for believing that the relevant concept of neutrality is not between consumption and savings but between consumption now and consumption in the future.

It is this neutrality in the impact of the tax system on the decision between current and future consumption which is achieved by tax systems of the EET or TEE type. Such systems offer the alternative of consuming now or deferring tax by means of saving and paying tax when the funds are withdrawn (EET) or paying tax now, but paying no tax on the return to saving or its withdrawal (TEE). Thus both present and future consumption are taxed on the same basis. And as noted above, the EET/TEE regime corresponding to the 'Expenditure Tax' maintains equality of pre- and post-tax returns, another reflection of the lack of distortion imposed on the decision as to whether to consume now or in the future.

The Comprehensive Income Tax or TTE/ETT approach, by contrast, reduces the post-tax rate of return on savings, discouraging the deferral of consumption. In an inflationary world with nominal investment income taxed, it could actually impose a penalty on deferred consumption. If fiscal neutrality between current and future consumption is desired, the appropriate tax system is an Expenditure Tax type system.

The second concept of fiscal neutrality which is of interest to us concerns the way in which different kinds of savings are taxed. Here, neutrality demands that all forms of saving are taxed in the same way. If not, more generously treated forms of saving will tend to attract greater flows of saving, regardless of their underlying economic efficiency. In general, different forms of saving are taxed very differently in countries across the OECD.

Although it is hard to make generalisations in this area, two forms of saving still stand out as being conceded relatively favourable tax treatment in many countries, being owner occupied housing and private pensions. Governments in the 1980s and 1990s made many statements to the effect that fiscal neutrality between forms of saving was an important goal, but progress towards this goal has been disappointing (OECD, 1994). There were two main reasons. First, although many statements were made in favour of a comprehensive income tax type treatment, nowhere was any serious attempt made to adjust investment income as well as capital gains for inflation. Second, very few governments had the courage to remove much of the 'privilege' associated with owner occupied housing or private pension plans. We have seen, for example, reduction in the value of tax relief on interest payments for house purchase in the United Kingdom, but no shift to taxing the return on saving in the form of house purchase, which comes in capital gains and the imputed income to owner occupation. House purchase in the United Kingdom is therefore still slightly more favourably taxed than TEE, while pensions are more favourably taxed than EET. Part of the reason for lack of action to remove privileges was the widespread belief that there are strong arguments for providing special incentives for certain types of saving. It is to a discussion of these which we now turn.

Two types of argument are often advanced to defend the special tax advantages of a particular form of saving, often pensions or housing, but also sometimes investment in small or new businesses, for example. First, that one particular form of saving is more important that other saving; second than saving in general should benefit from tax incentives.

Households save for a variety of reasons. They save in order to redistribute income over their lifetime to use it when they are old, sick, or unemployed, or when young children reduce the family's income and increase its outgoings. They save in order to accumulate assets from which they may derive benefits (housing services from owner-occupied housing) or that they might use to establish or develop a business. They save as a precaution against the unexpected. They may also save in order to leave money to their children.

It is not immediately easy to see why any one form of saving should be singled out in this list. They are all worthy motives, which is no doubt why, at one time or another, in one place or another, all have been singled out for fiscal privilege, although frequently in an uncoordinated manner. Several possible arguments exist.

First individuals may fail to perceive accurately their likely needs at a given time, and this failure of perception/information is more serious here than in other areas. This argument is often used with respect to retirement. It would be plausible to argue that this could be so simply because at the beginning of the period when saving for retirement might make sense, old age can seem very distant. This is a basically paternalistic argument that asserts that governments know better than their people what is good for them and should distort choices using the tax system in an attempt to correct the deficiencies of individual preferences.

A second argument for singling out savings is that they can be particularly significant in reducing other forms of state expenditure. If individuals fail to save for their old age, the state will have to provide incomes for them during that period. Certainly in most countries at least a part of the social security system that supports the elderly pays benefits that are related to income. If governments can encourage more people to save for their retirement, and also those who already are saving to save more, expenditure on means-tested benefits to the retired would fall. The importance of this argument will obviously vary from country to country, and can apply to savings to cover healthcare, education and child-rearing as well as retirement.

A third argument could simply be a distributional one. If a particular form of saving is especially important or convenient for some group within the population for whom there are special concerns, a case might be made for special treatment.

The remaining argument for tax incentives for particular forms of saving relates to the overall level of saving. Across much of the OECD there is concern that savings rates are too low. The United States, the United Kingdom, and Australia would be obvious examples, while in countries like Japan and Germany such a problem seems not to exist. Table 1.2 illustrates the diversity of personal savings rates. One of the longest-running debates in applied economics has been the extent to which new tax incentives for saving in a particular form will increase the overall level of saving. It is clear from the experience of Registered Retirement Savings Plans in Canada, Individual Retirement Accounts in the United States and 401(k) Plans, and Personal Pensions, TESSAs and PEPs, in the United Kingdom, for example (Carroll and Summers, 1987; Venti and Wise, 1986; National Audit Office, 1991, respectively), and the popularity of private pension saving in general, that new or existing generous tax regimes for certain types of saving can be enormously 'successful', if we measure success only in terms of amounts of money flowing into the favoured regime and the number of people involved.

Such a measure of success is of little help in assessing the impact of such schemes on overall saving levels. Of course, tax incentives for saving in a certain form will attract funds. We need to know what impact this has on funds held in, and flowing into, other forms of saving, and the impact of the new scheme on government tax revenue, since if we are concerned about any measure of saving it is likely to be national saving, which includes public sector saving, not simply personal sector saving.

It would be quite possible for a new savings incentive to appear to be successful while in fact reducing both personal sector saving and public sector saving, and thus diminishing national saving (Munnell, 1982). If we started from a world in which individuals had a relatively fixed demand for consumption at some future date but in which savings were harshly treated by the tax system, the introduction of tax incentives would allow a reduction in current saving without any reduction in the level of future consumption, thus reducing the level of personal sector saving. At the same time, since the tax incentive would reduce tax revenue, public sector saving would fall.

Table 1.2 Household Savings Rates as Percentage of Disposable Household Income

Country	1988	1993
United States	4.5	4.6
United Kingdom	5.7	11.5
Australia	6.5	4.2
Japan	14.3	14.6
Germany	12.8	12.1

Source: OECD *Economic Outlook*.

There has been a great deal of empirical work using microeconomic data to attempt to provide conclusive evidence on the likely effect of tax incentives. This is an extremely difficult area, since the data requirements are very severe: complete answers would require detailed information on all assets, incomes, preferences, and expectations for a large sample of individuals over a long period. To the extent that there is a consensus, it seems to be that in some circumstances tax incentives can increase personal saving, and that after taking account of the reduction in tax revenue there may be a small increase in national saving (Bovenberg, 1989; Feenberg and Skinner, 1989; Feldstein, 1992; Poterba and Wise, 1993; Venti and Wise, 1987, for some representative views). Some, however (e.g. Gravelle, 1991) cast doubt that even a small increase in national saving occurs. These results are still debated, and would tend to vary enormously from country to country as a function of the nature of the tax system and the determinants of saving. Introducing a tax favoured scheme for a type of saving, say pensions, which has previously been heavily taxed, but is likely to be important for individuals, seems to have the best chance of success. Certainly differences in tax systems can go only a little way toward explaining cross-country variation in saving.

All too often, it is simply assumed that more saving is a good thing, and that tax incentives for particular savings are an effective and appropriate way of achieving a change in the level of national saving. Even if we accept that there is some argument for higher saving, it is not obvious that tinkering with the tax system is a good way of raising national saving. But it does seem reasonable to assert that we would not want a tax system that imposed a post-tax rate of return on deferred consumption lower than the pre-tax return. If our concern is not to depress saving, than we must expect to impose a tax treatment for saving in general that does not tax the return to saving. Starting from a tax system that does tax the return to some or all forms of saving, moving to one that taxes the return to fewer or no forms of saving might increase national savings. But the taxation of savings in most developed countries is enormously variable (OECD, 1984) with some forms of saving having a post-tax rate of return higher than the pre-tax rate and some far lower than the pre-tax rate. Consequently, confident prediction in this area is very difficult.

The Taxation of Pensions

In this section we look in rather more detail at the taxation of pensions. As populations age, incomes rise, and governments become increasingly unwilling to provide generous tax-financed pensions, the already well advanced shift to further private pension provision seems likely to continue in those countries which have traditionally relied on state provision. In countries without such a tradition, private provision also seems likely to develop rapidly. Because of these trends saving in the form of pensions is now, and will continue to be, certainly one of the most important forms of saving, and arguably the most important. Pension saving is itself complex, often subject to extremely complicated taxation regimes, and because of its scale, also commonly thought of as a possible source of additional revenue. For all these reasons it seems appropriate to consider this area in greater detail. We begin this section by describing the current tax regime for pensions in a number of countries, and then discuss the scope for increasing revenue by changing tax treatment. Table 1.3 is inevitably a simplification.

Almost all of the countries shown impose upper limits on the level of contribution and/or benefits which can be paid, although typically these limits affect only a small proportion of the workforce. Many countries treat lump sum payments out of pension funds more generously for tax purposes than they do regular payments: Australia, Ireland, Japan and the

United Kingdom fall into this category. Some other countries such as Canada and France take quite the opposite route, disallowing lump sum payments out of tax privileged pension regimes, while the remainder subject lump sums to tax in broadly the same way as regular payments. It is clear from the Table that the bulk of countries operate systems most like the EET regime referred to above, which itself corresponds quite closely to the expenditure tax, and can also be thought of as a system of deferred pay. These apparently quite generous schemes have typically operated over lengthy periods.

Table 1.3 Taxation of Private Pensions

	Pension regime
Australia	ETT (approx)
Belgium	EET
Canada	EET
Denmark	EET (approx)
Finland	EET
France	EET
Germany	EET
Greece	EET
Ireland	EET
Italy	EET
Japan	ETT
Luxembourg	EET
Netherlands	EET
New Zealand	TTE
Norway	EET
Portugal	EET
Spain	EET
Sweden	ETT
Switzerland	EET
United Kingdom	EET
United States	EET

Source: Forman (1997).

It is worth noting that two countries which have reformed their taxation of pensions in the last decade, Australia and New Zealand, have both moved towards less generous systems, at least partly with the aim of raising extra revenue but also with the aim of improving the efficiency and equity of the tax system as a whole. New Zealand has taken the boldest steps, making all contributions taxable, taxing all fund income (with no allowance for inflation) and then leaving all pensions untaxed. As argued at the time in New Zealand, this puts pension saving on the same basis as saving in an ordinary interest bearing account.

The reforms in Australia moved in a similar direction, but have produced a substantially more complex system. Employer contributions continue to be deductible. Employee contributions are partially deductible up to certain limits contingent on employer support being below a given level, and all concessions are phased out beyond roughly average earnings. These limits discourage employers from increasing their contributions beyond the level at which employees lose their rights to deductibility and create a number of other distortions. Contributions which have been deductible are subject to a 15 per cent withholding tax. Investment income of the fund is taxed at 15 per cent, as are capital gains, but capital gains are taxed after adjustment for inflation, thus making capital gains far more attractive than income from the point of view of the funds. Lump sum benefits are taxed at 15 per cent beyond a threshold, and pension benefits taxed at the individual's marginal rate less 15 per cent.

Two other regimes deserve special mention since they do not fit so readily into the framework outlined above – those of France and Germany. Occupational pensions are provided in France through a pay-as-you-go system known as 'repartition'. Employers make contributions to a collective pension plan; these earn a certain number of points for the employee on whose behalf they are made. At retirement the worker concerned will have a points score to his or her credit that determines the pension to be received. The value of a pension point is reviewed annually and moves in line with earnings. The cost of a pension point is set by the annual outflow from the fund. Thus there is no funding of future liabilities, and hence no pension fund assets or liabilities of great significance. Contributions made by employers on this basis are deductible against corporation tax paid by employers, and employee contributions can be deducted from taxable income. Pensions are taxable as ordinary income, although subject to some special concessions.

The normal method of private pension finance in Germany is through the use of 'book reserve' accounting. There is no special fund; prospective pension liabilities are charged each year against the company's profit and loss account and balance sheet. Charges computed in accordance with bases agreed on by the tax authorities can be deducted in assessing corporation tax liabilities. Scheme members rank with other creditors in the event of insolvency of the parent company; hence legislation requires that vested benefits and pensions in payment should be insured. Premiums for such insurance are in turn tax-deductible. There is no charge to employees until pensions are paid. Pensions are then taxed as other income, subject to a lower rate of tax on small incomes. If a German employer does establish a segregated fund, the employees will be liable for tax on contributions made on his or her behalf. Such funds are correspondingly rare.

Although the French and German institutional arrangements are rather different from those in most countries, they fit into the hugely dominant group of countries for which the only significant source of tax revenue from pensions is the taxation of pensions in payment. The United States, for example, does deny relief to employee contributions to defined benefits plans, but the consequence is that there are few employee contributions.

The extent of international similarity of tax treatment of private pensions is very striking, with an enormous predominance of the EET type regime. But this regime seems at first sight to run somewhat counter to the 'broaden the base and lower the rate' refrain of much tax reform in the 1980s and 1990s. Hardly surprisingly, there has been much discussion of the scope for raising more revenue by moving away from an EET regime. Starting from a tax treatment of the EET type, there are three areas in which changes could be made in an attempt to raise more revenue: the taxation of contributions, the taxation of pension funds themselves, and the taxation of benefits paid out. We examine each in turn.

The Taxation of Contributions. One seemingly obvious way of raising revenue from taxing pensions is to give no relief, or only limited relief, to employees for contributions to pensions plans. Such relief could be abolished where it exists, or restricted to a low rate of tax, or be subjected to a maximum. Yet it would be pointless to make such a change without simultaneously reviewing the tax treatment of employer contributions. Indeed, it seems inevitable that all forms of contributions to pensions funds be given identical tax treatment. If not, employees, employers, and pension funds will so arrange their affairs as to make all contributions in the most tax efficient manner. The losers in such a position will be the ill advised, or those unable to take advantage of the most lightly taxed route. As we noted earlier, the general non-exemption of employee contributions in the United States means that very few employee contributions are made, not that large amounts of tax are raised.

If employees' contributions are to be subject to tax it seems that employers' contributions must also be. There are few practical problems in subjecting employees' contributions to tax; tax due would simply be calculated on income inclusive of contributions rather than exclusive of them. Difficulties do arise in the case of employers' contributions, however. In principle, contributions made by employers on behalf of their employees would be treated as a benefit to the employee, and taxed as income of the employee. This causes no problem where employers' contributions are clearly defined and linked to particular individuals, but difficulties arise in the much more common procedure where an employer makes general contributions to a fund related to aggregate payroll. Here the task of allocating the employer's contributions to employees is challenging. One possibility is simply to require employers to attribute general contributions to individual employees, but this would not be easy to implement.

An alternative would be to levy tax on employees who are members of defined benefit schemes on the value of their pension rights, rather than on contributions. Contributions to defined benefit schemes would remain tax-deductible, but the benefit in kind in the form of increased pension rights would be taxable. This route requires an answer to the question of what the value of the rights is; valuing such rights may be at least as difficult as allocating general contributions. Valuation is especially hard where the final pension is a function of years of employment and final salary. It is also worth noting that rights within pension plans are frequently defined quite narrowly, with pensions paid frequently far exceeding rights. If tax authorities imposed a tax on the annual increase in the value of an individual's pension rights, it is easy to imagine such rights would very soon be all but replaced by discretionary payments. The alternative of trying to tax as income the expected value of discretionary payments many years in the future is not a task that would appeal to many revenue authorities.

The problems outlined above are not insuperable; the difficulties of taxing general unallocated contributions, for example, can be dealt with, as in New Zealand, by imposing a flat rate tax. This solution is reasonably fair if most taxpayers face the same marginal income tax rates, and somewhat inequitable in countries with multiple-rate income taxes. And although calculating the value of accrued pension rights is hard, we must remember that such calculations are already made, for example, to determine transfer values. If a country is determined to tax pension contributions, it can certainly be done.

If there is no tax relief for pension contributions, then it is inappropriate to tax the whole of any pensions in payment as income, since part would already have been taxed. The easiest solution to this, adopted by New Zealand, is to tax the income of pension funds as well, making any further taxation of pensions in payment unnecessary. But if the income of funds is not to be taxed, full exemption from tax of pensions in payment produces a TEE regime equivalent in impact to the EET regime, although with the timing of tax payments advanced. If the aim is to move to a system that raises more revenue, without taxing contributions twice, rules to distinguish between the underlying contributions and the return on them would be needed, so that only the previously untaxed elements would be taxed. These rules would probably be quite complex, and inevitably cause some distortions. The Australian system, which imposes partial tax on contributions, fund income, and benefits illustrates some of the problems.

The Taxation of Fund Income. Taxing fund income is an alternative (or additional) route to raising revenue from pensions schemes. There is no obvious lack of logic in a system that taxes both contributions and fund income, as is done in New Zealand, although pensions in payment should then be relieved of tax. If not, pension funds would suffer a substantial fiscal disadvantage relative to other means of saving, and could be expected to decline rapidly in popularity and importance.

If the problems with taxing contributions outlined above are thought to rule out such a regime, the alternative of taxing fund assets or income while leaving contributions untaxed and benefits taxed is also open. This is the type of system that operates in Japan, although with a very low rate of tax. There is an apparent element of double taxation in a procedure that taxes the income of funds as it is received (or their assets) and imposes tax again when benefits are paid out. But it is the same element of double taxation that is intrinsic to the taxation of income in general, where both the capital and the returns on capital are taxed.

If fund income is to be taxed, a decision as to the rate at which it is to be charged is needed. The most obvious candidate is the marginal tax rate of the majority of members of the scheme, provided that this majority is a large one. If there is a wide divergence of tax rates among scheme members, then any single tax rate will inevitably be unfair, but the problems of attempting to allocate fund income to specific individuals and then tax it at their marginal tax rate seem likely to be too great to consider such a route seriously.

Perhaps, the greatest problem in this area is designing a system that deals properly with inflation, since a system that taxes full nominal income will be very vulnerable to inflation. In New Zealand and Australia no adjustment is made to fund income to account for inflation, producing a position where at high inflation rates the post-tax rate of return can become negative. This clearly makes little sense, but the difficulties of adjusting income for inflation would be very great. The area that is most frequently chosen for the attempt to adjust for inflation is capital gains; many countries now have capital gains taxes that adjust for inflation.

The combination of taxing full nominal fund income and taxing only real capital gains in the fund, as in Australia, provides a strong bias to the fund in favour of assets producing capital gains rather than regular income, and this bias is a function of the rate of inflation, being stronger the higher the rate of inflation becomes. This sort of distortion will tend to affect the portfolio behaviour of funds, and is clearly undesirable.

One further problem in this area relates to the way in which such a tax could be introduced if it did not already exist. One possible transition mechanism would be to close all existing schemes to new contributions, and allow these schemes to continue to accumulate tax free income and pay out taxable incomes. Such a transition would be challenging for pension funds, actuaries and tax authorities, but ought to be possible. An alternative route would simply be to subject fund income to a relatively low rate to begin with, reflecting the large share in the fund of 'old' contributions, perhaps increasing the rate steadily over time.

The Taxation of Pension Benefits. As already noted, the most common form of taxation levied on the activities of private pensions is of benefits in payment. While it is true that if contributions and/or fund income are taxed, it is not necessarily appropriate that all benefits be taxed; where relief exists for contributions, there is a strong case for taxing benefits.

The most significant area for debate over the taxation of benefits is the appropriate treatment of lump sum payments. In several countries (Australia, Ireland, Japan, and the United Kingdom, for example), lump sum payments are taxed more leniently than pensions. Given our belief that all forms of contributions to private pensions should be taxed in the same way, we might expect to believe that all forms of withdrawal should be taxed in the same way.

Two arguments in support of preferential tax treatment for lump sums are frequently advanced. The first is that such provisions are an accepted part of the regimes where they exist, and therefore should not be changed. This is a weak argument; although it is vital to avoid too great a disruption to established expectations, and thus avoid too dramatic a change for those approaching retirement, we cannot accept the status quo simply because that is what it is.

The second argument relates to personal capital accumulation and general capital formation and suggests that the availability of tax-free lump sums may encourage this. It is certainly the case that private capital accumulation may stimulate enterprise and risk taking in the economy. But a relief whose receipt is conditional on reaching retirement age seems somewhat inappropriate if this is the aim. There are arguments for supporting retirement savings, but these do not imply encouraging lump sum provisions – rather the reverse. There may be arguments for encouraging the accumulation of capital sums by individuals, but not especially individuals past retirement age – rather the reverse.

There seem to be no very strong reasons for treating the lump sums more favourably than pension payments for tax purposes. If lump sums are taxed, the question of whether they should be taxed in the year of receipt becomes relevant. Once more, the question is unimportant in a single-rate income tax, but significant with a graduated tax system. Under a graduated system, any lump sum might attract a marginal rate of tax well in excess of the recipient's expected average marginal tax rate during retirement. One possibility would be an averaging provision, but it could also be argued that the disincentive to lump sums caused by graduation is appropriate, and should be allowed to stay.

Most countries could raise more revenue from private pensions than they do at present. However, serious problems are associated with taxing both contributions and fund income; it is not an accident that neither are taxed in most regimes. The one area where increased taxation seems appropriate in many countries is lump sum benefits, but even here, entrenched expectations may make raising more revenue difficult in the short term.

This rather lengthy discussion of pension taxation serves to illustrate the potential complexity of savings taxation and the remarkable similarity of treatment of one of the principal forms of saving in a wide range of countries. Both these observations are relevant to any attempt to make more general statements about the taxation of saving.

Conclusion

The taxation of savings is a clear example of a policy area where what is actually done in most countries seems not to be what it first seems. Although the main direct tax is universally described as an income tax, the tax treatment of major forms of saving, especially housing and pensions, is generally far closer to an expenditure tax than an income tax, and often more generous even than an expenditure tax.

The arguments in favour of seeking to tax the return to all forms of saving equally seem powerful. If we do not have tax systems which achieve this we will see substantial distortion of saving towards the most tax favoured assets. While there may be some forms of saving which governments may seek to favour, great care should be taken both to be clear about why a particular form of saving is to be favoured, and in the implementation of any tax incentive.

The debate about whether the comprehensive income tax or expenditure tax route to achieving equal treatment of different savings forms has a long history. If we were to deliver a comprehensive income tax, tax regimes would need to:

- impose tax on real capital gains on all assets as they accrue, including owner occupied housing;
- impose tax on the imputed income to owner occupied housing;
- tax real, and *only* real, incomes of pension funds;
- remove any tax privilege associated with lump sum pension benefits;
- tax real, and *only* real, interest income of individuals;
- remove all other tax privilege so as to tax the real return to all savings.

This list presents such large political and practical problems that there is little surprise in the reality that no government has sought to move towards such a system.

Simply delivering on a part of this list enhances the incentive to save in the remaining tax favoured assets, worsening the distortion in the system. The taxation of saving is a good example of an area where policy makers may be readily tempted by the appearance of juicy, revenue laden bits of the tax system, ripe for reform, only to find that, in the act of grasping the revenue, it slips between their fingers. The most promising path for increasing revenue in relation to pensions is the judicious taxation of lump sum benefits where they are currently tax free.

The tax treatment of saving has far more to do with efficiency and equity than with revenue raising. It is little surprise that in much of the world the bulk of saving receives an EET or TEE type treatment, broadly in line with an Expenditure Tax. Achieving a perfectly neutral system may be too much to hope for, but arguments of both theory and practice suggest that further shifts in the EET/TEE direction are both likely, and probably desirable.

References and Further Reading

Banks, J. and S. Tanner, 'Savings and Wealth in the UK: Evidence from Microdata', *Fiscal Studies*, London May, 1996.

Broadway, R. and D. Wildasin, 'Taxation and Savings: a Survey', *Fiscal Studies*, Vol.15, No. 3, pp.19-63, 1994.

Bovenberg, A., 'Tax Policy and National Saving in the United States: A Survey', *National Tax Journal*, Vol.42, No. 2, pp.123-38, 1989.

Capital Taxes Group, *Neutrality in the Taxation of Savings: An Extended Role for PEPs*, Commentary No. 17, Institute for Fiscal Studies, London, 1989.

Carroll, C. and L. Summers, 'Why Have Private Savings Rates in the United States and Canada Diverged?' *Journal of Monetary Economics* Vol. 20, pp.249-80, September, 1980.

Carter Commission, *Report of the Royal Commission on Taxation*, Queen's Printer, Ottawa, 1966.

Dilnot, A., R. Disney, P. Johnson and E. Whitehouse, *Pension Policy in the United Kingdom and Economic Analysis*, Institute for Fiscal Studies, London, 1994.

Dilnot, A., 'The Taxation of Private Pensions' in *Securing Employer Based Pension*, Z. Bodie, O. Mitchell and J. Turner, Pension Research Council and University of Pennsylvania, Wharton, 1996.

Feenberg, D. and J. Skinner, *Sources of IRA Saving*, NBER Working Paper 2845, Cambridge MA, 1989.

Feldstein, M., *The Effects of Tax-Based Saving Incentive on Government Revenue and National Saving*, NBER Working Paper 4021, Cambridge MA, 1992.

Forman, J., 'The Tax Treatment of Public and Private Pension Plans Around the World', *American Journal of Tax Policy*, Vol.14, No. 2, 1997.

Gravelle, J., 'Do IRAs Increase Savings?', *Journal of Economic Perspective*, Vol.5, No. 2, pp.133-48, 1991.

Kaldor, N., *An Expenditure Tax*, Allen and Unwin, London, 1955.

Leape, J., 'The Impossibility of Perfect Neutrality: Fundamental Issues in Tax Reform', *Fiscal Studies*, Vol.11, No. 2, pp.39-54, 1990.

Meade, J., *The Structure and Reform of Direct Taxation*, George Allen and Unwin for IFS, London, 1978.

Munnell, A., *The Economics of Private Pensions*, Brookings Institution, Washington, 1982.

OECD, *Taxation and Household Saving*, OECD, Paris, 1994.

Poterba, J., S. Venti and D. Wise, *Do 401(K) Contributions Crowd Out Other Personal Saving?*, NBER Working Paper 4391, Cambridge MA, 1993.

United States Treasury, *Blueprints for Basic Tax Reform*, US GPO, Washington, 1977.

United States Treasury, *Tax Reform for Fairness, Simplicity and Economic Growth*, US GPO, Washington, 1984.

Venti, S. and D. Wise, 'Tax Deferred Accounts, Constrained Choice and Estimation on Individual Saving', *Review of Economic Studies*, Vol.53, pp.579-601, 1986.

CHAPTER 2

THE TAXATION OF TOBACCO

John O'Hagan*

Introduction

The effects of tobacco and the various measures used by government, including taxation, have been very much in the news in recent times. The Food and Drug Administration in the United States introduced a set of new regulations in 1997 intended to reduce smoking among young people. More damaging from the tobacco industry's point of view is a series of lawsuits that are coming to trial in the Unites States, some for medical expenses incurred by states, others for the suffering of individuals and groups of people. In some of these cases, deals have already been struck whereby some tobacco companies are prepared to admit liability and make large payments in exchange for immunity from further lawsuits, thereby requiring some tobacco companies to admit, for the first time in 40 years, that tobacco causes cancer and that it is an addictive substance (*Economist*, 1997).

In Europe, similar moves are afoot intended to reduce smoking, but especially amongst young people (Commission of the European Communities, 1996). Noteworthy, though, is the lack of progress in relation to the harmonisation of structures, let alone rates, for the taxation of cigarettes and other forms of manufactured tobacco products. One of the major reasons perhaps for the lack of progress is that decisions on such matters are initiated under Article 99 of the Treaty, which requires unanimity, as opposed to a qualified majority, for them to be carried.

A new study for the European Parliament in Strasbourg, in 1997, meantime has given an urgency to the tobacco tax issue not only in Europe, but across the world. It confirmed what many people have known for some time, namely that the very high levels of taxation on the consumption of tobacco products have created a huge illegal trade in cigarettes, with major criminal players involved.

* Associate Professor of Economics, Trinity College Dublin.

This is the background to the present chapter. A number of questions will be looked at. First, in Section 2 the rationale for government intervention in the tobacco trade, especially through the imposition of special taxes, will be examined in some detail. There has always been a rationale in relation to the provision of adequate information, but more recently the objective for some organisations has been explicitly to reduce tobacco consumption significantly. Even if such an objective is accepted, the issue then arises as to the role of taxation in achieving this objective and the consequential costs associated with the tax measure. This will be discussed in Section 3. There are the costs in terms of the effects on income distribution, and the large illicit trade in cigarettes that is resulting from the high levels of taxation on tobacco products. Section 4 will look at the issue of the structure of tobacco taxation, especially as it applies in the European Union (EU), and Section 5 will conclude the chapter.

Taxation and the Unaccounted for Costs of Smoking

The Idea of Social Cost

In attempting to answer the question why governments place special taxes on the consumption of tobacco, economists usually examine actual situations by relating them to an 'ideal type' – which essentially consists of a set of perfectly functioning markets, operated by rational individual actors. Government intervention is justified where some activity has a social cost: only then can the government intervene (assume for the moment there is no information problem), e.g. by imposing a tax.

The social cost argument runs as follows: before anybody does anything in the market, they weigh up the costs and benefits of any action they are considering. Because it is assumed that each individual is rational and self-interested, for a cost and/or benefit to be included in the calculation, it must satisfy two conditions: (i) it must be foreseen by him/her, and (ii) it must be an 'own cost' or 'own benefit' in that it will be borne by him/her. This individual weighs up all foreseen own costs and all foreseen benefits, and if the latter exceeds the former the action is carried out, but if the former exceeds the latter it is not. To use the example of smoking, the benefits would be, for example, the personal satisfaction from smoking and the social ease it permits in some situations, and the cost – assuming for the moment that there is only one relevant cost – the purchase price. Costs not borne by the potential smoker will not be included – and at first sight, the costs of 'passive smoking', or the public health costs, seem like classic examples of such an external or social cost.

It is quite possible that the smoker will foresee such costs to others, but will not include them in the calculations because they are not relevant. Thus the argument goes, the government must intervene by imposing a tax to the amount of the above costs to others of each cigarette, or more specifically the marginal external cost per cigarette. The cost to others enters as an own cost or private cost through the cost of the cigarette itself and if the new augmented cost still does not exceed the benefits of smoking, the person continues to smoke.

The translation of this principle in its pure form into reality is, however, almost impossible. The marginal external cost associated with the consumption of each cigarette depends on who smokes it, under what circumstances it is smoked, and where it is smoked. Apart from the fact that information on the marginal external cost for each circumstance simply does not exist, there would be the rather ludicrous administrative problem of applying these different rates. The best practical equivalent of this approach is the 'insurance' approach to taxing external costs of tobacco consumption – smokers as a group should meet all of the costs to the exchequer of smoking through a uniform general tax on the consumption of all tobacco. In this sense, tobacco tax can be regarded as a premium, similar to motor insurance, in that it is related to the overall costs imposed, as measured by the numbers of cigarettes consumed.

Passive Smoking

The insurance approach to tobacco taxation, though, does not deal with the passive smoking issue. The external or social cost of passive smoking is not borne by the individual or the exchequer, but involuntarily by a third party. This cost of smoking has been given enormous publicity in the last two decades or so and one consequence is that, in many public places, smokers tend to be segregated from non-smokers, or else smoke alone. Indeed, the World Health Organisation (WHO) has the aim of reducing smoking to the status of a private activity of a minority of adults who are unable to give up the habit (Chollat-Traquet, 1996).

The difficulty with this cost is that it cannot really be dealt with through taxation. Apart altogether from the link between passive smoking and the incidence of cancer (which, while queried strongly in the past, is rarely challenged today), the existence of other people's smoke can cause irritation and watery eyes, and in general pollutes the environment for others present through the existence of unpleasant smoke and odours in the air.[1] The fact that smokers may be paying high levels of taxation to the exchequer to compensate for these and other costs of their smoking is no consolation to those present, as these particular costs are very specific to the individual and affect no other taxpayer. They could leave the area where the smoking is taking place, but why should they if the area is a public area, or if there is no part of the public area where they can go to undertake their work or pursue their leisure interests?

Regulation and legal instruments, not taxation, are the main ways to deal with such issues. In the European Union (EU) a Resolution of 1989 has led to major changes, particularly in relation to the banning of smoking in enclosed premises open to the public and in all forms of public transport (Commission of the European Communities, 1996). It is noteworthy that in this Resolution it was agreed that clearly defined areas should be reserved for smokers, including in public transport on long journeys. This allayed the fears of some that smoking might be banned in all areas of a public building or a public transport carrier, even though over 40 per cent of the adult population of the EU still smoke. In areas other than those reserved for smokers, though, the right to health of non-smokers was to prevail over the right of smokers to smoke. Such measures have gone a lot further in the United States (Fritschler and Hoefler, 1996). For example, no smoking rules for certain areas were introduced there as far back as 1972, and Congress, in 1989, banned smoking on all commercial domestic airline flights, regardless of duration. In 1994, McDonalds decided to ban smoking in all of its 9,000 chain-owned restaurants, with other similar organisations following suit.

An outright ban on smoking in public places is the polar opposite position to allowing smoking at will in all public areas. Neither policy is optimal, as in many public areas the costs imposed on non-smokers is as much to do with the quality of the air-conditioning as on the fact that someone is smoking. It is also possible that the loss of welfare to smokers through the imposition of the ban may not be compensated by the gain in welfare to non-smokers. It may be that people have a right to clean air in public places, but why then is this not applied with the same vigour to air near public thoroughfares or to noise created by third parties in both private and public areas? 'Smoking today, what we wear tomorrow' may

---

[1] It is interesting to note that in Elizabethan times the smoke from tobacco was considered desirable as it smothered odours resulting from the then reluctance to take baths!

be overstating the situation, but it is this type of fear that has bred pro-smoking lobbies in countries such as the United Kingdom in recent years (Nicholson, 1994). Despite this, it is now generally accepted that people have the right to clean air, both in their work environment and in their leisure activities especially where they take place in confined spaces.

Public Health and Other Exchequer Costs

An external or social cost that is susceptible to correction through tax policy is the public health and other costs of treating the victims of smoking. Smokers tend to use public health facilities more often than non-smokers and thus, in the absence of special taxes, are in effect being subsidised by non-smokers to smoke. However, this is only true in a system where medical care is provided by the state completely free of charge. Thus the problem may not be due to the fact that people smoke, but rather the institutional health arrangements of that particular state. In fact, however, a system of completely free medical care rarely exists and for many people there is usually at least a partial private insurance element in health care costs. Thus, to this extent, smokers do not burden non-smokers with the additional health care costs resulting from the fact that they smoke. In large part though it is the case that the health care costs of smokers, in the absence of special taxes, would be subsidised by non-smokers.

If the principle were introduced that smokers should pay for their treatment, either through special taxes or by being rejected for treatment in public hospitals, because their illness is willingly self-inflicted, then there seems to be no reason why it should not be extended to any victim of a risky undertaking, e.g. to someone who eats a lot of butter or someone who is injured when playing rugby football or skiing. Another issue is that if smoking does affect health in the manner alleged, then smokers should die younger and thus cease to draw on state pensions, geriatric care, etc. It is quite possible that the costs of treating age-related diseases is greater than that of treating smoking-related diseases, or at least that they balance out. In short, if one looks at life-cycle health costs, then the argument that smokers impose a burden on non-smokers may have little foundation. Atkinson and Townsend (1977) found that the actual cost savings to the exchequer from a hypothetical 40 per cent reduction in cigarette smoking were relatively small. Indeed, as new non-smokers aged they would consult general practitioners more, resulting in a net increase in consultation costs within 25 years. In fact, the major savings would not be in health costs at all, but in the non-payment of sickness benefit and widow's benefit.

Lost output due to the effects of smoking on a worker is often quoted as a social cost of smoking – but if workers are being paid on an output or time basis, then any lost output will be reflected in a lower wage packet, i.e. it is a cost that will be foreseen by them and be borne by them, and is thus not a social cost. For many workers this is not the case though, and there is in fact a cost to the state arising from their inability to work, through the payment of sickness benefit etc.

Increasingly in the United States and Europe, the financial costs imposed by smokers on non-smokers are being internalised (Chollat-Traquet, 1996). Differential mortality rates for smokers and non-smokers have led to actuarial studies demonstrating a fiscal basis for different risk ratings for life insurance. All life assurance companies in the United States offer discounts to non-smokers and thus the differential cost of life assurance is now borne by smokers themselves. In addition, some countries offer non-smokers discounts for health insurance and property insurance, not just to individuals but to companies. This and other considerations could mean that, all things being equal, employers will favour hiring non-smokers. The outcome of all of these developments is that the costs of smoking that were once borne by third parties are now borne by smokers themselves.

These though are costs borne by others through the existence of non-differential premiums for private insurance. The insurance principle to taxation is still broadly applicable where costs are imposed by smokers on the exchequer. However, apart from the broad issue discussed above, there is the issue of measuring precisely what these net costs are and thereby setting the 'correct' level of special tax that will recoup them for the state. It is possible that the existing tax rates in some EU countries in particular are at levels way above those required to recoup such costs. Whatever the true situation, it is difficult indeed to explain the variation in the rates of special taxes on tobacco in different countries (see later) in terms of varying exchequer costs.

Lack of Information

As mentioned, for a cost to be included in the cost-benefit calculation of a smoker, the cost must be foreseen and be borne by the smoker. So far costs that will quite possibly be foreseen but will not be borne by the smoker have been discussed. There remains the possibility of a cost which, although it will be borne by the smoker eventually, does not enter the cost-benefit decision at the purchase stage. An illustration would be if a smoker bought a packet of cigarettes unaware of the health risks of such cigarettes and was later afflicted with cancer. At the time of purchase, known costs and benefits are not accurately reflecting true costs and benefits and a 'wrong' decision is being made. Thus, in principle, a significant cost is being overlooked, if (i) there was a causal link between smoking and ill health, and (ii) smokers did not know about such a relationship. This, of course, is the basis of many of the lawsuits in the United States.

Nowadays, information about the ill health resulting from smoking is almost impossible to avoid and tobacco products in many countries are now forced to carry health warnings, and extensive anti-smoking advertising and educational campaigns are commonplace. The emphasis recently has been on providing information and protection for young people, especially as around 1 per cent of those aged 11 years in the EU are already smoking, a figure rising to as high as 30 per cent for those aged 15 years. The early age of starting smoking, combined with the addictive nature of smoking, suggests that particularly active measures must be taken to 'protect' younger age groups from persuasive advertising and promotion of a product the costs of consumption of which they are too young to assess and comprehend until it is too late. Particularly strong measures have been adopted in 1997 in the United States. For example, cigarette vending machines are to be restricted to places where those under 18 never go, cigarette billboards are to be banned from within 300 metres of schools and cigarette advertisements are to have no colour (leaving them only the aptly named 'tombstone' format of black words on white paper), except in magazines which have few young readers or in places where youngsters never go (*Economist*, 1997).

Few economists would question this public information function of the state, especially in relation to a product which is addictive and whose adverse effects are so long-term in nature. However, if lack of information is the central problem, there is clearly little role for taxation. It could be argued of course that young people will disregard all information provided, but that given their relatively low incomes they are price sensitive and that the best way to 'protect them from themselves' is by raising the price of cigarettes so high, through taxation, that they simply will not be able to afford to purchase them until they have reached an age when they can make a more informed decision. This brings us into the domain of paternalism, which we consider next.

Paternalism

It is possible to go outside the economist's framework and decide that, despite the fact that each individual, including young people, might possess all relevant information, and that present levels of taxation are covering all possible costs on the exchequer imposed by smokers, the 'correct' decision is still not being made and that the tax instrument, through raising prices, must be used to bring it about. This philosophy raises some well-known problems such as: What is the 'correct' decision? Who decides what it is? Why stop at smoking? These of course are the problems associated with the philosophy of paternalism, which is implicitly invoked by any decision to proceed despite the arguments that have been put forward. It may be claimed, as mentioned earlier, that the possibility of habitual use provides a rationale for intervention of this sort. However, if smokers are aware of the possibility and costs of habitual use, these too will be internalised in their decision. Doubtless this will not satisfy many in the anti-smoking lobby – but, as will be argued later, in the case of habitual use, raising price, through increasing taxation, is both the least effective and most unfair way of coping with the problem for those who already have become habitual users.

Taxation, Demand and Income Distribution

Smoking and Price

It is an odd position to adopt, that in order to discourage younger people from smoking, the price of the product must be raised by imposing higher taxes, thereby penalising all habitual smokers, the nature of whose habit makes it extremely difficult for them to cease consumption in response to the tax hike. This raises the issue of smoking and price and the effect of the latter on the former.

According to the genetic hypothesis, certain factors in a person's make-up may determine a person's psyche and, in turn, the likelihood that they will smoke. In other words, some people may have an underlying tendency to habitual usage of certain substances. If this is true, then it is possible that banning smoking or raising the price of cigarettes, through increased taxation, may simply have the effect of causing smokers to switch to some other such habit, especially the consumption of relatively lower-priced alcohol or soft drugs. Thus the motivations to smoke are varied and complex and it may be that price simply is not a key factor in the decision whether or not to smoke.

It is well known that, at least for small price changes, the demand for tobacco products is inelastic, which means that the percentage fall in quantity demanded resulting from a price rise will be less than the percentage rise. In other words, demand tends to be unresponsive to price – meaning that if a reduction in tobacco consumption is desired, as opposed to simply recouping exchequer costs, then altering the price may not be an effective way of doing it. Indeed, often tax is imposed on these products by governments precisely for this reason, namely that if the tax is increased tax revenue will increase. Habitual use is simply an extreme form of non-price sensitivity – an habitual user will pay large sums to get what he/she wants and as Shoup says: 'If...we put aside the problem of negative externalities, there seems to be no acceptable principle that justifies higher taxation of addicts' (Shoup, 1983, p.263). Payment of such a tax may not be voluntary and, moreover, to maintain expenditure on tobacco, the habitual user will have to spend less on something else, which for the poor will mean less consumption of necessities – which may be unjustifiable on equity grounds (see later).

Demand being inelastic does not of course mean that there will be no fall in demand following a tax-induced price increase: a 10 per cent increase in price for example is likely to lead to a 4 to 6 per cent decline in consumption, *ceteris paribus*. Everything else in the real world, though, is not equal. At the same time as prices might be increased, incomes may be increasing, thereby providing a countervailing force pushing up demand for smoking. It is also possible that if taxes go too high, people may switch from the consumption of legally-sold tobacco to the illicit tobacco trade, with no net reduction in overall smoking, the main effects being a loss of tax revenue to governments and the encouragement of smuggling and illegal selling of tobacco products.

Cross-border and Duty-free Purchasing, and Smuggling

There are three ways an individual can continue to smoke manufactured tobacco and avoid paying the special taxes imposed in his/her place of residence. Under the Single European Act of the EU, residents in one member state can effectively purchase unlimited amounts of tobacco, provided it is for personal use, duty paid in another member state. As the duty paid varies very substantially across EU member states (see below), this clearly provides a legitimate way for someone to avoid paying the high tobacco tax in his/her country. There is considerable evidence of such activity in the EU, especially in border areas, something that, in the absence of EU agreed harmonisation of rates, has prompted market-driven alignment of duty rates in neighbouring member states.

Those travelling across EU boundaries, by air or sea, do not have to pay any duty at all on a fixed quantity of tobacco purchases, thanks to the existence of duty-free shopping. The higher the special tax rates, the more incentive there is to purchase duty-free tobacco. An extension of duty-free shopping beyond the introduction of the single market in 1992, to June 1999, was provided for in the VAT Systems Directive (91/680/EC) and the Excise Directive (92/12/EC). The issue of a further extension, at least for some countries, is still a possibility. The rationale for introducing duty-free purchases is hard to find, but now that a whole duty-free business and an associated rent-seeking lobby have grown up in the interim, its removal will inevitably be hotly contested. Whatever the rationale for imposing special taxes on tobacco, it is hard to see why that rationale would not apply when people are purchasing tobacco as part of a holiday or business trip abroad. Its existence simply undermines the suggested rationale for the existence of the special taxes, adds to the inequitable nature of the taxes, as lower income people would have less opportunity to purchase duty-free tobacco, and lessens the case for a clamp down on the illegal sale of tobacco across the EU.

As with duty-free purchasing, the incentive to sell and buy illegally supplied tobacco is a function of the level of the special taxes that apply. As will be seen later, these levels are exceptionally high in some European countries. Smuggling of tobacco has become big business. Tobacco duty in the EU is only payable at the final destination of the cargo, implying that it can be bought duty-free in another EU state or in a non-EU state, and then sold, if undetected crossing borders, duty-free in the streets or through illegal outlets. Because of the high duty levels that apply, huge profits can be realised through this illegal activity, which for organised crime must be considered a low-risk venture. There are a number of reasons for the low risk. The product is legal and around 40 per cent of EU citizens consume it; people are prepared to purchase contraband because of the huge saving to themselves and because of the perception, perhaps, that since you can buy tobacco duty free at an airport or on a boat, it cannot be that 'illegal'; the scale of the operation, the large number of people involved in the sale of contraband and the relatively low penalties make a major crackdown on the trade unlikely. Smuggling of tobacco, of course, is not just an EU phenomenon but is worldwide (Nicholson, 1994).

All of these outcomes arise from the high level of tobacco duty, and to a lesser extent from the differential tax rates applying in neighbouring countries. They do not necessarily provide a case against high special taxes on tobacco, but they certainly act as a major constraint on the operation of a high tobacco tax policy in any country.

Income Distribution

The biggest constraint on the use of high special taxes on tobacco in some people's opinion arises from the adverse distributional consequences that such a policy entails. It is well known that taxes on tobacco are among the most regressive forms of taxation available to a government. This is because the poor spend a higher proportion of their income on tobacco, and thus any taxation-induced price rise hits them harder than other groups.

Data for the United Kingdom show that expenditure on tobacco products as a proportion of expenditure on all commodities comes to 6 per cent for the poorest 10 per cent of households, but less than 2.5 per cent for the richest 10 per cent of households. Looking at it differently, professionals smoke the least (14 per cent), while unskilled manual workers smoke the most (42 per cent of them smoke). As many as 46 per cent of those unemployed smoke (Nicholson, 1994). This is an EU-wide phenomenon, as evidenced by the following: 'A notable trend is the higher prevalence of smoking in lower socioeconomic groups as better educated, better paid and more health conscious individuals increasingly avoid smoking. This has very important socioeconomic implications. Persons on lower incomes spend a disproportionate amount on tobacco as, due to its addictive properties, it often takes priority over other household expenditure. Expenditure on other items important to health, such as food and housing, suffers accordingly' (Commission of the European Communities, 1996, p.3). Why then, it may be asked, is the European Commission favouring a policy of increases in tobacco tax above the rate of inflation for the foreseeable future?

Contrasts with other forms of taxation highlight the regressivity of tobacco tax. It is quite possible for some of the poorest households in the high-tax countries such as Denmark, Ireland and the United Kingdom to pay as much in tobacco taxes as they do in VAT on all other products, and more than they do in pay-related social insurance and income tax combined. It could be argued of course that examining one particular tax is not relevant because it is the regressivity or otherwise of the overall tax system that counts, and that in particular a progressive income tax will balance out any anomalies on the tobacco side. However, what the poor gain from the progressivity of the income tax system they may lose, many times over, on the excise front. Such effects lessen considerably the supposed redistributional impact of the state welfare system.

The above paragraphs dealt with the issue of vertical equity, the principle being that the higher your income, the higher should be the percentage of your income that is paid in tax. There remains a less well-documented issue – that of horizontal equity – involving the principle that people on similar incomes and in similar circumstances should pay the same tax. That this principle is very seriously violated in the case of tobacco can be seen by examining the different taxes paid by people on similar income levels, assuming different levels of consumption of cigarettes. Take two people each on the average industrial wage, of whom one does not smoke and the other smokes 40 cigarettes a day: the non-smoker clearly would pay nothing in excise duties whereas the smoker could pay as high as 8 per cent of his/her total income in such taxes.

The inequity of tobacco taxes is seen at its clearest when politicians claim that six or seven out of ten people are in favour of increasing taxes on tobacco. This is not surprising: six or seven out of ten people in the EU do not smoke and therefore do not pay tobacco tax. Increasing tobacco tax therefore is an 'ideal' tax for them: if it is increased the burden will not fall on them. It could of course be argued that, as seen earlier, the tax on tobacco is simply a premium to pay for the costs that smokers impose on the exchequer. As such, the issue of equity does not arise at all, as smokers are not being taxed to fund general expenditure but simply expenditure that arises directly as a result of their consumption. As noted earlier, though, it is not clear at all that over, say, 30 years, smokers do impose a significant net cost on the exchequer: there may even be a net saving. Moreover, given the addictive nature of tobacco consumption and the fact that the better educated and higher income persons are best able to cope with quitting the habit, is it equitable to make lower-income smokers effectively pay for their health care in full, through the imposition of high excise taxes on the consumption of tobacco? The real reason for special taxes on tobacco appears to lie elsewhere: the revenue raising potential of such taxes.

The Structure and Level of Taxation and EU Harmonisation

At present three principal forms of taxation are levied on tobacco products in the member states of the EU – value added tax, a fixed specific excise duty and a variable *ad valorem* excise duty. It is only the last two that are special to tobacco, as VAT is applied to most consumer goods and services.

One thing that is evident from Table 2.1 is the enormous variation in price across the EU of the most popular category of cigarette. As can be seen, it varies from a high of 181 Ecu in Denmark to a low of 36 Ecu in Spain. These differences are largely explained by the different tax levels applying in each country, but not wholly so. Column 2 of Table 2.1 outlines the non-tax price of the most popular brand and as may be seen this varies from 38 Ecu in Ireland and the UK to 12 Ecu in Portugal and Spain: these differences could be explained by three factors: variation by country in the quality (and therefore cost) of the most popular brand, variation in ex-factory price for the same cigarette quality, and variation in retailers' margin. These differences are not the concern of this paper though they are relevant to the tax issue where the taxes are *ad valorem*, as is the case with VAT and the *ad valorem* tobacco duty. The lower the non-tax price, the lower will these taxes be in absolute terms, even when the rates are the same across countries.

Table 2.1 Cigarette Prices and Taxes in EU Countries, 1994

Country	Current most popular price category per 1,000 cigarettes in Ecu	Net of tax price	Total tax yield, in Ecu per 1,000 cigarettes	Specific excise in Ecu
Belgium	111	28	83	9
Denmark	181	28	153	79
France	10	42	67	84
Germany	128	36	92	44
Greece	82	23	59	3
Ireland	152	38	114	62
Italy	78	21	57	3
Luxembourg	79	25	54	3
Netherlands	103	29	74	37
Portugal	66	12	54	7
Spain	36	12	24	2
United Kingdom	161	38	123	67

As may be seen in Table 2.1, the total tax yield varies from 24 Ecu in Spain to 153 Ecu in Denmark, and this is mostly explained by the different specific excise duty (2 Ecu in Spain and 79 Ecu in Denmark). There is a huge variation in the specific excise rates across member states, and there has been almost no progress in harmonising these rates over the last twenty-five years, despite efforts to do so. Failing this, the EU has tried to harmonise the structure of cigarette taxation, again with very limited success.

The first two columns of Table 2.2 illustrate that the reliance on *ad valorem* and specific excise duties varies hugely by member state. However, looking at Column 3 it can be seen that when the two taxes are taken together, they vary relatively little when expressed as a proportion of the selling price: from a low of 55 per cent in Spain to a high of 67 per cent in Portugal. It is on this ratio that there has been some progress in the EU: it has been agreed that this ratio should not fall below 57 per cent, Spain having been given an extension beyond 1994 to achieve this figure. However, there has been almost no progress on the split of this ratio between specific and *ad valorem* elements and the huge variation across member states remains. It was agreed that the specific tax as a proportion of the total tax take on tobacco should fall within a set range (see last column of Table 2.2), but this range was set at such a broad level, between 5 and 55 per cent, it is almost meaningless. As may be seen all countries fall (just) within this range, but no progress has been made in the last twenty-five years in narrowing the permitted range.

Table 2.2 Cigarette Taxes in EU Countries, 1994

Country	*Ad valorem* excise as % of retail selling price	Specific excise as % of retail selling price	Sum of first two columns	Specific excise as % of total taxation (excise plus VAT)
Belgium	50	8	58	10
Denmark	21	43	64	51
France	55	4	59	6
Germany	25	34	59	47
Greece	53	3	56	5
Ireland	17	41	58	55
Italy	53	4	57	5
Luxembourg	54	4	58	5
Netherlands	21	36	57	50
Portugal	56	11	67	14
Spain	49	6	55	9
United Kingdom	20	42	62	54

The issues that the structure of tobacco tax between *ad valorem* and specific elements raises were examined in detail by Kay and Keen (1982) over 15 years ago and most of what they wrote then is still relevant given that almost no change has been effected in the intervening years in the structure of tobacco tax. Their conclusions were clear. The EU should attempt to harmonise the *ad valorem* tax rate (i.e. Column 2 in Table 2.2) but given that each country relies to a different extent for tax revenue purposes on tobacco tax the EU should let the specific tax element vary across countries. The reason Kay and King favoured the harmonisation of the *ad valorem* rates is that it is this aspect of tobacco taxation, they argue, that affects market structure and conduct in the tobacco trade and that it is desirable to harmonise these aspects of the industry across member states in order to ensure a single market. The issue why there should be an *ad valorem* element at all, though, was not addressed. However, if the view is taken that it is appropriate to tax tobacco because of its detrimental effects on health, then it would appear that specific excises are more appropriate given that it is the quantity rather than the value of the product that matters most from a health point of view.

Conclusion

This paper has addressed a number of issues. The rationale for special taxes on tobacco was considered and it was illustrated that the case is not nearly as clear-cut as is sometimes assumed. There are clearly informational problems in relation to smoking, given the long-term nature of some of the costs and the addictive nature of the product. These, however, do not suggest any role for taxation, but point to better information on packaging, restrictions on advertising and promotion, and educational programmes, in particular for young people. If people still choose to smoke given these measures, then their free choice to do so must be recognised and not penalised through special taxation measures. If it is felt that taxation, and therefore higher prices, discourage young people, because of their limited incomes and the fact that they are not yet addicted to the product, a more sensible approach would be to ban altogether the sale of cigarettes to those under a certain age and not add further to the financial problems of those already addicted to the product, mostly people on lower incomes.

The fact that smoking confers costs on non-smokers was also considered. The major such cost are costs to the exchequer in terms of increased health bills and disability benefits, but because smokers die younger these must be offset by reduced pension and other payments by the state. Hence, no precise measure of the exchequer cost of smoking, if any, appears to be accepted. The main rationale in practice for the special taxes appears to be to raise revenue. One cost, though, that is real and has caused considerable controversy, is the cost of passive smoking: not just the increased risk of cancer from passive smoking, but the general unpleasantness of the atmosphere created for non-smokers by the presence of smokers, especially in a confined space. There have been several legal and other measures introduced to reduce the level of such costs to non-smokers, but here again there is no real role for taxation measures.

The real reason for special taxes on tobacco in most countries appears to be the fact that they provide a relatively easy source of tax revenue. Demand for the product is relatively inelastic and politically they appear to be a popular tax. Herein lies the first real problem with tobacco taxes as a revenue-raising device: they are paid for entirely by smokers, thereby allowing non-smokers to avoid completely paying any of these taxes. This is hugely inequitable between smokers and non-smokers, and also across income groups, as those who smoke come predominantly from the lower income classes. Another problem with relying on tobacco taxes as a revenue source is that, if set at too high a level, they may lead to cross-border purchasing, legal and illegal. It is the latter that is now of particular concern, especially in Europe.

Apart from the level of the taxes, the chapter concluded with some discussion about the structure of tobacco taxes in the EU. It was seen that not only is there huge variation in the rates of specific taxes on tobacco, but that there is equally large variation in the structure of tobacco taxes as between specific and *ad valorem* rates. Any country seeking to reform its tobacco taxation needs to take account of the complex range of issues outlined above.

References and Further Reading

Atkinson, A., and J. Townsend, 'Economic Aspects of Reduced Smoking', *Lancet*, Vol.3, 1977.

Chollat-Traquet, C., *Evaluating Tobacco Control Activities: Experiences and Guiding Principles*, World Health Organisation, Geneva, 1996.

Commission of the European Communities, *Communication from the Commission to the Council and the European Parliament* (Com. 96, 609 final), Brussels, 18 December, 1996.

Council of the European Communities, 'Council Directive 95/59/EC', *Official Journal of the European Communities*, 6 December, 1995.

Economist Newspaper, 'Tobacco Outclassed', *Economist*, London, 15 February, 1997.

Fritschler, A., and J. Hoefler, *Smoking and Politics* (fifth edition), Prentice Hall, New Jersey, 1996.

Kay, J., and M. Keen, *The Structure of Tobacco Taxes in the European Community* (Report Series No. 1), Institute for Fiscal Studies, London, 1982.

Nicholson, M., *Smugglers' Charter*, Forest, London, 1994.

O'Hagan, J., 'The Proposal for Upward Alignment of Tobacco Taxes in the European Community: A Critique', *British Tax Review*, No. 8, 1988.

Shoup, C., 'Current Trends in Excise Taxation', in ed. S. Cnossen, *Comparative Tax Studies*, North Holland, Amsterdam, 1983.

CHAPTER 3

THE CARBON TAX: A TAX WHOSE TIME HAS COME?

Stephen Smith*

Introduction

An issue of rising importance in tax policy is the possible use of taxation to promote a cleaner environment. Taxes might be designed in such a way that, as well as raising revenues, they also act to discourage activities which pollute or otherwise damage the environment. In many countries there have been both official and independent reports and studies investigating whether the fiscal system could be modified to operate with this dual role. A major study by the OECD (1993) reviewed the advantages and disadvantages of environmental taxation, and concluded that, in a number of areas of environmental policy, taxes could make a positive contribution.

One attractive property of taxes is that – in comparison with certain forms of direct 'command-and-control' environmental regulation – they offer greater flexibility in how pollution abatement is achieved, and may thus be able to achieve a cleaner environment at lower economic cost. In addition to this 'static' efficiency gain from the use of environmental taxes there is also a potential 'dynamic' efficiency gain, in that they may stimulate more innovation in pollution abatement technologies. Thirdly, they raise revenues, permitting reforms to the tax structure in which existing taxes on labour and capital could be reduced. Some have argued that such tax reforms might offer a 'double dividend', in terms of both environmental gains and lower economic costs from revenue-raising, although the economic theory underpinning this claim is controversial (Goulder, 1995).

One of the environmental problems which is, in principle, most amenable to the 'eco-tax' approach is the problem of global climate

*Professor of Economics, University College, London.

change ('global warming'). In very broad terms, this problem is arising as a result of the rapid growth in emissions of 'greenhouse gases' into the atmosphere; scientists believe that the accumulation of these gases in the global atmosphere will lead to substantial (though probably quite unpredictable) climate changes, as they increase the proportion of the sun's radiation which is trapped by earth's atmosphere (the same phenomenon that warms a domestic greenhouse). Greenhouse gases are emitted as a result of a number of different human activities, but in quantitative terms the most important man-made contribution to the greenhouse effect is the emission of carbon dioxide from the use of fossil-fuel energy. Coal, gas and oil contain carbon, and combustion of these fuels releases this carbon into the atmosphere as carbon dioxide.

Reducing emissions of carbon dioxide sufficiently to halt the rise in atmospheric carbon dioxide concentrations would require far-reaching changes in patterns of energy use, and, more fundamentally, in patterns of human activity. The 'baseline' trend in carbon dioxide emissions is strongly upwards, reflecting rapid industrialisation in many developing countries, and spiralling energy use in transport throughout the world. Achieving the major changes that would be needed in patterns of production and consumption activities in order to halt the rise in global emissions will require both improvements in energy efficiency (the amounts of energy used per unit of production, for example), and a shift in individual consumption away from energy and products which are energy-intensive in production. A range of policy instruments can be applied, but 'pricing' measures such as higher taxes on energy have particular advantages, given that the use of fossil fuels so comprehensively pervades the whole range of human production and consumption activities. Put bluntly, reliance on the conventional instruments of environmental policy alone, such as direct regulation of emissions or technologies, financial incentives to develop or adopt new technologies, and various forms of encouragement and exhortation, runs the risk of being wholly inadequate to the scale of the changes needed in carbon dioxide emissions. Alternatively, if such instruments are to be used to achieve changes in fossil fuel use on the scale required, they would require such extensive regulatory intervention into the detailed workings of the economy that the efficient working of the market economy could be undermined.

To date, however, few countries have made much use of tax measures as part of their policies to reduce carbon dioxide emissions. Many have preferred to stick with more conventional instruments of environmental policy, for a range of reasons. The principal exceptions are the Scandinavian countries which have introduced tax measures specifically directed at carbon dioxide emissions. These 'carbon taxes' vary in terms of tax rates and the precise detail of the tax base, but the basic structure of the tax is similar in each case. They tax carbon dioxide emissions indirectly, by taxing the carbon content of individual fuels, a tax base which is a close proxy for the carbon dioxide which will be emitted when the fuels are used. A similar 'carbon/energy tax' was proposed by the European Commission in 1991, although it met with strong opposition from some member states, and has not been implemented.

This chapter considers the issues surrounding the possible design and use of a 'carbon tax' to reduce carbon dioxide emissions. It is in three main sections. The first discusses the optimal control of carbon dioxide emissions, and the required level of a carbon tax; the second considers the design and implementation of a carbon tax; and the third reviews possible objections and obstacles to the use of carbon taxation.

The Efficient Carbon Tax

This section begins with the logical first step in the design of a carbon tax – identifying the goal to be achieved through its use. What reduction in carbon dioxide emissions should we aim to achieve? From the answer to this first question, we may then move to a second question: what rate of carbon tax should accordingly be set?

Economists would naturally tend to think of global warming policy in terms of a conceptual framework which draws together the various relevant costs and benefits.

On the one hand, we need to weigh up the 'damage' costs of global warming, in terms of the consequences of higher global temperatures, increased climatic volatility, etc. How large would these costs be if global warming were to be allowed to continue unchecked, and by how much would these costs be reduced if carbon dioxide emissions were to be reduced by various given percentages?

On the other hand, we need to assess the 'abatement' costs of controlling the carbon dioxide emissions that are the source of the problem; these may include higher production costs of more energy-efficient equipment, reductions in household living standards if certain energy-using activities such as travel and tourism have to be curtailed, a greater risk of catastrophic accidents if we switch away from fossil fuels towards nuclear power, etc.

The issue of emissions control is not, of course, a simple all-or-nothing choice, but involves a range of possible degrees of stringency. If we decide to do anything at all about global warming, how much should we do? The economist's approach would be to look at this question in terms of the relationship between 'marginal' costs and benefits, in other words, the costs and benefits of each successive tightening of the policy. The conclusion (given certain conditions about the relationship between marginal costs and benefits and the level of abatement) would then be that policy should be tightened (i.e. emissions reduced) up until the point where an extra unit of emissions reduction is more costly than the benefits it yields. So long as all relevant costs and benefits are included in the analysis, this would be the optimal reduction in carbon dioxide emissions.

Although it is relatively straightforward to set out this conceptual framework, it is much harder to operationalise it in practice. Estimating the benefits from abatement, in particular, is far from easy. The scientific and environmental issues surrounding the carbon tax debate have been extensively researched, and a major effort by the Intergovernmental Panel on Climate Change (IPCC) has provided a consensus analysis which has been broadly accepted by governments as the basis for policy intervention. Despite all this work, enormous uncertainty still surrounds both the magnitude and timing of the various climatic effects (on global temperatures, climatic volatility, and the climate of particular regions). There is, likewise, uncertainty about the consequent economic costs and risks involved. Even quite basic questions about the efficient policy towards global warming remain unclear, such as whether, if global warming takes place, the necessary adaptations (such as building sea walls to combat sea level rise, and moving activities to reflect the change in climate patterns) might actually prove much cheaper than the costly abatement expenditures that would be needed to reduce greenhouse gas emissions.

However, despite the great uncertainty about the basic facts and forecasts of global warming and its consequences, it may not be possible to postpone policy action until conclusive evidence has been obtained, without in the meantime risking irreversible changes in climate and in the global environment. Although it could turn out that gradual adaptation of the pattern of economic activity and human settlement might be far cheaper than prevention, the risk of catastrophic and irreversible climatic effects would justify some level of precautionary policy to restrict greenhouse gas emissions. Where policy measures can be taken which have low cost (including any 'no-regrets' measures), immediate action would avoid the risk of irreversible damage, whilst leaving the full range of policy options open, should future studies make major revisions to the scientific and economic assessments of the risks of global warming. This, then, would imply that some policy action should be taken now, if for no other reason than as an insurance policy against the eventuality that the most pessimistic forecasts of global warming turn out to be right.

Timing

The design of policy measures to control carbon dioxide emissions involves an added complexity not present in many other pollution control problems, which is that both the environmental effects of carbon dioxide emissions and the impact of policy measures to control emissions are spread out over time. Determining the optimal level of emissions control is thus not simply a matter of comparing marginal costs and benefits of abatement in a single period. Instead the policy problem is one of dynamic optimisation, to determine the optimal time profile of emissions abatement. Global warming is a function of the accumulated stock of CO_2 and other greenhouse gases in the atmosphere. Since the rate of decay of any addition to the stock of atmospheric CO_2 is slow, current emissions have an effect which extends into many future periods. Likewise, policy measures taken now potentially confer benefits on future generations as well as the current one. Given the length of the time horizon involved, balancing the interests of present and future generations in climate change policy raises unusually difficult philosophical issues (Broome, 1992) concerning the treatment of large gains and losses in the distant future, which conventional discount rates could render of negligible current value.

Also there is likely to be a substantial adjustment lag to climate change policy, since the level of energy use in the economy will be partly governed by the speed at which the existing capital stock is replaced. The scope for changing the energy intensity of production using existing capital equipment is likely to be much lower than when existing machinery is being replaced. As Ingham, Maw and Ulph (1990) show, the average life of plant and machinery may be of the order of 15 years. Regulations or tax incentives requiring immediate compliance with more stringent CO_2 emissions limits may thus have heavy costs, if they require immediate replacement of relatively new capital equipment, or costly retrofitting of modifications which could be accomplished more cheaply when the capital stock was renewed. Ideally, therefore, policies to control carbon dioxide emissions should be introduced gradually rather than abruptly, so as to give energy users sufficient time to adapt in the most efficient way, and they should be pre-announced, for the same reason.

The Need for Coordinated Action

To be effective, action to combat climate change has to be taken by all countries (or, at least, a large part of the world economy), acting in concert. Since global warming is a function of global emissions of greenhouse gases, the impact on global warming of national policy measures taken by any individual country acting alone will be negligible, since they can at best reduce that country's carbon dioxide emissions, and the emissions of any individual country (other perhaps than the United States, China and the former Soviet Union) constitute a small percentage of the global total.

International discussions have led to agreement amongst a large number of countries on the Global Convention on Climate Change, signed at Rio in 1992. This commits developed countries to taking the measures necessary to return their emissions of greenhouse gases to 1990 levels by the year 2000. Achievement of this target alone will not, of course, be sufficient. Even if emissions are cut back to 1990 levels by the turn of the century, continuing (and increasingly stringent) restraint will be required, if economic growth is not to lead to a resumption in the upward trend in emissions.

The international agreements on climate change have, to date, set targets for emissions levels for the countries signing the agreement, but have not specified the policy measures which should be taken in order to meet these emissions levels. This might be argued to be a sensible approach. Individual countries may be in a better position to judge the measures needed to meet their particular national target, and they may have a much better awareness of the political constraints on policy, so that they can avoid measures which would be liable to face excessive domestic opposition. However, it does have a drawback which needs to be noted. This is that individual countries may not necessarily act in the interests of the global community in their domestic implementation of an international agreement on climate change policy. Since the impact of any individual country's emission reductions on the global climate is small, the benefit to the country itself from its *own* domestic carbon dioxide control policy will generally also be small. The country may gain significantly from the coordinated international policy, but may perceive its own actions as involving large domestic costs (of abatement measures, etc.) but negligible domestic benefit. In these circumstances, there is an incentive for the country to free ride, if it can, on the international agreement, by taking no action itself to control carbon dioxide emissions, but still hoping to benefit from the actions taken by other countries. Such a strategy is, of course, more attractive if other signatories to the global agreement cannot see when free riding is taking place.

It is at least arguable that an international agreement which specifies targets, but which does not specify the policy measures which should be taken to meet these targets, will be particularly prone to free riding by individual signatories. Countries face an emissions target for a date in the future, and their compliance with the target can only be fully judged when the future date is reached. They may fail to meet the target despite trying to do so, if their policy was knocked off-course by unexpected events; alternatively, they may meet the target even without trying, if other factors reduce their emissions over the period[1]. Achieving the target, *ex post*, is therefore a poor indicator of the *ex ante* adequacy of the measures taken. Compliance monitoring may therefore be difficult. At the same time, countries face considerable temptation to put little effort into meeting the targets. If the date is sufficiently far in the future, the current generation of politicians may expect to have retired, and, even if they expect to be still in office, they may place higher weight on the immediate domestic opposition to the costs of abatement policies than on the costs of international disapproval if they do not meet their target. In these circumstances, where compliance is costly and non-compliance cannot easily be observed by other signatories to the agreement, the risk that countries will try to free ride on the actions of others is high.

By contrast, an international agreement which specifies the measures to be taken may have the attraction that compliance with the agreement can be readily verified. This will be particularly true where the policy measures required are of a straightforward, transparent, and non-discretionary form. A carbon tax has these characteristics, and it may be relatively straightforward for countries to observe whether or not all of the signatories to an international agreement on carbon taxation have indeed

---

[1]The United Kingdom finds itself in this position in relation to global climate change policies, since the Thatcher Government's policies to reduce reliance on electricity generated from coal and to liberalise the electricity market, introduced for reasons unrelated to environmental policy, have had the fortuitous effect of reducing the United Kingdom's carbon dioxide emissions.

introduced a tax in compliance with the terms of the agreement. Where they can do this, the chance is increased that individual countries will comply with the agreement.

Tax Rates

Control of carbon dioxide emissions is liable to require high tax rates, because energy demand tends to be relatively unresponsive to price, and because large behavioural adjustments may be required. Using the OECD 'GREEN' model, Burniaux *et al* (1991) estimate that a carbon tax averaging $215 per tonne of carbon across all countries ($308 per tonne in the OECD countries) would be needed to keep aggregate global emissions at 1990 levels over the period until the year 2020. To give some indication of the scale of this tax, $215 per tonne of carbon would be equivalent to roughly $25 per barrel of oil.

To achieve longer-term targets for emissions reduction or for stabilisation of atmospheric concentrations of carbon dioxide, more substantial carbon taxes would be required, although their level will depend critically on the prices at which new sources of non-fossil fuels eventually become available. Thus, for example, Manne and Richels (1991) estimate that in order to reduce carbon dioxide emissions by the United States to a long run level 20 per cent below current emissions, a long-run carbon tax of $250 per tonne of carbon would be needed; over the first few decades of the policy the tax would have to be even higher, peaking at $400 in the year 2020. These estimates perhaps lie towards the upper end of the likely range, and other studies have suggested that emissions might be more responsive to a carbon tax, and the required tax rates correspondingly lower than indicated by Manne and Richels. Cline (1992) summarises the results of four key studies in terms of the marginal carbon tax required to achieve a one percentage point reduction in year 2050 emissions below their level in the absence of policy intervention; the marginal tax rates range from $5.9 per tonne of carbon (Manne and Richels, 1991), $4.9 (Edmonds and Reilly, 1983), $2.8 (Nordhaus and Yohe, 1983), to $1.2 (Jorgenson and Wilcoxen, 1991).

These rates of carbon tax translate into substantial tax burdens for industrial and household users of energy, and correspondingly high tax revenues. As discussed in the following section, this raises important policy issues of industrial competitiveness and the distributional incidence of the tax. However, high rates of carbon tax also mean that the revenues from environmental tax measures might conceivably be sufficiently large to facilitate major tax reform elsewhere in the fiscal system, a feature of a carbon tax which has increased its attractions to some fiscal policy-makers. In Sweden, for example, carbon tax revenues were used to finance a tax reform package involving substantial cuts in Sweden's high income tax rates.

The Design of a Carbon Tax

From an environmental point of view, the purpose of a carbon tax is to discourage carbon dioxide emissions. The carbon tax, in effect, levies a charge for each kilogram of carbon dioxide emitted, and industry and households thus face an incentive to take actions to reduce emissions of carbon dioxide.

As noted above, the way in which the charge is levied on carbon dioxide emissions is indirect. There is no attempt to measure individual emissions of firms or households, and to levy the charge directly on emission measurements. Instead, the tax is levied on the carbon content of fuels, on the basis that this is a close proxy for the carbon dioxide emissions which result when the fuel is used.

Thus different fossil fuels bear a tax which reflects the carbon content of each fuel; fuels with a higher carbon content per unit of energy (such as coal, for example) bear a higher tax burden than fuels with a lower carbon content per unit of energy (such as natural gas). The price of each fuel is increased by the carbon tax, and the increase in price is higher for fuels with higher carbon content (and consequently higher emissions of carbon dioxide when used). By raising the price of energy relative to other industrial inputs, and relative to other household spending, the carbon tax acts to discourage energy use in general. Also, by raising the price of fuels differentially, in proportion to their carbon content, the tax encourages substitution away from high-carbon energy sources towards lower-carbon fuels. Both the reduction in overall energy use and the substitution towards lower-carbon fuels have the effect of reducing carbon dioxide emissions.

Using a tax on the carbon content of fuels to discourage carbon dioxide emissions depends for its effectiveness on a close linkage between the tax base (carbon content) and the emissions (of carbon dioxide). The key requirement for this is that the main scope for reducing carbon dioxide emissions should be through reductions in the carbon going into combustion processes, either through substitution to lower-carbon fuels, or through reductions in the amount of fuel used. There should be no significant ways in which the linkage between the taxed carbon content of fuels and the carbon dioxide emissions from combustion can be broken. If there are, then the tax may encourage costly (and hence socially-wasteful) actions which reduce tax liability without conferring any environmental benefits, and/or it may lead to abatement measures which result in tax savings being preferred over abatement measures which do not result in tax savings (even if the former abatement measures might be more efficient).

The latter danger would be present if, for example, emissions could be 'cleaned', so that fuels containing carbon can be used without leading to carbon dioxide emissions. In practice with carbon dioxide emissions this is not currently a problem, since there is, at present, no cost-effective method of removing carbon dioxide from combustion emissions through end-of-pipe 'cleaning' technologies. In this respect, the technologies for carbon dioxide emissions abatement are very different from those available for reducing sulphur dioxide emissions from combustion, and taxing the carbon content of fuels may be expected to contribute to efficient carbon dioxide emissions abatement, whilst taxing the sulphur content of fuels would be liable to encourage inefficient abatement choices for sulphur dioxide emissions, with insufficient use of the available effluent cleaning technologies such as flue gas desulphurisation.

Point of Imposition of a Carbon Tax

In the European countries (Sweden, Norway, Finland, the Netherlands and Denmark) which have actually introduced carbon taxes, these have taken the form of extended systems of fuel excises. Rates of tax are defined separately for each fuel, in terms of fuel quantities, and relative tax levels on different fuels are set so as to equate the implicit rate of tax per unit of carbon across fuels. This requirement is not, however, always observed; in Denmark and Norway, for example, some fuels are not subject to the carbon tax. Also, the level of tax can vary across types of energy user; in Sweden and the Netherlands, for example, much lower rates of tax apply to industrial energy users than to energy use by private households. However, the basic principle has been to extend fuel excises to cover all relevant fossil fuels, and to structure the relative tax rates on these fuels (for the carbon tax component of the excise) according to the relative carbon content.

Likewise, the carbon/energy tax proposed in 1991 by the European Commission would most probably have been implemented by adding to the rates of existing fuel excises, and extending the scope of fuel excises to cover fuels previously untaxed. This proposal was, in fact, not for a pure carbon tax, but for a two-part tax, reflecting both the carbon and energy content of fuel. Fossil fuels such as gas, coal and oil would have borne a tax comprising two components, one related to their carbon content, the other related to their energy content. Non-renewable forms of energy other than fossil fuels (mainly nuclear power) would have been subject to the energy-related part of the tax, but not the carbon component. The tax rates per tonne of carbon and per joule of energy would have been set so that on a barrel of oil the carbon and energy components would have been weighted 50:50.

As Pearson and Smith (1991) discuss, the logic behind introduction of the energy component to the proposed EC tax was unclear and poorly justified. It would have reduced the strength of the incentive to switch from high-carbon to low-carbon fuels compared with a tax of the same overall scale levied purely on carbon content. One possible explanation for including the energy element in the tax base was to avoid giving undue preference to nuclear power, or to avoid giving an undue competitive advantage to those member states (France, especially) which already generate a substantial proportion of their electricity from nuclear sources.

The EU carbon/energy tax would have been introduced in stages, starting at the equivalent of $3.00 per barrel of oil in 1993 and increasing by $1.00 per barrel annually, to $10.00 per barrel of oil in the year 2000. According to Commission estimates of the price effect of the tax at its final level, it would have increased the price of fuels used by industry by between 30 per cent (gas) and 60 per cent (coal). The price increases for domestic fuels and petrol would have been lower in percentage terms, because they already cost more per unit of energy (substantially more in the case of petrol) than industrial energy. Domestic fuel prices would have risen on average by some 15 per cent, and the price of petrol by only 6 per cent.

An alternative to implementing a carbon tax as an extension of existing fuel excises would be to levy a 'primary' carbon tax, levied on primary fuels (e.g. crude oil, coal, and gas) where they are mined, extracted or imported. Pearson and Smith (1991) discuss the merits of this approach compared with the extended excise approach, under which carbon tax would be levied on final fuel products (such as coke, anthracite, four star petrol) sold to industrial users or households. Although there are advantages and disadvantages associated with each form of carbon tax, the 'primary' carbon tax has two significant attractions. The first is that it would involve fewer taxable individuals than a 'final' tax, and no need for fiscal supervision of the energy chain beyond the first point; administrative costs would be expected to be low, and there would be scope for tight supervision to prevent evasion. The second is that it would be better able to tax the full contribution of individual fuels to carbon dioxide emissions, taking account of emissions during fuel processing as well as their carbon content when finally sold. A carbon tax in the form of excises on refined fuels has to make assumptions about carbon dioxide emissions during processing; these can vary greatly between different refining technologies, and using 'average' values for these processing emissions can be a poor approximation.

It will be noted that levying a 'primary' carbon tax at an earlier stage in the production chain would not necessarily imply that it would have different economic or environmental effects from an equivalent excise-type carbon tax, levied on refined fuel products. The incidence, for example, of the carbon tax on fuel consumers could be largely invariant to the stage at which tax is formally incident; some part of the burden of a primary carbon tax would be passed on in the prices of fuel products according to their carbon content, so that the prices of fuels purchased by industry and consumers would be much the same as if an equivalent excise-type carbon tax had been levied.

Similar issues arise in the choice of arrangements for the taxation of electricity under a carbon tax. Electricity can be taxed either by taxing the fuels used in electricity generation, or by exempting fuels used in electricity generation from the carbon tax and taxing sales of electricity at a rate reflecting average fuel inputs. Generally it will be more efficient to take the former route; taxing electricity at a rate reflecting average carbon emissions during generation provides no incentive for generators to use low-carbon fuels for generation. However, in considering how the European carbon tax might operate, the Commission was strongly tempted by the second approach. One reason is that if electricity is traded between member states, the excise approach makes it easier to attribute tax revenues to the country of final sale. Another possible reason might again be to avoid giving any fiscal advantage to electricity generated from nuclear power.

Obstacles and Objections

Carbon taxation has proved controversial, and, despite the growing political priority accorded to the issue of global climate change, most countries have so far fought shy of using taxation in pursuit of carbon dioxide emission reductions. There was initial resistance to the idea both from environmental policy-makers (fearing that the tax will not be able to deliver the necessary emissions reductions), and from fiscal policy makers (concerned that over-complication of the fiscal system will increase costs and reduce its effectiveness as a mechanism for raising public revenues). In the process of public debate some of these initial positions have perhaps softened, but carbon taxation – like 'eco-taxation' more generally – still has some way to go before being accepted as a routine element in fiscal and environmental policies.

The European Commission's 1991 proposals for a carbon tax foundered because of opposition from a number of directions. The United Kingdom opposed the proposals largely as a matter of principle – the then United Kingdom Government had begun to oppose all proposals for restrictions or limitations on domestic tax policy as a matter of 'sovereignty'. The negotiations also contained an element of free riding, in that some countries, especially Spain, sought to have the proposal modified so that they would be less affected by its provisions.

However, the public policy debate over the European proposal included two major areas of controversy over and above the issues of European competence and burden-sharing. First, would a carbon tax be liable to harm industrial competitiveness? Second, an argument prominent in the United Kingdom debate especially, would it be a burden on the poor? This section considers each of these in turn.

The 'Competitiveness' Argument

Concerns about the impact of carbon taxes on industry's costs and international competitiveness figured prominently in industry's response to the EC proposal. The Commission suggested various measures to try to limit the impact of the tax on industrial competitiveness, including exemptions for energy intensive industries and firms. For the same reason, it was decided at an early stage in the discussion that the European tax should not be introduced unless similar measures were taken by other major industrial countries. (The subsequent failure of the United States Government's proposals for a new energy tax, the 'BTU tax', effectively ended hopes that this might occur.) Likewise, in those countries such as Sweden which have introduced carbon taxes on a unilateral basis, application of the tax to industry has tended to be limited by competitiveness concerns; the Swedish carbon tax was modified soon after its introduction to reduce sharply the level of taxation on industrial energy use.

The impact on competition could, of course, be offset, on average, by exchange rate movements. A devaluation by a country imposing a carbon tax could offset the impact of the higher taxation on industrial competitiveness. Much the same effect could be achieved by returning the revenues from the tax to the industrial sector through reductions in other taxes (such as corporate profits or payroll taxes). In each case, the net impact of the carbon tax would be to worsen the relative position of carbon-intensive sectors, whilst improving the competitiveness of sectors of industry with low carbon intensity.

Indeed, it is worth noting that these mechanisms to offset the initial impact of a unilateral carbon tax on industrial competitiveness are not simply policy options which are available to governments, but are part of the automatic process of market adjustment. Indefinite disequilibrium in the balance of payments, in which all domestic industries are permanently disadvantaged in international competition by the imposition of a carbon tax, is not a feasible situation; at some point, economic adjustments would have to take place which would restore the balance of payments to equilibrium. These could either take the form of exchange rate changes, or changes in the domestic wage and price level, which would offset the impact of the carbon tax on the prices of domestically-produced goods in international trade. The result would be that the long-run impact of a carbon tax on competitiveness is predominantly an issue concerning the relative impact on different industries, rather than concerning overall industrial competitiveness; there would be sectoral 'gainers' and 'losers'.

In the long run, some contraction of carbon-intensive sectors might be one of the desired outcomes from policies to reduce carbon emissions. However, whilst other countries do not impose the tax, these sectors may be liable to contract too much, in the countries which do impose the tax, relative to the final desired equilibrium where all countries impose similar carbon taxes. Part of this contraction may represent 'carbon leakage' – international displacement of carbon-intensive production when a carbon tax is implemented without full international coordination – and this may impose adjustment costs and loss of profits, without any corresponding environmental gain.

One possible way of limiting this would be by exempting particular sectors in the tax structure. This was proposed for the six most energy-intensive sectors in the European Commission's 1991 plans for a carbon tax (Commission of the European Communities, 1991) and has been a feature in some of the countries which have unilaterally introduced carbon taxes, especially in Sweden following the recent revisions to the system.

An alternative approach which might reduce the extent of international displacement to countries which do not impose the carbon tax would be to levy compensatory border tax adjustments for the carbon contained in traded goods, although it is unclear whether such border tax adjustments would be compatible with the rules of the World Trade Organisation.

The 'Regressivity' Argument

A further issue, which has been especially prominent in the United Kingdom debate about the taxation of energy, concerns the distributional impact of the carbon tax burden, in the sense of the distribution of tax payments across households at different levels of income. In the United Kingdom, spending on household energy for heating and other domestic uses forms a considerable proportion of total spending by households in the poorest income groups, and household energy spending rises little with increasing income. Taxes on domestic energy spending are therefore sharply regressive, an observation which played a decisive role in opposition to the Conservative Government's plans to extend standard rate VAT to domestic energy.

The distributional incidence of a carbon tax would, however, be less regressive than taxes on domestic energy spending alone, since the carbon tax would also apply to motor fuels, which are not a large part of the spending of the poorest income groups, and also to industrial energy use (and, if passed on in prices, this component would be broadly proportionate to household non-energy spending). The estimates shown in Table 3.1, drawn from Smith (1992), suggest that the European carbon tax would have had a markedly greater regressive distributional impact in the United Kingdom than in Germany or Italy. Quite apart from this difference in the objective situation, it also appears clear that the issue of the distributional effects of the carbon/energy tax has had much greater political resonance in the United Kingdom than in other European countries, where the distributional aspect has been quite a minor part of the public debate.

In principle, even where the burden of carbon tax is found to be regressively distributed, it would be relatively straightforward to devise policy measures which could offset this effect. The fact that one element of the tax system is regressive matters much less than the overall distributional incidence of the tax system. Using the revenues from the carbon tax, it would be possible to make adjustments elsewhere (for example in tax-free allowances against income tax, and also in the rates of pensions and other social security benefits) so as to leave poorer households at least as well off, on average, as before the imposition of the carbon tax. Nevertheless, although this can be done, the experience of the United Kingdom in introducing VAT on household energy suggests that the political arguments over the impact on the poor and the elderly may still have considerable political resonance. Also, there may be genuine difficulties concerning the impact of high energy prices on households with particularly high energy needs, for whom compensation based on average energy consumption may prove inadequate.

Table 3.1 Carbon Tax Payments, by Decile and Quartile Groups of Gross Household Income, in the United Kingdom, Germany and Italy.

	UK ECU per annum	UK	Germany	Italy
		percentages of total household spending		
All households	161	1.19	0.86	0.78
Decile groups				
Poorest 10 per cent	94	2.58	1.06	0.81
Second 10 per cent	115	2.03	1.01	0.76
Third 10 per cent	128	1.74	0.96	0.81
Quartile groups				
Poorest 25 per cent	108	2.10	1.01	0.78
Second 25 per cent	145	1.45	0.94	0.81
Third 25 per cent	173	1.16	0.87	0.79
Richest 25 per cent	219	0.92	0.77	0.77

Source: Smith (1992)

Conclusion

Introduction of a carbon tax would be a major fiscal reform, harnessing the tax system in pursuit of the major changes in the level and pattern of energy use which will be needed if the world economy is to prevent an acceleration in global warming and climate change. Like other 'eco-tax' measures, it has the attraction that it allows the private sector flexibility in the choice of abatement measures. Compared with command-and-control regulatory policies, it may therefore reduce the economic costs of environmental protection. Unlike most other environmental taxes it would raise substantial revenues, both because the rate of tax necessary is likely to be high, and because all fossil fuels used in industry and by households would (in principle, at least) be taxed.

Determining the optimal level of control of carbon dioxide emissions requires a complicated calculation of costs and benefits, with the added complication that many of the benefits from reducing climate change would probably accrue to future generations, a long time in the future. This is, of course, true for any policy to combat global warming and not a difficulty peculiar to a carbon tax. Even in the absence of clear answers on the balance of costs and benefits of control, there is a case for action, to reduce the risks of large and unpredictable climate changes, with potentially catastrophic effects. Such action, to be effective, needs to involve coordinated measures by a large part of the global economy.

Although the purpose of a carbon tax would be to discourage carbon dioxide emissions, the tax itself would be levied on the carbon content of fossil fuels, and would rely for its effect on a close linkage between carbon content of fuels and carbon dioxide emissions from combustion. The carbon taxes in Scandinavia have generally taken the form of extended systems of fuel excises, with the relative tax rates reflecting relative carbon content of the different fuels.

The principal obstacle to adoption of a carbon tax probably is the perception that the substantial carbon tax burden on industry would adversely affect industrial competitiveness, unless all major countries were to adopt a similar tax at the same time. This is more a difficulty of short-term adjustment, and a problem of public perception, than a matter involving long-term costs. Since the carbon tax would raise revenues, these could be used to reduce other taxes paid by industry, thus offsetting the initial tax burden on the industrial sector as a whole. In the absence of compensating tax reductions of this sort, exchange rate adjustments would have a similar effect. The carbon tax would then lead to a shift in the relative competitiveness of different sectors, with carbon-intensive activites declining, but an offsetting improvement occurring in the competitive position of less carbon-intensive sectors.

References and Further Reading

Broome, J., *Counting the Cost of Global Warming*, The White Horse Press, Cambridge, United Kingdom, 1992.

Burniaux, J. M., J. P. Martin, G. Nicoletti, and J. O. Martins, *The Costs of Policies to Reduce Global Emissions of CO_2: Initial Simulation Results with GREEN*, OECD Economics and Statistics Department Working Papers No. 103, OECD, Paris, 1991.

Cline, W. R., *The Economics of Global Warming*, Institute for International Economics, Washington, 1992.

Edmonds, J. and J. Reilly, 'Global Energy and CO_2 to the Year 2050', *The Energy Journal*, Vol. 4, No. 3, pp.21-47, 1983.

Goulder, L. H., 'Environmental Taxation and the Double Dividend: a Reader's Guide', *International Tax and Public Finance*, Vol. 2, No. 2, pp.157-184, 1995.

Ingham, A., J. Maw and A. Ulph, 'Empirical Measures of Carbon Taxes', *Oxford Review of Economic Policy*, Vol. 7, No. 2, pp.99-122, 1991.

Jorgenson, D. W. and P. J. Wilcoxen, *The Cost of Controlling US Carbon Dioxide Emissions*, mimeo, Harvard University, 1991.

Manne, A. S. and R. G. Richels, 'CO_2 Emission Limits: An Economic Cost Analysis for the USA', *The Energy Journal*, Vol. 11, No. 2, pp.51-85, 1990.

Nordhaus, W. D. and G. W. Yohe, 'Future Carbon Dioxide Emissions from Fossil Fuels', in National Research Council, *Changing Climate*, pp.87-153, National Academy Press, Washington, 1983.

OECD, *Taxation and Environment. Complementary Policies,* OECD, Paris, 1993.

Pearce, D., 'The Role of Carbon Taxes in Adjusting to Global Warming', *The Economic Journal*, Vol. 101, No. 407, pp.938-48, 1991.

Pearson, M. and S. Smith, *The European Carbon Tax: An Assessment of the European Commission's Proposals*, The Institute for Fiscal Studies, London, 1991.

Smith, S., 'The Distributional Consequences of Taxes on Energy and the Carbon Content of Fuels', *European Economy*, Special Issue No 1/1992, 'The Economics of Limiting CO_2 Emissions', pp.241-268, 1992.

FURTHER KEY ISSUES IN TAX REFORM

PART II
TAX REFORM – ADMINISTRATION

CHAPTER 4

MINIMISING CORRUPTION IN TAX AFFAIRS

Roger Bowles*

Introduction

The corruption of officials responsible for collecting taxes has been a problem for just about as long as rulers and states have sought to collect funds. Elaborate methods were devised in ancient civilisations to control the opportunism of those who were given the task of tax collection. In contemporary times sophisticated methods are used by some administrations to detect cheating by tax officials and punishments for those convicted of corruption continue to be severe.

Tax systems lend themselves particularly well to creating temptation for officials to abuse their position for private gain. In most economies a substantial proportion of GDP creates tax liabilities, and a significant proportion of citizens may be paying large amounts of tax. Incomes of tax officials, by contrast, may account for only a very small part of national income. In the United Kingdom in tax year 1995-6, for example, Inland Revenue had total staff costs of just over a billion pounds representing 1.03 per cent of the total they collected in the form of taxes and duties (Inland Revenue, 1996). The comparable ratio for Customs and Excise, responsible primarily for indirect taxes, was even lower at 0.63 per cent (Customs & Excise, 1996). The taxes and duties collected by these two departments amounted to 27.1 per cent of money GDP during the tax year.

The sums 'at risk' are thus huge, and the scale of the difference between tax liabilities and tax officials' incomes is such that diverting only a small fraction of revenue into his own pocket may transform the financial position of an official. Persons (or corporate entities) obliged by law to pay taxes may stand to benefit individually from tax evasion, and may be quite happy to compound evasion offences which come to light by

---

*Reader in Economics and Director of the Centre for Fiscal Studies at the University of Bath, United Kingdom.

offering bribes. Poorly paid officials might perceive themselves to have little to lose from taking bribes, particularly since neither side will want the transaction to be brought to public notice. Provided they can be reasonably confident of avoiding detection, taxpayers and tax officials alike might regard corruption as an attractive option.

The potential losses to government from corruption of the tax administration are thus very great. The capacity to fund infrastructural development, education and so on may be undermined by corruption and thus for many countries there is a real sense in which the prevention of corruption is essential if economic development is to occur. Our purpose in this chapter is to review some of the recent work by economists on corruption, and to derive some implications for the design of anti-corruption policy. The approach we take is based on two main assumptions or propositions. The first assumption is that corruption is primarily a problem of asymmetric information and its exploitation. In a world of perfect information there would be no opportunities for corruption of the type with which we are concerned here. The second proposition is that contemporary economic theory can be used to illuminate many issues in tax administration, even though it has not as yet been widely applied in this area.

Corruption and Information

The essence of tax collection is information. A tax administration with perfect knowledge of the business of all taxpayers will have little, if any, difficulty in identifying everyone's tax liability. Conversely an administration which knows little about its taxpaying population will struggle to raise tax revenue. But collecting information is time-consuming and costly, so that an administration will want to weigh the costs of collecting further information in relation to the increased tax revenue which can be expected to result. These high costs are likely to have two critical consequences, namely:
(1) self-imposed limits on the amount of information the tax administration sets out to gather; and
(2) implications for the way in which tax administrations set out to collect information.

Let us consider, as an example, the use of collateral information as a means of checking on the reliability of declarations of personal incomes. In some countries where government databases are well developed it has become conventional to cross check lists of persons acquiring immovable property against taxpayer income tax returns. But if the property register used to generate the list is in its early stages of development or is unreliable, this would be an extremely costly exercise to do and probably not worth the effort. As a second example, consider the move to self-assessment of personal income tax. This is a means by which the tax administration can pass on some of its costs to taxpayers. But this delegation is only likely to be worthwhile if the administration has reliable ways of verifying the information it receives and is able to threaten credible punishments for taxpayers whose returns are scrutinised.

An asymmetry of information between the taxpayer and the tax administration may be sufficient to explain tax evasion, but it is unlikely to be enough to explain the possibility of corruption of a tax administration. The pursuit by tax officials of their own private interests at the expense of government revenues is much more likely to be the result of an asymmetry of information either *within* the tax administration itself or *between* the tax administration and the legislature or body to whom the administration is accountable. Corruption of tax officials can be interpreted, in some instances, as collusion between the official and a taxpayer against higher tiers of the administration. In other cases, the higher tiers in the administration may collude themselves in the collusion between the junior official and the taxpayer.

Of a different order altogether from this 'bureaucratic corruption' is the 'political corruption' which might run in parallel with it, or which may drive it. Politicians with positions in the legislature to influence the course of events within the administration may, unless there are very strict safeguards, misuse this influence for personal gain. A capacity to issue instructions to officials to desist from investigating particular taxpayers suspected of evasion may be a tremendously rewarding asset. Where the corruption pervades the whole government machinery in this way the notion of asymmetry of information begins to lose some of its meaning. But this is straying into an altogether more 'political' field. For present purposes we will be confining ourselves largely to the bureaucratic corruption case, where the notion of asymmetric information undoubtedly has a central contribution to make.

A number of models have been developed in the public economics literature over the past decade or so which explore corruption by exploiting the idea of collusion between taxpayers who are discovered, on investigation, to be evading tax and the officials who investigate them. These models do, of course, rely on the argument that the investigating official has an informational advantage over the administration employing her, and that she can gain personally by failing to report the findings of her investigations truthfully. Auditing of junior officials comes to play an important role in these models, because it quickly becomes clear that the work done by officials to collect information about taxpayers is of little value unless it can be verified elsewhere in the organisation. For otherwise when an official takes steps to investigate a taxpayer the information advantage passes from the taxpayer to the bottom tier official but travels no further. This leaves the tax organisation at the mercy of the most junior official who may be able to exploit the informational asymmetry for private advantage. Before illustrating the structure of some of these models we pause to consider the logically prior question of why it is that we might worry about corruption.

Why Worry about Corruption?

Our model, like others, does of course prompt the question of exactly why we choose to worry about the corruption of tax officials. Without wanting to dwell on a full taxonomy of possible reasons we still find it useful to identify at least some of the possible consequences of corruption in such a setting, namely:
(1) it increases the amount of revenue lost to the government which is going directly into the hands of tax officials;
(2) it increases the amount of revenue lost to the government which the taxpayer is keeping for herself;
(3) it harms the credibility of government institutions;
(4) it involves the use of time and effort on the part of both taxpayers and tax officials in the process of attempting to conceal information, negotiating bribes and so on.

The revenue loss under (1) and (2) might be dismissed as a 'mere transfer payment' and as not representing a real resource cost. For purposes of social welfare, there may not be much to choose between a bribe of $100 going into an official's pocket and the same money going as a tax payment to help fund public expenditure. Seen from this kind of perspective, corruption may seem somewhat lacking in allocative significance. This argument has close parallels with the argument in the literature on the economics of crime that the gain of the criminal should be taken into consideration as well as the loss to the victim when weighing policy options or when computing the cost of crime. But the counter to this in the tax corruption context is to argue that where revenue cannot be raised from one source (because of the bribe loss) it has to come from some other source. This may well involve a rather greater loss or distortion: in the technical jargon, the shadow price of tax revenue may be greater than unity.

The argument that corruption can be associated with 'lower private investment and slower economic growth' (World Bank, 1996) is not in any way inconsistent with this view. As more revenue is siphoned off by corruption, so governments will be forced to take other measures to maintain their spending capacity. This might entail printing money, with the obvious side-effects of inflation this will create, or it might entail an increase in interest rates in an effort to raise public borrowing at the expense of private borrowing, and this is very likely to impinge on private sector investment and thus in turn on the rate of economic growth.

From an economic point of view, it is (4) which may be the most tangible. Tax policy analysts have come, in recent years, to treat much more seriously the compliance and administrative costs of the tax system (Sandford, 1995, Pyle, 1989). But just as it is costly for taxpayers to comply with the tax system, so too is it costly when they seek to avoid or corrupt the tax gathering process. These latter costs are just as surely the consequences of raising taxes as are the costs to the government of enforcing the tax system or to the taxpayer of complying with it. By developing a model of evasion and corruption it is possible to begin to explore the links between tax policy, tax administration and the costs of corruption.

Corruption Pathways

As we have already implied above, there are various forms corruption can take in the context of taxation. In essence this is because different parts of government machinery are involved to some degree in the process of tax administration, and each may have its weaknesses and vulnerabilities. It is not our purpose here to explore all the possibilities, but rather to illustrate some of the more obvious pathways through which corruption may work. Figure 4.1 sets out a simple schema which summarises some of the best known types of corruption in the tax field. By distinguishing three groups working for the government (politicians, tax officials and judges) in addition to taxpayers we have four groups whose interests and interactions have to be considered in any serious analysis of corruption. We look now briefly at each of the four corruption pathways.

Figure 4.1 Corruption Pathways

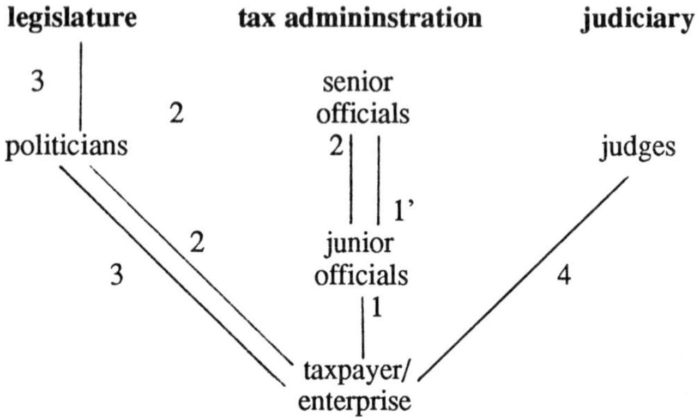

```
    legislature        tax admininstration        judiciary
         |
         3                    senior
         |         2          officials
    politicians               2| |                    judges
              \                | |
               \               | | 1'
                \       2      junior                /
                 3 \           officials       / 4
                    \             | 1
                     \            |
                      \       taxpayer/  /
                              enterprise
```

Pathways: route 1: bureaucratic
route 2: political-administrative
route 3: political-legislative
route 4: judicial

Bureaucratic Corruption

This is perhaps the most obvious form of corruption, involving the taxpayer paying a bribe to a junior tax official. The bribe may be in return for ignoring any irregularities the official uncovers or threatens to uncover. Underdeclaration of income or undervaluation of the value of a consignment of goods and so on might be involved, but failure to register as a taxpayer may equally enable an official to ask for money. In all these cases the official discovers some information which the taxpayer would prefer to remain unknown. In informational terms, the taxpayer loses her advantage to the junior official who now has an advantage over the tax administration. The official trades a promise to preserve the secret in return for cash or favours. Such promises may not be legally enforceable but they are self-enforcing. The taxpayer knows that the official who has taken a bribe is compromised, and cannot afford to disclose the offence subsequently because of the strict laws in most countries forbidding officials to take bribes.

For this simple form of corruption to survive the junior official has to prevent 'leakage' of information to more senior officials in the administration. An important function of these more senior officials is to ensure that junior officials do not fall prey to temptation. If junior officials are corrupt, however, they may try to implicate their more senior colleagues by offering to share the bribe revenue. In Figure 4.1 we represent this possibility as route 1. As we argue below in the analysis of route 2, it is possible that senior officials might have their own corruption agenda and agree to overlook the petty corruption of juniors in exchange for occasional favours. This is represented in Figure 4.1 by the extension of pathway 1, labelled 1'.

Political-Administrative Corruption

This second type of corruption involves a breakdown in the independence of the tax administration from political influence. If politicians are able to bring pressure to bear on senior tax officials, perhaps through influence on promotions and sackings, then they create for themselves the possibility of abusing this influence. Politicians seeking funds for their campaign activities or for their own pocket may find it very lucrative to take bribes from taxpayers if they can deliver 'cooperation' from tax officials. Senior tax officials may thus want to persuade their junior colleagues to 'play the game' and in order to achieve this may either persuade (by overlooking the junior's petty corruption) or threaten (by wielding powers to transfer officials to bad postings and so on).

Political-Legislative Corruption

This form of corruption may be entirely legal and may more closely resemble tax avoidance than anything else. It occurs where legislative powers are used to provide 'special' tax treatment for certain groups or interests. These moves will, of course, only class as 'corruption' if the politician or party expressly receives money or some other reward for promoting the legislation. More commonly the link will be only rather indirect, and thus this area is a rather grey one. From the point of view of the taxpayer seeking to minimise tax liabilities, however, this may be a rather attractive avenue. Collective efforts, via lobbying and the development of trade association pressure groups may enable the costs of tax avoidance via this route to be kept down to a minimum. Whilst this might be good news for the battle against corrupt offficials, whose own capacity to collect bribes might be weakened by it, it is not good news for the regular taxpayer who finds herself contributing more heavily to fill the revenue gaps the 'special arrangements' have created.

Judicial Corruption

Pathway 4 to corruption entails paying bribes to judges. This may not be very subtle, but there are certainly anecdotes suggesting that there are countries where taxpayers will find it worthwhile contesting tax liabilities through the courts because the judiciary are known to be corrupt.

There is, unfortunately, nothing to prevent the coexistence of some combination of these different pathways in a country. Indeed it seems often that knowledge that one form of corruption is occurring encourages the development of other forms. As we have already hinted, there is a sense in which this might be a good thing in that it encourages competition between the pathways and thus drives down the capacity of any one group to hold the taxpayer to ransom. But this is not a virtuous circle, because the cheaper corruption becomes, the more attractive it becomes to the taxpayer.

A Basic Model of Bureaucratic Corruption

In order to develop a framework for thinking about anti-corruption policy, it is convenient to begin by looking at a model of the taxpayer-tax official interaction outlined in the section on bureaucratic corruption (above). We make just about the simplest assumptions possible to create a situation in which the two parties may find it worthwhile entering corrupt negotiations. Since the tax official contemplating a corrupt transaction with a taxpayer will, in many jurisdictions, be committing a crime, it seems natural to apply a variant of the Becker model of crime to this decision (Becker, 1972). The fact that the standard Allingham-Sandmo (1972) model of tax evasion uses this same starting point lends the model a natural symmetry which has been exploited by many researchers in this field in recent years Basu *et al* (1992), Benson and Baden (1985), Chander and Wilde (1992) and so on. Evasion, on this approach, is a prerequisite of, and the motivation for, corruption.

In the model we develop here, tax evasion decisions and decisions about corruption are made jointly. The reason for this is that taxpayers contemplating evasion will want to anticipate the possibility of 'buying their way out of trouble' in the event that their evasion is detected. If the taxpayer can figure out both the probability of being detected by an official who turns out to be corruptible and the size of the bribe which will be demanded, then evasion becomes a three way gamble rather than a two way gamble. By making some assumptions, it is possible to argue that taxpayers will indeed be able to infer both the probability of encountering a corrupt official and also the size of the bribe for which they will be asked if they do 'hit lucky' in this way.

The key assumptions we make are as follows:
(1) the taxpayer knows the distribution of punishment costs for officials in aggregate but cannot identify the cost for any individual investigating officer;
(2) taxpayers and tax officials are both risk neutral;
(3) an investigation by a tax official will reveal a taxpayer's true income for sure.

The model has a simple recursive structure, similar to that used by Cadot (1987) and Bowles and Garoupa (1997). It is solved backwards, because the taxpayer will want to begin by figuring out the likely consequences of strategies such as underdeclaring true income. The corruption decision is explored first, because the outcome of the corruption analysis is used as an input for the evasion analysis. Since we will be assuming that taxpayers are risk neutral, it is sufficient to observe that each of them will choose either to declare their full income (Y) or to declare none at all. We return to this choice below.

The tax official investigating a taxpayer is assumed to discover the true income, Y, in which event the taxpayer becomes liable to pay a penalty of zY, where z may bear some fixed relation to the tax rate e.g. z is twice t. The official is then assumed to have discretion in reporting this income level. An official's report will be audited with probability q, in which event we assume the full story will emerge (again, for sure). If the official is discovered to have been taking bribes she will be punished. The cost this punishment inflicts on the official will be assumed to have two components. First, there is a common element representing loss of job, fine, imprisonment or whatever. Secondly, there is a subjective component, which might be termed generically 'loss of face'. This component which we label S, varies across individuals with the result that we can characterise the total loss across officials as a distribution, across values of S.

Corruption Decision

The first step is to explore the corruption decision. Given our assumption about the distribution of attitudes towards corruption on the part of officials, the likelihood is that some officials will be corrupt and others will not. The condition that must be satisfied for an official to be corrupt is that the bribe, b, must exceed the expected punishment; i.e. b > qS. If this condition were not met and the bribe were less than the expected punishment the official confronts, then the official will refuse the bribe. At the margin, the 'last' official prepared to take a bribe has a punishment cost we denote as $S^{\sim}$: all officials with costs below this level will take a bribe and all others will refuse it.

This last official will not, however, want to reveal to the taxpayer that he is the 'marginal' one. Although it might seem that the official has something to gain from revealing that he 'only just' finds the bribe worthwhile, since that will prevent the taxpayer from trying to offer a lower bribe, this will not work. We have assumed that the taxpayer has no way of discerning the subjective cost to the official of falling prey to temptation, and thus there is no way in which the official can credibly signal that he really is the one at the margin. All the officials tempted by the bribe will make the same claim and the taxpayer cannot distinguish.

The consequence is that we can argue that the size of the bribe which emerges will be common to all corrupt tax dealings. We can argue further that this size can be inferred by considering the position of the marginal official. This official has punishment cost $S^{\sim}$. At the time when the bribe offer is made the official does not yet know whether she will be investigated, and thus assigns to it the probability of audit, namely q. This expected cost of taking a bribe (qS) provides a minimum level (or 'threat point') below which the official would stay honest.

From the point of view of the taxpayer, it is possible to derive the maximum size of bribe it will be worth their paying. The penalty on unreported income is given by the product of the penalty rate z and the unreported income level, and it is this amount which will constitute the maximum they will be prepared to pay as a bribe. In bargaining terminology, this amount represents the 'threat point' of the other side.

Corruption will occur so long as there are at least some officials prepared to accept bribes of the size some taxpayers will be prepared to offer. The size of bribes will, in general, depend upon the degree to which taxpayers and tax officials are informed about each other. We have assumed here that both sides know the distribution of views of the other side, but cannot identify the position in the distribution taken by any particular individual. This assumption could be modified. The size of bribes will depend also on the kind of bargaining which is assumed to take place between two corruptible parties. We make what is, in most respects, the most obvious assumption, namely that the bribe level will settle at the mid-point between the minimum the official will accept and the maximum the taxpayer will pay.

Once the size of the bribe has been inferred in this way, we have sufficient information to infer also both the proportion of taxpayers who will evade and the proportion of officials who will be corrupt. That is because the size of the bribe fixes the 'payoff' to taking bribes, which each official can compare with their subjective disinclination to behave corruptly. For the taxpayer, this is important because it determines the proportion of officials taking bribes, and thus the payoff to the taxpayer from underdeclaring their income. The taxpayer filing a return has basically two choices, namely:

Strategy 1: declare true income and pay tax. With the tax rate at t, the taxpayer with income Y will pay tY in tax and enjoy after-tax income of Y(1-t) irrespective of whether she is investigated.

Strategy 2: declare true income as zero. This is equivalent to entering a lottery with three possible outcomes, namely:
(1) Remain undetected and thus retain post-tax income of Y. This will happen with probability (1-p).
(2) Experience investigation by an honest official who will refuse any bribes offered. The probability of investigation is p and the probability that the official will be honest is (1-s), giving a probability p(1-s) for this outcome.
(3) Experience investigation by an official who proves susceptible to overlooking the evasion in exchange for a bribe b.

The various possible outcomes are summarised in Figure 4.2. The taxpayer will decide to make an honest income declaration if and only if the payoff from strategy 1 exceeds the payoff from strategy 2. Taxpayers will differ in this decision because of the assumption we have made that they differ in the degree to which dishonesty will entail subjective costs or losses for them. Any aversion to risk-taking on the part of taxpayers is a further source of differences in the strategy taxpayers will choose when in otherwise similar positions, but is not something we pursue here. This distinguishes our model from those used in much of the tax evasion literature, making it simpler but better adapted to incorporating corruption.

76 *Further Key Issues in Tax Reform*

Figure 4.2 Evasion and Corruption Outcomes

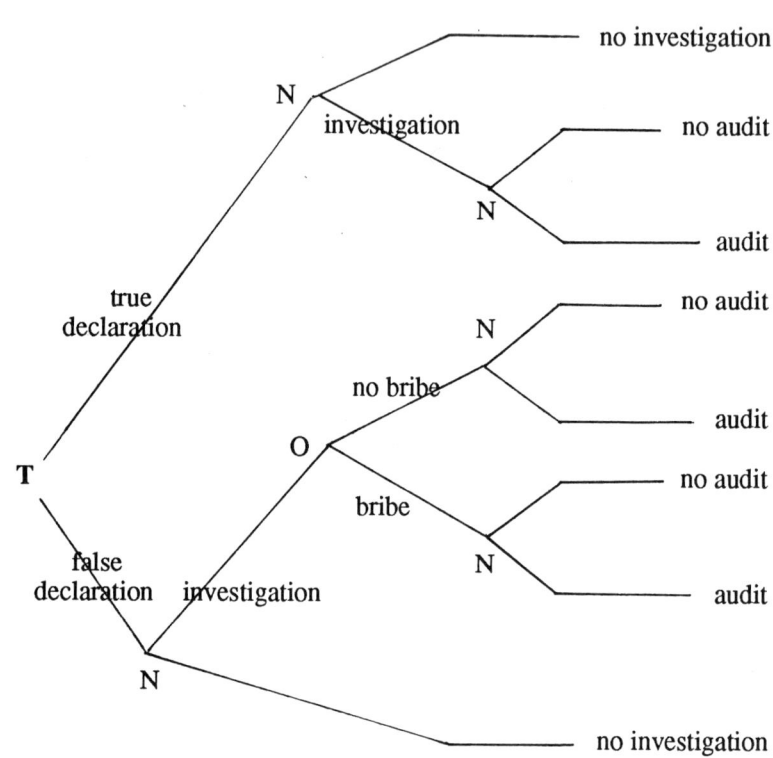

The players:

T Taxpayer

O Tax official

N Nature (i.e. random)

Anti-Corruption Policies

The structure of our model makes the evasion and corruption decisions interdependent, and this has the implication that the assessment of any policy change will have to consider the impact on both. There are various areas which the model suggests for purposes of identifying policies which might reduce corruption.

The proportion of officials finding corruption the best policy, (s), depends on the gains and costs to the official implied by the various parameters in the model. A high tax rate, for example, gives the taxpayer more to gain from evasion and also more to gain from collusion with an official who investigates and discovers the evasion. Raising the penalty rate z the taxpayer is charged on underdeclarations might be a disincentive to evasion in the first place, but it will raise the potential benefits from collusion after investigation for the taxpayer who decides the evasion risk is worth taking. This will be reflected, at least in part, by a rise in the size of bribes, with the result that more officials might be expected to become corrupt. An important implication of this is that a 'tough' policy designed to attack one problem may make something else worse. It is important therefore that the policy change be carefully considered.

At this point it is useful to ask the question: What is the objective of the government? Is it to maximise net tax revenue, or to minimise evasion or corruption, or what? The most likely response is that the government is pursuing the maximisation of a social welfare function in which these, and possibly other, arguments appear. That is certainly the conclusion of Shavell and others who have explored the question of the optimal pattern of sanctions to employ in the area of criminal law. It is only by confronting such questions explicitly that it is likely to be possible to make any progress on 'difficult choices' such as the decision between policies which differ in the amounts of corruption and revenue they can be expected to deliver.

The model we have developed here will, for any given set of parameters, generate evasion and corruption levels and an amount of tax revenue. It is possible also to use it to identify the response of any of these variables to policy change. For present purposes we might suppose that an 'optimal' anti-corruption policy is being sought, irrespective of whether it is the one which generates the greatest possible volume of revenue. On this presumption, we can return to our expression for the proportion, s, of officials who will respond positively to an invitation to take a bribe, and seek a policy which will minimise this proportion. Even this might not be quite what we are interested in, since the proportion of taxpayers who end up paying bribes will depend upon the proportion of taxpayers who evade. This evasion decision anticipates the 'bribe' position, so there might be policies which would depress the taxpayer's inclination to evade sufficiently to offset any increase in the propensity of an official to accept a bribe after an investigation.

Implications

By characterising corruption in the way we have, it becomes natural to think of the costs of corruption as 'agency costs'. In much of the contemporary work on corruption in theoretical economics, the government is treated as a 'principal' holding the rights to the proceeds from taxes. The government's problem is to devise a tax administration to act as its 'agent' in collecting taxes. As in most principal-agent models, the principal can only monitor the behaviour of the agent in an approximate way. The problem is for the principal to construct a 'contract' which rewards the agent in such a way as to ensure that the agent expends the greatest achievable effort in its tasks and diverts as little of the proceeds as possible into its own pockets.

An 'agency' approach to corruption offers further insights. In many countries the tax administration is very much part of the government bureaucracy. The degree of institutional flexibility implicit in a model of an 'optimal incentive contract' between the government and the administration so as to minimise agency costs may thus be missing. Other barriers, such as rigid working practices, preservation of public sector employment and so on may severely constrain the government's capacity to reconstruct incentives within the tax administration itself.

The agency model has two particularly illuminating points to make. First, it raises the possibility of there being a 'selling the store' equilibrium. Historically, corruption of tax administration has been a continuing and pervasive problem. The solution in the classical world was for governments to engage in 'tax farming', in which the state would grant franchises to individuals or corporations to collect tax proceeds which they themselves keep, in return for payment of a fixed fee: for a fascinating account see Webber and Wildavsky (1986). In the contemporary jargon, this is equivalent to using a 'high powered incentive contract' (Laffont and Tirole, 1993). It is a means of giving incentives to private sector agents acting on behalf of the government to behave efficiently. Any cost savings (or revenue gains) a tax farmer makes will, in principle, be reflected in the profits the agent makes from the contract. Ultimately, of course, the gains may not persist for very long because the improved working methods (or whatever) can be copied by prospective competitors in the next round of franchise auctions. As the franchises become more profitable, their price at auction will increase and the improved profitability will be capitalised in higher fees for the government.

Secondly, the agency model can be used to 'deconstruct' the tax administration itself. Instead of treating a tax administration simply as a unified agent acting (imperfectly) on behalf of the government, the administration can be treated as a hierarchy having a series of tiers (at least two). This approach is very valuable, for the stylised facts about corruption of tax administrations suggest strongly that it is often a much more pervasive and systematic force within an organisation than the more 'casual encounter' kind of model outlined above.

The use of multi-level hierarchy models enables a distinction to be drawn between at least two layers of officials within a tax administration as well as between the administration and the taxpayer on the one hand and the administration and the (legislative branch of) government on the other. The advantage of doing this is that it allows control mechanisms to be incorporated.

There are two themes in contemporary analysis of corruption which fit quite neatly into this hierarchical picture. First, a number of authors, including Shleifer and Vishny (1993), have argued that it is competition between officials which can prevent much of the petty bureaucratic corruption encountered amongst government officials in some countries. They propose allowing a 'multi-channel' approach for citizens wherever there might otherwise be scope for officials to behave opportunistically. They argue that it is the monopoly element, which often characterises exchanges between citizens and officials, which creates the possibility for officials to demand bribes. By attacking the monopoly, and giving the citizen choice, the corruption becomes unsustainable via a kind of Bertrand price-cutting process.

Quite closely related to this competition argument is the call for transparency in government dealings (see for example World Bank, 1996). In terms of our hierarchical analysis, this generalisation of the 'openness' argument is very appealing because it permits one (at least in principle!) to deal with the most deeply entrenched corruption. The central idea is essentially an attack on informational asymmetries, which we argued earlier are really a precondition for corruption. The argument is that steps to improve access to information can weaken the position of corrupt officials, citizens or politicians. By opening up access to files it becomes much easier to question the way an official has handled matters. If the official has exercised discretion should it not be possible for third parties to question the basis on which a decision has been made?

An important weakness of this approach is that the volume of information held by a tax administration may be huge, and any effort to improve transparency may founder simply on the volume of material. Unless systematic efforts are used to review information and performance it is unlikely that irregularities will come to light. Even if such efforts are made, it will be essential to ensure that it does not just result in less information being recorded within files. Just as unscrupulous traders may keep one set of books for tax purposes and another for private purposes, so unscrupulous officials may keep a second set of files for private consumption only.

Another limitation is that, in many countries, large numbers of transactions are never formally recorded. If literacy of the population is limited or if there is deep-seated distrust of officialdom, it may be very difficult for the tax administration to compile much of a database. A corrupt administration will, of course, have an interest in maintaining a high degree of opacity. If politicians are conniving in the corruption, then unless there is external pressure on the country via loan conditionalities or whatever, it may be very difficult to create a will to improve information collection and transparency.

As usual in this field, more careful scrutiny of the behaviour of tax officials working in the field will not be sufficient. At higher levels within the tax administration, and particularly at the interface between the legislature and the tax administration, there may be particularly strong grounds for wanting effective scrutiny of the behaviour of both civil servants and politicians. The tax officials must be able to act independently of political control if the executive branch of government is to work properly. A famous illustration of this principle breaking down was the dismissal by the Minister of Finance of the head of the tax administration in Brazil after an incident with the Brazilian football team on return from victory in the World Cup some years ago. When the team arrived, customs officials wanted to search the huge amount of baggage with which they had returned. The head of the tax administration had supported his officials but was dismissed by the Government. Although politicians do carry some responsibility for the behaviour of the tax administration it is essential that the methods in place to ensure accountability are not misused. Properly independent audit authorities and an independent judiciary are essential if officials are to be reassured that their integrity will be defended.

Anti-Corruption Policy

As well as saying something about the broader issues of corruption, the model of bureaucratic corruption developed here has at least some pointers for the design of policy to counter evasion. In this concluding section we consider some of these pointers in relation to corruption problems in different kinds of economies, ranging from less developed countries through transitional economies to developed countries.

The model we have developed gives prominence to the role of two kinds of variables. The first group is essentially about attitudes, via the psychic costs of evasion for taxpayers and the subjective costs of corruption for officials. The second group of variables includes the various policy levers at the disposal of the legislature and the tax administration, such as the choice of tax and penalty rates and also the administration's decision about how to split its budget between investigations of taxpayers and audits of the work of its own officials. The model enables the analyst to trace through the impact of changes in any or all of these variables on the amount of evasion and the prevalence of corruption. The propositions which emerge include the following:

(1) increases in tax administration salaries give the tax official more to lose from dismissal, provided that the frequency of audit is sufficient to ensure that there is some possibility of a corrupt official being identified;
(2) improving the morale of tax officials may be a powerful weapon, particularly if corruption is widespread, through the harnessing of 'peer pressure';
(3) methods of raising the psychic costs of evasion to taxpayers may be valuable, not only because of the improvement in the honesty of taxpayer reporting behaviour but also because of the depressing effect on the opportunities for corruption;
(4) a judicious choice of the administration's allocation of resources between investigation and audit work can have a substantial payoff, because if either activity is neglected revenue loss may be very great;
(5) high tax rates and high penalty rates both tend to encourage anti-social behaviour, with high tax rates being conducive to evasion and high penalty rates tending to increase the scope for corruption.

These implications are rather general but can be applied at some level in most types of tax administration. We consider briefly their relevance in different types of country.

Less Developed Countries

In many less developed countries the corruption of tax administrations is a very serious problem. There are many reasons for this, although of course each country's administration has its own variant on the more general position. In many cases political corruption is at least as serious an issue as corruption of the tax bureaucracy. Low salaries for officials, political protection of prominent tax evaders, poor monitoring of junior officials, high tax rates, high levels of discretion for the tax official, and poor information generally are some of the reasons commentators are inclined to give for the persistence of extensive corruption in many countries in Africa, Asia and Latin America. It is difficult to argue with the diagnosis. The more pressing matter is whether it is possible to construct ways to escape the corruption cycle.

There is certainly no instant solution. Many countries have had committees of enquiry and governments which have promised to put an end to corruption. Few of them have had great success. Quite rightly, many of the international bodies have tried to improve matters. The Overseas Development Agency have made 'good governance' a key priority whilst the World Bank and IMF have tried to impose on borrowers loan conditionalities designed to improve the tax collection effort. Many of these policies are inspired by the sorts of arguments we have looked at in earlier sections. Higher salaries for officials are essential if they are to have anything to lose from being caught taking bribes. Greater independence from government for tax administrations via the construction of Revenue Authorities, greater transparency within administrations and reduced discretion and tax rates have all been urged on the governments of less developed countries. But corruption remains for many a real obstacle to the effective mobilisation of revenue badly needed for the provision of basic public services and for infrastructural development.

Economies in Transition

In economies in transition, where the relation between the taxpayer, the tax official and the politician have changed, often very radically, but where weaknesses in the definition of property rights and accountabilities remain, it seems particularly vital that ways be found of ensuring that taxes are administered fairly and efficiently. Fiscal crises can prompt responses which only intensify problems for the tax administration. Increases in tax rates and penalty rates may raise the propensity of the taxpayer to evade and increase the amount of corruption. Moves to reduce the operating budget of the tax administration meanwhile may reduce the amount of investigation and auditing work which can take place, thereby reinforcing the increase in both evasion and corruption. The net result will be an even worse fiscal crisis. An approach which seeks to reduce tax rates and penalty rates may appear to some to be a sign of political weakness. But provided that it is accompanied with serious efforts to improve tax administration and to seek greater transparency, particularly at the interface between the tax official and the political world, it may contribute to improved tax administration and reduced tax evasion over the longer term.

Developed Countries

Corruption of tax administration is an issue in a number of developed countries. In most of these countries a much higher proportion of the population is liable for personal income tax than in less developed countries. Methods of data collection and processing used by tax departments tend to be more sophisticated and more automated and routinised, with the result that corruption can be easier to detect. Despite this there are some developed countries where corruption is nevertheless thought to be still comparatively commonplace.

In countries such as the United Kingdom, however, where officials are well paid and systems are highly computerised, the scope for corruption is limited and the chances of being detected appear to be quite high. The instances where corruption have been found have mostly involved abuse of discretion by officials working in rather specialist fields with taxpayers who have a high tax liability, the exact size of which is open to interpretation. There are some sectors where evasion is alleged to be more common, including football, construction and some services such as taxi cabs, but there does not seem to be any suggestion that this is accompanied by corruption. At a political level there seems to be no suggestion of politicians exercising undue influence over tax departments. If there is an area where there is a question mark, it is the grey area of the third type of corruption identified above, namely the use of influence to manipulate the legislative agenda to help ease the tax burden of particular groups.

Concluding Remarks

Corruption of tax administration is a serious problem for countries where it occurs, because it causes distortions of tax burdens and impedes the financing of public activity. In many countries this corruption is deep-rooted and is found alongside widespread corruption in many other spheres of life. Our concern in this chapter has been to identify some of the pathways through which corruption can travel and the incentive and information structures in which the various participants in the tax gathering process are embedded. A better understanding of these two elements seems essential for the development of any effective anti-corruption policy. Over recent years there can be little doubt that some progress has been made in areas such as making tax administration more transparent and putting tax officials in a position where they feel they have something serious to lose if they are caught taking bribes. But equally there can be no doubt that in many countries a very large amount of tax revenue goes uncollected and that some proportion of this revenue finds its way into the pockets of corrupt tax administrators.

References and Further Reading

Allingham, M. G. and A. Sandmo, 'Income Tax Evasion: A Theoretical Analysis', *Journal of Public Economics*, Vol. 1, pp.323-38, 1972.
Basu K., S. Bhattacharya and A. Mishra, 'Notes on Bribery and the Control of Corruption', *Journal of Public Economics*, Vol. 48, pp.349-59, 1972.
Becker, G. S., 'Crime and Punishment: An Economic Approach', *Journal of Political Economy*, Vol. 76 No. 2, pp.169-217, 1968.
Benson, B. L. and J. Baden, 'The Political Economy of Governmental Corruption: The Logic of Underground Government', *Journal of Legal Studies*, Vol. 14, pp.391-410, 1985.
Bowles, R. and N. Garoupa, 'Casual Police Corruption and the Economics of Crime', *International Review of Law and Economics*, Vol. 17, No. 1, pp.75-88, March 1997.
Brickley, J. A. et al, *Organizational Architecture: A Managerial Economics Approach*, Irwin, Toronto, 1996.
Cadot, O., 'Corruption as a Gamble', *Journal of Public Economics*, Vol. 33, pp.223-44, 1987.
Chander, P. and L. Wilde, 'Corruption in Tax Administration', *Journal of Public Economics*, Vol. 49, pp.333-49, 1992.
Customs and Excise, *87th Report of the Commissioners of Her Majesty's Customs and Excise for the Year Ended 31 March 1996*, The Stationery Office, London, 1996.
EBRD, *Transition Report*, October 1994, EBRD, London, 1994.
Economic Trends, *Economic Trends: Annual Supplement 1996/97*, Office for National Statistics, HMSO, London, 1997.
Feige, E. and K. Ott, *Underground Economies in Transition: Tax Evasion, Corruption, Criminality and Organized Crime*, Edward Elgar, Cheltenham, forthcoming 1998.
Inland Revenue, *Report of the Commissioners of Her Majesty's Inland Revenue for the Year Ending 31 March 1996*, The Stationery Office, London, 1996.
Kofman, F. and J. Lawarre, 'On the Optimality of Allowing Collusion', *Journal of Public Economics*, Vol. 61, pp.383-407, 1996.
Laffont, J-J. and J. Tirole, *A Theory of Incentive Procurement and Regulation*, MIT Press, 1993.
MacMullen, R., *Corruption and the Decline of Rome*, Yale University Press, New Haven, 1988.
Mauro, P., 'Why Worry about Corruption?', *Economic Issues*, Vol. 6, IMF, Washington, 1997.

Pyle, D., 'The Economics of Tax Compliance', *Journal of Economic Surveys*, 1989.
Sandford, C. T., M. R. Godwin and P. J. W. Hardwick, *Administrative and Compliance Costs of Taxation*, Fiscal Publications, Bath, 1989.
Shleifer, A. and R. W. Vishny, 'Corruption', *Quarterly Journal of Economics*, Vol. 108, pp.599-617, 1993.
Tanzi, V., 'Corruption, Governmental Activities and Markets', *Finance and Development*, Vol. 32, No. 4, pp.24-26, December 1995.
United Nations, *Corruption on Government*, United Nations, New York, 1989.
Webber, C. and A. Wildavsky, *A History of Taxation and Expenditure in the Western World*, Simon and Schuster, New York, 1986.
World Bank, *From Plan to Market: World Development Report 1996*, The World Bank/OUP, New York, 1996.

CHAPTER 5

TAX LAW SIMPLIFICATION IN THE UNITED KINGDOM

Geoffrey Howe*

Introduction

The simplification and better management of every kind of legislation (and not just tax) is a topic in which I have long been interested. The problem of the volume and quality of legislation is one of great seriousness. It is also a problem of very long-standing. It was Tacitus who said, 'Whereas formerly we suffered from crimes, now we suffer from laws'. Unfortunately the criticisms of our legislation in general apply equally – indeed perhaps even more – to our tax law.

Eighteen months ago, in a Foreword to a report published by the Tax Law Review Committee (TLRC, 1995), I reflected on some comments I had made as long ago as 1977, in a talk to the Addington Society. In that talk, I had denounced the 'incoherent drift towards a tax system that is incomprehensible, unrespected, unenforceable – and spinning like a top'. Nearly twenty years on, I noted that nothing had changed. This was not through want of trying – but we did not try hard enough. I welcomed the TLRC Report, not only as a refreshingly clear description of what needed to be done but also as a convincing demonstration that it is possible to write tax legislation in plain English and in a form which can actually be understood. I expressed the hope that 'this strikingly clear Report will inspire a fresh generation to try again'.

In parallel with the TLRC work, the Inland Revenue were carrying out their own review into this question. Their report (Inland Revenue, 1995) came to very similar conclusions, '... that the language of existing tax law can be simplified; that the benefits should substantially outweigh the

---

*Rt Hon Lord Howe of Aberavon, CH, QC, Chancellor of the Exchequer 1979-1983, Chairman of the Steering Committee for the Inland Revenue's Tax Law Rewrite Project.

costs; and that a rewrite of most of the existing code could be accomplished over a period of about five years'. That judgement had been foreshadowed in the then Chancellor of the Exchequer's statement, in his Budget Speech of 28 November 1995, that he hoped to 'make a start on a major project to simplify tax legislation' in 1996.

This announcement was generally very well received. But, before a final decision could be taken, a number of important practical issues needed to be clarified. The Final Report by the TLRC (TLRC, 1996), published in June 1996, reaffirmed their support in principle for work to proceed. A month later, the Financial Secretary to the Treasury, the Rt Hon Michael Jack MP, announced the publication of an Inland Revenue Consultative Document (Inland Revenue, 1996a), which set out detailed proposals for taking the project forward. After a very constructive and worthwhile round of consultations with the main interested parties, the Inland Revenue published a Response Document (Inland Revenue, 1996b), in December 1996. This outlined how, in the light of comments received, the Revenue project team would take forward the rewrite work and set out its provisional programme for 1997.

The project is now fully under way. Among the many innovative aspects to this work is the extent of consultation, something which I have long championed, particularly in my time as Chancellor of the Exchequer. In addition to the general public consultation which I am pleased to see is more and more becoming the norm with fiscal legislation, two largely private sector committees dedicated to the rewrite project have been established. The first is a strategic, high level Steering Committee to oversee the project and to ensure that its aims are met; the second a Consultative Committee of taxpayers and the professions to enable full consultation with all the relevant private sector interests. Given my long-standing interest in this whole area, I was delighted to be asked to chair the Steering Committee and thereby to make my own contribution to this long overdue and potentially far-reaching task.

Let me begin by briefly considering the factors that have led to the need for simplification of United Kingdom tax law. I will then move on to review the current position on tax law simplification in other countries, and the TLRC initiative to examine the way tax legislation is drafted. Finally, I will address the detail of the Revenue project to rewrite United Kingdom tax law so that it is clearer and easier to use.

The Need for Tax Law Simplification

The volume of tax legislation in the United Kingdom, both primary and secondary, has increased tremendously over the past 36 years. Figure 5.1 shows the new Inland Revenue legislation (both primary and secondary) added each year since 1960. In 1970, there were roughly 2,000 pages of primary legislation. Now, up to Finance Act 1996, there are over 6,000 pages of primary legislation. Table 5.1 shows the growth in the total volume of Inland Revenue primary and secondary tax legislation since 1952. On the whole, this growth is not because many new taxes have been introduced, but because existing taxes have become more elaborate. That reflects a number of factors including:

- tax reform initiatives (e.g. independent taxation, self assessment);
- the need to take account of an increasingly global and sophisticated business environment (e.g. rules on foreign exchange gains and losses, taxation of manufactured dividends);
- the need to respond to changes in the general legal framework within which businesses and other taxpayers operate (e.g. developments in company law have led to provisions for open-ended investment companies, and the demerger provisions); and
- the increasing desire for tax law to be detailed and precise, to ensure it is certain in its application (e.g. the detailed rules for relocation expenses).

As the modern world has become more complex, tax legislation – which both reflects and responds to that world – has also increased in complexity. This is true not just of the United Kingdom, but of other developed economies also. Over the last 10 years, for instance, the volume of Australian tax legislation has more than doubled and in New Zealand it has increased by 80 per cent.

The complexity of underlying tax policy adds to this even further, driven by the desire to ensure an equitable outcome in an increasingly diverse economy. This continual elaboration of existing rules to deal with changes in the outside world feeds upon itself. As the tax code becomes bigger and more complex, even a simple change may interact with a large number of existing provisions. So getting that change to fit in properly will lead to legislation which is not easy to follow. Through the annual Finance Bills, it is often the case that the same legislation is amended year after year, making the code ever more complex and difficult to use.

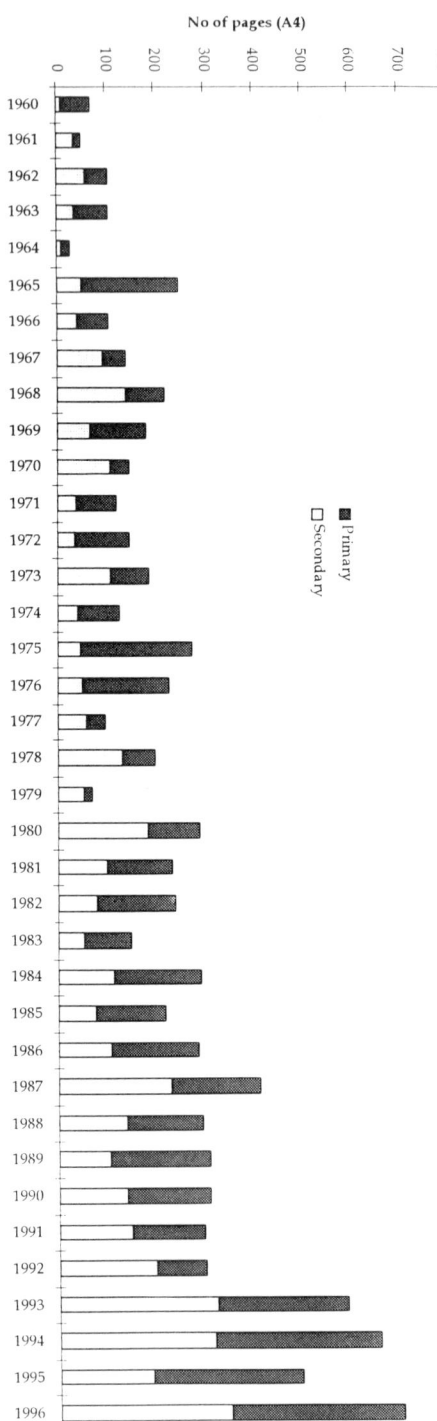

Figure 5.1 New Inland Revenue Legislation (Primary and Secondary)

Crown copyright 1997. Published with the permission of the Inland Revenue on behalf of the Controller of HMSO.

Table 5.1 – Total Volume of Inland Revenue Primary and Secondary Tax Legislation[1] – no of pages[2]

YEAR[3]		1952	1970	1988	1989	1990	1991	1992	1993	1994	1995	1996[4]
Income Tax, Corporation Tax & Capital Gains Tax	Primary[5]	687	1297	2796	3070	3091	3237	3251	3733	4159	4580	4983
	Secondary	168	171	629	692	764	797	1018	1075	1114	1444	1829
Petroleum Revenue Tax	Primary[6]	—	—	405	403	462	494	515	563	605	630	639
	Secondary	—	—	46	52	63	64	62	74	132	129	134
Inheritance Tax[7]	Primary	601	534	412	415	415	415	416	420	421	423	431
	Secondary	168	85	28	45	103	108	109	111	137	147	167
Stamp Duty	Primary	150	214	307	314	321	327	329	331	336	329	362
	Secondary	—	—	11	27	27	27	35	34	37	37	49
Profits Tax	Primary	146	—	—	—	—	—	—	—	—	—	—
	Secondary	7	—	—	—	—	—	—	—	—	—	—
Double Taxation Orders	Primary	322	1024	1810	1814	1822	1896	1917	1991	2126	2208	2304
TOTAL[8]	Primary	1584[9]	2045[10]	3920	4202	4289	4473	4511	5047	5521	5962	6415
	Secondary	665	1280	2524	2630	2779	2892	3141	3285	3546	3965	4483
GRAND TOTAL		2249	3325	6444	6832	7068	7465	7652	8332	9067	9927	10898

Crown copyright 1997. Published with the permission of the Inland Revenue on behalf of the Controller of HMSO.

1Sources – HMSO Taxes Acts series where available, and double taxation orders. HMSO Taxes Acts series include legislation repealed within the previous 6 years. Figures also include closely related non-Revenue legislation. Figures for Estate Duty and Stamp Duty are estimated as this legislation is not currently available in consolidated form.
2Page size is Royal Octavo as per HMSO Taxes Acts – which is thought to give the best indication of the total size of the 'tax code' including footnotes. This means, however, that the figures are not directly comparable with those in the table of new Revenue legislation.
31952 and 1970 selected for comparison as these were years in which the main tax legislation was consolidated.
4Figures as at 31 December 1996.
5Includes Capital Allowances Act 1990.
6Includes Corporation Tax legislation which is specific to North Sea Oil.
7Estate Duty for years 1952 and 1970.
8Some parts of the tax code (e.g. Taxes Management Act 1970) apply to more than one tax. These have been included within the figures for each tax to which they apply. This means that the 'total' figures include some double-counting, although this does not significantly distort the figures. Figures exclude tax rules in other legislation such as privatisation Acts (approx 55 pages in total).
9Excludes number of pages of Land Tax legislation for which information is not available.
10Excludes legislation (81 pages) on tithe redemption annuities which the Inland Revenue took over from HM Treasury in 1960 and which was repealed in Finance Act 1977.

The volume of legislation and the frequency with which it is amended are not the only factors at work. The language, structure and organisation of tax law have contributed. The structure of the existing legislation makes it difficult either to get an overview of the law or to find where particular concepts are dealt with.

In common with those countries with the same sort of annual Budget and Finance Bill cycle, the quality of tax legislation in the United Kingdom is not helped by the tremendous time constraints this imposes. In practice it often leaves too little time to develop policy thoroughly and to draft in the clearest possible way. This in turn stems from an overall timetable which is dominated by the needs of the Budget, rather than the Finance Bill which follows. There is therefore little time to produce draft legislation which is not just technically correct, but also user-friendly.

All of these factors, rather than any one or two of them, have made our existing tax code almost unintelligible to any but the skilled expert. Tax legislation which is difficult to understand leads to uncertainty, which may hinder business transactions; will mean higher compliance costs for business and other taxpayers; and gives rise to extra costs in administering the tax system.

The project to rewrite the United Kingdom's tax law has developed against this background.

Tax Law Simplification in Other Countries

As I noted in the previous section, the United Kingdom is by no means unique in facing these pressures. Some other countries with similar legal systems to ourselves are taking steps to improve their tax legislation.

Australia

Australia is engaged in a tax law rewrite project. The Tax Law Improvement Project (TLIP) was announced by the Australian Government in December 1993. The aim of the project is to improve the structure and arrangement of the law and to express it in language which readers can more easily understand.

Many of the criticisms of Australian tax law which led to the establishment of the TLIP are similar to the criticisms of United Kingdom law, focusing on complexity and impenetrability. The law of both countries is broadly comparable in length. In addition, however, Australia's Income Tax Assessment Act 1936 has never been consolidated and the process of amendment over 60 years has produced an extremely unwieldy document. For example, in more than one part of the code over 100 sections have been inserted over the years between two of the original consecutively numbered sections. This leads to statutory references such as Section 59GZZZZA(2)(b)(iii)(B).

The rewrite of Australian income tax laws is not intended to make significant policy changes. The TLIP's approach to these is to identify such changes early so that they can either be dropped completely or hived off to be dealt with through the normal policy channels.

The rewrite aims to replace the 1936 Act progressively. In doing so it will:

- **restructure** – the new structure is described as a three-level pyramid of core provisions to provide a conceptual framework, general provisions which apply across a wide group of taxpayers, and specialist topics affecting particular groups of taxpayers;
- **renumber** – a two-part numerical system has been adopted. The parts indicate the division and section, with section numbers recommencing at 1 at the start of each division. Gaps have been left between section numbers to allow for later insertions; and
- **rewrite** in clearer language.

The first tranche of replacement legislation was enacted as the Tax Law Improvement (Substantiation) Act 1995 which dealt with rules on expenses claims and the records required to substantiate them.

The Income Tax Assessment Bill 1995 having fallen at the 1996 general election, an improved and extended version was reintroduced as the Income Tax Assessment Bill 1996. This runs to 396 pages and is the beginning of the new structure. Part I contains all the core provisions. The later Parts are fragmentary, with large gaps in the numbering to be filled up by further rewritten blocks of legislation. The Bill has now been enacted as the Income Tax Assessment Act 1997. A second substantive Act is the Tax Law Improvement Act 1997 (550 pages) which inserts a further 16 rewritten substantive divisions into the Income Tax Assessment Act 1997. This approach leaves the TLIP free to tackle blocks of work as and when convenient, inserting the rewritten text into the largely empty 1997 Act and repealing the old law as they go along.

The style of Australian legislation in general has become more plain language orientated over the last 10 years or so. This began with the publication of a number of working papers by the Victoria Law

Commission in the early 1980s. The federal and state drafting offices all use plain language and are experimenting with different styles of lay-out and editorial aids. That said, the TLIP legislation is at the leading edge of the movement. It is consciously expressed in a colloquial style and uses second-person drafting extensively (addressing the taxpayer as 'you'). There is frequent use of tables and graphics. There is a great deal of non-operative, editorial material on the page.

The TLIP is separate from the Australian Tax Office and consists of a team of about 40 people (broadly comparable to the size of the United Kingdom Simplification Project Team). Because most Australian tax inspectors are qualified lawyers, there is a large majority of lawyers in the team. Members of the Australian Office of Parliamentary Counsel have been seconded in to the team to do the drafting work. There is also one private sector accountant. To assist the TLIP in its work, a Consultative Committee of experienced individuals drawn exclusively from outside the public sector was also set up. The Committee reviews the work of the TLIP and provides it with feedback from the professions and business.

New Zealand

The impetus for the New Zealand simplification project can be traced back to recommendations made in 1992 by an independent committee, the Valabh Committee, that the Income Tax Act 1976 – which had not been consolidated – should be reorganised. A *Working Party on the Reorganisation of the Income Tax Act 1976* reported on how this could be done, and in the light of this, the New Zealand Government issued a consultative document in 1994. The rewrite project was then established with a view to improving the structure of the legislation, making interrelationships between different provisions explicit and adopting a plain language style of drafting. The rewrite is being undertaken in three main stages:

- reordering and renumbering of the existing legislation to give a better structure;
- the addition of new 'core provisions'; and
- progressive rewriting of the remainder of the Act.

The first stage – reordering into a logical structure and renumbering using an alpha-numeric system – was achieved in 1994 with the Income Tax Act 1994. The second stage, the core provisions, was completed in

1996. They are now part way through the rewriting phase which should be completed in 1999. Policy change is not part of the rewrite. When a policy issue arises it is taken out of the work of the rewrite team and dealt with as part of the government's ordinary programme of fiscal legislation.

The rewrite is being undertaken by a combined team of New Zealand Revenue and Treasury officials, numbering approximately 12 people. These are organised into a team of 3 drafters (who are responsible for 'business-as-usual' legislation in addition to the rewrite) plus a rewrite team whose role is to research the history and interpretation of each section and then to instruct the drafters.

United States of America

There is currently no specific project in the United States to simplify the language of tax legislation. Although the Internal Revenue Service has guidelines for effective drafting which incorporates plain language techniques, drafting is carried out within the context of traditional legal expression.

The United States tax code was extensively reformed in 1986, in an attempt to increase fairness and simplicity. The increase in simplicity was sought through a review of underlying policy. Despite these changes, the United States tax system remains complex. One factor which may have some bearing on this is that individual legislators in the United States have much more freedom than in some other countries to introduce Bills and provisions on their own. While there is some homogenisation in the legal language used, legislation produced in this way can never be completely standard.

Recently some of the regulations which govern the implementation of the statute have been relaxed. In April 1997, the United States Treasury Secretary, Mr Robert Rubin, released a new administration tax simplification package. This contained over 60 proposals to simplify the tax code for individuals and business. He also issued the 'Taxpayer Bill of Rights 3' to provide taxpayers with new rights.

Canada

There is no designated policy of tax simplification in Canada, and no current plans for a plain English rewrite of the Income Tax Act. The main changes in recent years have been in the procedures for enacting tax legislation.

Since 1990, there have been two separate tax Bills each year, a budget Bill and a technical Bill. The budget Bill deals with changes in policy whereas the technical Bill is for amendments to existing legislation (both minor and major) that stop short of a significant change in policy. The budget Bill is published after the budget announcement, although some parts of the Bill may be issued as draft legislation for consultation. The technical Bill is published in draft form and 9-12 months are usually allowed for consultation. Explanatory notes are published for each section. These have apparently been well received by tax practitioners who generally find them helpful. The notes do not have any statutory status and Revenue Canada does not regard them as binding.

The Tax Law Review Committee Initiative

Returning to the United Kingdom, I have already referred to the increasing concern among the users of tax legislation about the way in which it was developing. This concern manifested itself in the autumn of 1994 in the establishment by the United Kingdom Institute for Fiscal Studies of the Tax Law Review Committee (TLRC), a private sector body independent of government but with cross-party support. I readily accepted the Committee's invitation to be its President and it has been ably chaired by Graham Aaronson QC, one of the United Kingdom's leading tax barristers. It brings together a distinguished range of people – lay men and women as well as tax experts – from all walks of life: judges, politicians, accountants, lawyers, industrialists, academics, retired government officials and so on.

The TLRC's role is to take a careful, balanced look at particular aspects of the tax system. It does not seek to question government policy, but it does examine whether policy is being achieved in a satisfactory and efficient manner and, if not, how this could be improved. As I have already said, one of the first projects it undertook in late 1994 was to examine the way tax legislation is drafted. The TLRC published its preliminary findings in its Interim Report on Tax Legislation in November 1995 and followed this with its Final Report in June 1996. The TLRC's main conclusions were as follows.

First, tax legislation should be drafted in a plain English style using shorter sentences and a clearer structure. The TLRC argued that it was possible to write precise and accurate tax law, providing the certainty which taxpayers need, without resort to the complex and impenetrable style which the draftsman has traditionally used. It demonstrated this was so by rewriting two blocks of existing legislation into plain English. The TLRC recognised that drafting in a wholly new – plain English – style would represent a very substantial culture change for everyone involved in producing and using fiscal legislation. But it had no doubt that such a culture change should be made.

Second, the TLRC proposed that legislation should be accompanied by explanatory memoranda. These would contain explanations of each clause of a Bill, including background information, the purpose of the clause, how it would operate and other details to help users understand and interpret the legislation.

These first two proposals principally related to future legislation. If fully implemented they would halt the rapid spiral of decline into ever deeper complexity. But they could not be expected to reverse that decline. This could only be done by rewriting existing tax legislation in plain English. The TLRC wanted to be sure that the costs of such a rewrite would be justified by the benefits. It did not feel able to make this judgement without further information and therefore recommended a pilot project to test the proposition.

The TLRC's final proposal was that, in the longer term, tax Bills should be drafted in more general terms, not elaborated in great detail as tends to happen now. But the primary legislation would need to be supported by secondary legislation to fill in some of the consequences flowing from the general principles. The TLRC was concerned that the current parliamentary processes for scrutinising secondary legislation are inadequate for the task. Nevertheless, it was optimistic that changes in parliamentary procedures might be achievable. If a new parliamentary committee were created with powers to review and amend drafts of Statutory Instruments for tax, the TLRC believed it would become possible to draft primary fiscal legislation in general principles.

The United Kingdom Tax Law Rewrite

As I have already indicated, in parallel with the TLRC review the Inland Revenue were carrying out their own review. Their Report was presented to Parliament in December 1995. Following further consideration of the main issues, the decision to proceed with a major project to rewrite some 6000 pages of direct tax legislation, over a period of five years, was confirmed in July 1996.

Objectives of the Project

The project will rewrite all (or most) of the United Kingdom's existing primary tax legislation in order to make it clearer and easier to use, without changing or making less certain its general effect. The project relates to Revenue taxes only and does not affect Customs and Excise legislation. Customs and Excise have initiated their own project, known as 'Legis', which is looking at the potential to standardise their business processes across all the taxes for which they are responsible – mainly VAT and the various excise duties. It will then move on to simplify (as far as possible) and consolidate Customs and Excise legislation.

The work to rewrite Revenue taxes is organised on established project lines, and the project team has identified six 'critical success factors' which must all be fully achieved if the project is to be adjudged a success. In some cases, the project team will not be solely or even mainly responsible for ensuring that these are met, but it will have a contribution to make to all of them at appropriate times. The six critical success factors are as follows.

(1) The rewritten legislation must be accepted by all the main users as clearer and easier to apply and as preserving the effect of the present legislation apart from minor agreed changes in policy.

(2) Parliament must be able to scrutinise and enact the rewritten legislation in accordance with clearly defined and appropriate parliamentary procedures and an agreed timetable.

(3) The main users, both inside and outside the Department, must be kept fully informed about progress throughout the life of the project and, when appropriate, properly consulted in good time for their views to influence the rewrite work.

(4) The operational implications of the rewrite work for the Department must be identified and properly addressed.

(5) The lessons learned from the experience of successfully rewriting the legislation should be developed, in close consultation with the main users, into new 'best practice' for producing tax legislation in the future.

(6) The project – including all the people in the Project Team - must be managed effectively and efficiently and all the project's objectives must be achieved within the agreed programme and budget.

From these high-level objectives, a detailed project plan has been developed and this is used to keep track of progress.

As the first critical success factor makes clear, the project is about simplifying the language and structure of tax legislation. There is no intention of changing the underlying tax policy. Such policy changes will continue to be dealt with in the normal way through the Budget and Finance Bill process. However, in the course of the rewrite, there will be instances where further clarity of the law can be achieved by simplifying minor rules, subject of course to the approval of Ministers and Parliament. In other cases, it will be desirable to enact current Extra Statutory Concessions or Statements of Practice and to discard provisions which are obsolete. In general, such minor changes to enable the legislation to be further clarified will be proposed in the relevant rewrite Bill. But, before any decisions are taken, they will be flagged up clearly for full public consultation.

The key points of the tax law rewrite are:

- a clearer and more logical structure for tax legislation;
- the use of plain language and other techniques to make the rewritten legislation more user-friendly; and
- more consistent and better signposted definitions.

The Structure of Rewritten Tax Law

The structure of the rewritten legislation is important for two reasons.
- At a lower level, a good structure makes the rewritten legislation more user-friendly. Users need to know where to start and a good structure makes the point of entry obvious. It gives a logical flow to the finished product which makes the rules easier to follow and easier to find. It also reduces (to some extent) the need for cross-referencing.
- At a higher level, the way in which the rewritten tax legislation is divided into separate Acts and grouped and ordered within those Acts also helps users. And it enables the work of rewriting the legislation and subsequently enacting it to be more effectively organised.

The United Kingdom project team considered various ways in which the present structure might be improved upon. A major structural point in this discussion was whether the current Income and Corporation Taxes Act (ICTA) should be split into separate Acts for income tax and corporation tax. The provisional view that emerged at the end of the consultation process in 1996 pointed towards:

- separate Acts covering income tax and corporation tax, possibly both including the appropriate capital gains charging provisions;
- individual Acts for each of the other main taxes;
- separate Acts for capital allowances and for capital gains computational provisions; and
- a separate Act for various general administrative provisions currently in the Taxes Management Act 1970.

These and other issues relating to structure and ordering will be considered more closely as the rewrite work proceeds. For the present, the provisional planning assumption is that the rewrite might result in the following main Acts:

- Income Tax (either tax- or individual-based);
- Corporation Tax (either tax- or company- based);
- Capital Allowances;
- Capital Gains (computational provisions);
- Stamp Duties;
- Inheritance Tax; and
- Administration.

The project team considered very carefully whether, within this framework, it would be helpful to attempt to establish in advance the structure of each Act. They were obviously aware that both the Australian and New Zealand projects had adopted an approach on these lines. However, they concluded that this approach would not be appropriate for United Kingdom legislation. Although they have developed a number of planning assumptions about how an Income Tax Act might be structured, the team has retained complete flexibility to change any of these assumptions if necessary.

The Tax Law Rewrite Work Programme for 1997

The decision not to establish the structure of an Act before the detailed rewriting work is well advanced has an important consequence for the organisation of the rewrite work. It effectively means that it will only be feasible to bring forward complete (or substantially complete) Bills for enactment by Parliament. This suggests that the project should, at one time, focus largely on a single tax, completing work on that before moving on to the next. Accordingly, the project's work programme for 1997 (and probably 1998) will concentrate primarily on income tax. At the time of writing, work is currently in progress on the following blocks of legislation:

- the main charging provisions for trading income of individuals;
- the main charging provisions for employment income;
- the main charging provisions for income from savings and investment;
- capital allowances; and
- a smaller, more technical, topic (single company trading losses).

In tandem with the rewriting of the legislation on company losses, an experiment in one or more methods of 'purposive or general principles drafting' is currently being carried out.

The project team is aiming to bring forward a first rewrite Bill for enactment in the 1997-98 parliamentary session. On present plans, this is likely to be the capital allowances legislation.

The project team intends to publish each batch of rewritten legislation in the form of draft clauses with a full commentary when it is ready. The first such Exposure Draft *Trading Income of Individuals: Part 1* was published on 31 July 1997. Further Exposure Drafts are due to be published later in the year. The general presumption is that, when these drafts have been fully considered and amended in the light of comments received, the rewritten legislation will be included in the relevant Bill for subsequent enactment.

The project team also proposes to publish a series of Technical Discussion Documents on general issues arising from the rewrite work. These may include draft rewritten legislation, but it will not be for immediate enactment. The first of these, testing out whether the basic rewrite techniques work when applied to the fairly complex Single Company Trading Loss provisions, was published in November 1997. A further Technical Discussion Document, likewise focusing on the single company trading loss provisions, will follow early in 1998. But, because these are corporation tax relevant provisions, they will not be enacted until the corporation tax Bill is ready.

Drafting the Rewritten Tax Law

Apart from the key question of structure, the rewrite project raises a number of important questions about the way in which the legislation is drafted, the design and layout of rewritten tax law, and the numbering system to be adopted.

The Inland Revenue Consultative Document, *Tax Law Rewrite: The way forward*, published in July 1996, outlined various drafting issues for further discussion. These included:

- the use of short sentences;
- the possibility of second-person drafting – addressing the taxpayer as 'you';
- avoiding archaic terms, legal jargon and drafters' shorthand;
- more consistent and better signposted definitions;
- gender-neutral drafting; and
- greater use of explanatory material.

In October 1996 the Inland Revenue published some illustrative examples of rewritten legislation which sought to employ many of these techniques, including an experiment in second person drafting.

The general response varied, although most commentators welcomed any move towards shorter sentences, clearer and more consistent use of definitions and (provided legal accuracy was not inadvertently affected) more up to date language. Many of the terms in the existing law have been interpreted by case law and this clearly might constrain the scope for changing the existing wording in some instances. The intention within the project is to make full use of these techniques but also to apply a large measure of common sense. The overall objective is to rewrite the tax law in the clearest and simplest terms that can be achieved.

There was little enthusiasm for second person drafting. Although some commentators agreed that the experiment clearly demonstrated the direct impact such an approach could have, they felt that it would be confusing where provisions affected more than one party. They also considered that the other examples – which were drafted in the third person – achieved a suitably direct impact. I have myself considered whether second person drafting would assist clarity and impact in the rewrite context. In some (mainly advisory) documents, it can certainly help. But I concluded that in substantive, generally directed legislation, it can create more problems than it solves.

There was also relatively little enthusiasm among the main users of the legislation for gender-neutral drafting. Most of those who commented felt that such an approach could often make the text less clear and precise than it would otherwise be. I do not find this altogether surprising, not least because the consultees are mainly male. But the other side do feel very strongly about it. They have my sympathy and have had it for years (I started us down the road to separate taxation). But this is an area where classically absolutism – either way – is inappropriate. I draw the line at 'person-hole'. So my preference would be to go for gender-neutral drafting, save where it generates significant or unacceptable problems from other points of view. Once adopted, this approach is much less troublesome than many fear.

It was agreed, at the end of the public consultation process, that the rewrite would adopt a multi-character numbering system, and that the proposal to leave gaps in the legislation would not be helpful. Leaving gaps would make the legislation messy and no-one can predict how fiscal legislation will develop in the future. Wherever the gaps were placed it would be impossible to be sure that they would turn out to be where most needed.

The project team is also considering possible improvements in the format of the rewritten legislation that it will publish, taking full account of the work which has already been done in this country and elsewhere. The question of how, and in what format, the rewrite Bills will be published is of course a matter for Parliament to decide.

Enactment and Implementation of the Rewritten Tax Law

The project to rewrite tax law raised the crucial issue about how Parliament would handle tax simplification Bills intended to enact the rewritten tax law. These Bills would not, in the technical sense, be consolidation Bills. However, neither would it be possible for Parliament to handle them under the ordinary Public Bill procedure. It seemed clear that a new, tailor-made procedure would be required to enable Parliament to scrutinise the rewritten legislation properly but without opening up the debate on the full range of fiscal policy matters. Affecting as it does the quality of the eventual legislation, this is a topic in which I have long had a particular interest. So I was very happy to chair a working party set up by the TLRC to look at how Parliament might resolve this question.

Helpfully, from our review of the historical precedents, it became clear that a reasonably close analogy to the tax simplification Bills was to be found in the Customs and Excise Act 1952. This Act was designed to consolidate customs and excise law – which at the time was spread across 200 separate Acts enacted over more than 150 years – with amendments to simplify it and bring it into conformity with modern practice. The draft Customs and Excise Bill was examined by an independent committee – chaired by a peer, the first Lord Kennet, and including users of customs and excise legislation – which consulted very widely and made various changes to the Bill. An *ad hoc* parliamentary procedure was adopted under which the Bill was referred – exceptionally for a tax Bill, but with impressive success – to a joint committee of both Houses which heard evidence and made further amendments. Thereafter, the Bill passed through its remaining parliamentary stages with minimal debate and amendment.

Taking into account our review of historical precedent, the report of our working party (TLRC, 1996b) proposed that tax simplification Bills should be introduced in the House of Commons, accompanied by explanatory memoranda to help Parliament understand their nature and direct its attention. We also felt that there would be a real advantage in enabling peers to play an active part in the consideration of these Bills. Our fundamental proposal was therefore that each tax simplification Bill should be referred, after Second Reading in the House of Commons, to a Joint Committee of both Houses. We regarded it as axiomatic that the entire tax code could not be enacted in a single Bill, and our report assumed that the rewritten legislation would be enacted in a series of Bills.

Ministers of the previous Government broadly endorsed the general approach outlined in our report. The Chancellor of the Exchequer, the Rt Hon Kenneth Clarke, QC, MP, in his Budget Statement of November 1996, invited the House of Commons Select Committee on Procedure to consider our recommendations. The Committee reported in February 1997 and endorsed our main recommendation that after second reading in the House of Commons, tax simplification Bills should be referred to a Joint Committee of both Houses, with a Commons majority and a Commons Chairman. A Standing Order was passed by the House of Commons on 20 March 1997, setting out the broad procedure for the enactment of the rewrite Bills. However, the details of the Terms of Reference and membership of the Joint Committee were left to be resolved by the new Parliament.

Tax Law Rewrite Project Team

The Inland Revenue have set up a separate project team to carry out the rewrite of tax law. The team has the following structure:

- an Inland Revenue Project Director;
- a drafting team headed by a senior Parliamentary Counsel on secondment to the project;
- a series of small mixed-discipline rewrite teams, each responsible for a different area of legislation;
- a small policy team;
- a project management and support team; and
- secretarial support.

One member of the drafting team will work closely with each rewrite team on the actual rewriting of the legislation. Each rewrite team will have three members from the Inland Revenue – a tax inspector, a lawyer and someone with a tax policy background – and also someone from the private sector who will provide vital input from an outside perspective.

The project team is therefore adopting an innovative approach to the work in several ways. It is unusual for members of the Revenue's Solicitor's Office to be involved on a day to day basis, working alongside policy and technical specialists, in the preparation of legislation. It is a new departure for people with a private sector background to be involved in such work in precisely the same way. And there are no precedents of which the Revenue are aware for parliamentary drafters to be so closely involved, on a day to day basis, in the process. Many will perhaps be surprised that all this has never happened before. In my view, the project team's approach deserves to be commended.

Steering Committee

A very high degree of user involvement is essential to the success of the tax law rewrite, and it is good to know that everyone involved in the project is determined to proceed with it on the basis of full consultation with all interested parties. The Steering Committee for the rewrite – of which I am the Chairman – is an important element in this process. The main role of this Committee is to provide strategic guidance to the project. It needs to satisfy itself that the project is meeting its objectives of clarity and user-friendliness and is taking full account of private sector concerns.

The Committee clearly will not be able to scrutinise the rewritten legislation line by line to testify to its accuracy. Ultimately that is the responsibility of the project team. But the endorsement of the Steering Committee that the project is being properly managed and has in place all the necessary processes to ensure that these objectives can be met will assure Ministers, Parliament and the outside world about the quality of the rewrite – which should make the passage of the rewrite Bills in Parliament a smoother process.

The other members of the Committee are the Rt Hon Sir John Balcombe (a Lord Justice of Appeal from 1985-95); Mr Ian Barlow (Head of Tax at KPMG, Chartered Accountants); Dr John Avery Jones CBE (Senior Partner at Speechly Bircham, Solicitors, and a Deputy Special Commissioner); Mr Steve Matheson CB (Deputy Chairman, Board of Inland Revenue); Dr John Marek MP (Labour Member of Parliament for Wrexham); Mr Nick Gibb MP (Conservative Member of Parliament for Bognor Regis and Littlehampton); Ms Sheila McKechnie OBE (Director of the Consumers' Association); Sir John Shaw (Deputy Governor of the Bank of Scotland); and Mr David Swaine (former Group Taxation Manager for Royal Dutch Shell).

Consultative Committee

As I mentioned at the beginning of this chapter, all rewritten legislation will be exposed as drafts for public comment. In addition, representative bodies of taxpayers and the professions (accountants, lawyers, etc.) will be involved in the rewrite through the Consultative Committee. This will have three elements:

- a core group of representative bodies who will be involved throughout the project and who will be invited to attend all the meetings. This group will include representatives of the main tax professional and business bodies plus some others;
- a group of specialist representative bodies who will receive all the papers of the Committee and who will be invited to attend meetings when a subject relevant to their interests is being discussed; and
- Inland Revenue and other government officials. The officials attending will vary depending on the subject matter being considered.

The core membership of the Consultative Committee is about 20 members, with nearly three-quarters coming from the private sector. To spread the work load, the Committee may choose to delegate some of its work to sub-committees. The Committee is chaired by the Inland Revenue Project Director.

The role of the Committee is to ensure full consultation on the rewritten tax law with all the relevant private sector interests before the high level Steering Committee comes to a final view on it. To provide a link between the two Committees, a representative of the private sector side of the Consultative Committee will attend meetings of the Steering Committee as a deputy chairman of the Consultative Committee, together with the Inland Revenue Project Director.

Costs and Benefits of the Rewrite of Tax Law

There is no United Kingdom precedent for this sort of project, which inevitably means that at this early stage the costs are somewhat easier both to identify and quantify than the likely benefits.

For both the public and private sectors, the costs imposed by the rewrite of tax law should primarily be short-term only with little, if any, long-run costs. These costs will mainly be those of adapting to the new rewritten tax law, learning new statutory references and so on. For the public sector, the biggest element is the cost of the project team, although there will also be some costs from the need to update Inland Revenue guidance material and training products.

The benefits of the tax law rewrite will come from the clarification of existing law and the scope for future changes to that law to be expressed more clearly. However, it is impossible at this stage to quantify these benefits (as the Australians and New Zealanders have already found). Their value will depend on how effectively the rewrite is done and what behavioural changes occur thereafter. In general, however, it seems difficult to argue against the proposition that rewritten legislation which is easier to understand and use should lead to:

- lower compliance costs for taxpayers;
- more accurate application of the law;
- fewer disputes between the Inland Revenue and taxpayers and their advisers; and
- better customer service from the Inland Revenue.

Most commentators believe that the benefits of the tax law rewrite will outweigh the costs of moving to the new rewritten legislation. But it seems clear that these benefits will probably not start to come through until a substantial part of the rewritten tax law has been enacted.

Conclusion

Many people will share my delight that after a great many years of struggle, it has been possible to mobilise the huge political will which is essential if we are to effect the fundamental changes in the way our tax law is expressed. There is, today, a strong head of steam in support of the case for change. We need to ensure that this is maintained and kept up. We must not lose sight of this very worthwhile project in the excitement of a new government and a competing set of legislative priorities. So I am pleased that the early indications from the new Government, notwithstanding their many other pre-occupations at the present time, are all supportive of this.

Plain language law, law which is clear and user-friendly, is obtainable. Everyone is agreed on the key components: a clearer structure of what it is intended to achieve; much shorter sentences; clearer and better signposted definitions; modern design and layout and headings that help the user.

There is no dispute that plain language law can bring huge benefits. It can bring about a reduction in compliance costs. It was estimated a few years ago that the cost of compliance for Inland Revenue taxes alone amounts to some £4 billion per year. It can help us to ease the process of future policy reform if we enable future Finance Bills to be simpler and clearer. But, if all this is to be achieved, it will require a very substantial culture change from everyone involved in producing fiscal legislation. Based on my experience of working with all those involved in the United Kingdom tax law rewrite project, I am confident that we have made a successful beginning.

I hope that it is a legitimate summation on which to close this chapter by quoting three more sentences from my 1977 speech to the Addington Society:

> 'It is the politician who must bear the responsibility for changing the system, whether as ministers or parliamentarians. It is we who are in charge. Only we can change the system.'

References and Further Reading

House of Commons Select Committee on Procedure, *Legislative Procedure for Tax Simplification Bills*, The Stationery Office, London, February 1997.

Inland Revenue, *Tax Law Rewrite: The way forward*, London, July 1996.

Inland Revenue, *Tax Law Rewrite: Plans for 1997*, London, December 1996.

Inland Revenue, *The Path to Tax Simplification: a report under Section 160 Finance Act 1995 and Background Paper*, London, December 1995.

Tax Law Review Committee, *Interim Report on Tax Legislation*, Institute for Fiscal Studies, London, November 1995.

Tax Law Review Committee, *Final Report on Tax Legislation*, Institute for Fiscal Studies, London, June 1996.

Tax Law Review Committee, *Parliamentary Procedures for the Enactment of Rewritten Tax Law*, Institute for Fiscal Studies, London, November 1996.

CHAPTER 6

DEALING WITH COMPLAINTS – THE ADJUDICATOR: A UNITED KINGDOM EXPERIMENT

Elizabeth Filkin*

Introduction

'The might of the Inland Revenue fills taxpayers with dread – but a tax watchdog can help turn the tables... The Revenue Adjudicator is one of many financial watchdogs receiving a record number of complaints...'[1]

Any operation which has human beings in it will find that things go wrong from time to time. The United Kingdom Inland Revenue is no exception. It is a large organisation which deals with a great many people. And, no matter how well the Inland Revenue deals with its customers, and runs its systems, there will always be some people who are unhappy with the service they have received.

The Citizen's Charter

In 1991, the United Kingdom Government launched the Citizen's Charter, an initiative designed to improve the standard of public services and to make them more responsive to users. The Charter contains six principles of good public service. The fifth of these is 'Putting Things Right'. This is defined as meaning that, if things go wrong, the organisation should give an apology, a full explanation and a swift and effective remedy; and that there should be well-publicised and easy to use complaints procedures, with independent review wherever possible.

*The Adjudicator for the United Kingdom Inland Revenue, Customs and Excise and the Contributions Agency of the Department of Social Security.

[1]*Daily Mirror*, 25 April 1995.

In response to this initiative, the Inland Revenue created the post of Revenue Adjudicator. I took up the post in June 1993. From 1 April 1995, I also started looking at complaints about Customs and Excise and the Contributions Agency of the Department of Social Security. To reflect these changes in my role, my office became known simply as the Adjudicator's Office, and I as the Adjudicator.

Before the Adjudicator's Office

United Kingdom taxpayers who are unhappy with the amount of tax they have to pay have always had the right to take disagreements about their liability to independent tribunals, known as the General and Special Commissioners. But the actions of the Inland Revenue that upset and frustrate some people often have nothing to do with the amount of tax they have to pay. Instead, they are unhappy about the way the Inland Revenue have handled their tax affairs or the way they have been treated.

Before my office opened, the Inland Revenue carried out its own review of such complaints. Understandably, some taxpayers were sceptical about the impartiality of such reviews. If they were unhappy with the Inland Revenue's review of their complaint, their only other course of action was to ask a Member of Parliament to consider referring it to the Parliamentary Commissioner for Administration (more commonly known as the Ombudsman). This is a statutory appointment, and the Ombudsman has wide responsibility for the investigation of administrative action throughout government departments.

The Parliamentary Commissioner for Administration, then Sir William Reid, said in his 1994 Annual Report:

> 'The way in which [the Adjudicator's Office] has developed shows clearly that there is a need for someone to handle complaints dealing with particular departments of government without the complainant initially having to invoke my help'.

The Adjudicator's Remit

What I Consider

I investigate the way the Inland Revenue, Customs and Excise and the Contributions Agency have handled their customers' affairs. I look at such matters as: delay; mistakes; staff behaviour (for example, rudeness and harassment); poor or misleading advice; and the exercise of discretion.

Throughout this chapter, I will often refer solely to the Inland Revenue. They represent the bulk of my work. But my procedures and my agreements with the Inland Revenue, Customs and Excise and the Contributions Agency are broadly the same.

What I Do Not Consider

I do not look at matters of law or disputes about the amounts of tax that someone has to pay. There are statutory procedures for resolving these problems that are already well established; for example, the General Commissioners and VAT Tribunals. The decisions of these tribunals are binding, and for me to look at the same issues would be a waste of public money.

I also do not look at complaints about government policy (which is a matter for Ministers and Parliament), complaints that have already been investigated, or are currently under scrutiny, by the Parliamentary Ombudsman, and matters that are, or have been, before the courts.

In the case of the Contributions Agency, I do not look at appeals against decisions made by the Secretary of State for Social Security about someone's National Insurance liability.

The Adjudicator's Role

Approach

My approach to, and the underlying principles of, my work are the same for the Inland Revenue, Customs and Excise and the Contributions Agency. My role is to act as an impartial referee where people feel they have been badly treated by any of these three organisations. When someone complains to me, I consider all the arguments and, if I think the complaint is justified, I make recommendations about how the organisation should put things right.

Staff

I have recruited a team of skilled staff to assist me in carrying out my work. The Adjudicator's Office currently has over 40 staff. Some have been seconded to the office after experience working in various parts of the Inland Revenue, Customs and Excise and the Contributions Agency. Others have come from outside the Civil Service, bringing complementary skills and a different viewpoint; for example, we have accountants, barristers, solicitors and other advice workers. Staff in the Adjudicator's Office are responsible to me.

The Work of the Adjudicator's Office

The Adjudicator's Office provides assurance for the public, for Parliament, and for the managers and staff of the organisations concerned that the considerable powers of those organisations are not being misused, and that the organisations are trying to ensure that their staff have high standards of behaviour and provide good customer service.

In June 1993 the United Kingdom Government set up a Citizen's Charter Complaints Task Force to undertake a wide-ranging review of public service complaints systems and to ensure that they operate in line with the principles of the Citizen's Charter. The Task Force has drawn up a list of principles which they think good complaints systems should follow. The seven principles are that complaints systems should:

- be easily accessible and well publicised;
- be simple to understand and use;
- allow speedy handling, with established time limits for action, and keep people informed of progress;
- ensure a full and fair investigation;
- respect people's desire for confidentiality;
- address all the points at issue, and provide an effective response and appropriate redress; and
- provide information to management so that services can be improved.

These principles form the basis of the way in which my office works.

We Aim to be Accessible and to Publicise Our Work

If genuine complaints are to be encouraged, it is clearly important that anyone with a complaint should know how to make it and to whom. We do a lot of work promoting the Adjudicator's Office. I and my staff frequently speak to a wide variety of organisations, both private and public, at seminars, meetings and conferences.

We have published leaflets telling people how to complain about the Inland Revenue, Customs and Excise and the Contributions Agency. These leaflets are available in a number of the main minority languages in the United Kingdom, as well as in English, and our Customs and Excise leaflet is also available in most of the main European languages. This helps to ensure that visitors travelling to and from the United Kingdom, who might for example wish to complain about the way they have been treated by Customs and Excise, know where to find us. All our leaflets are widely available, for example in libraries and public offices.

The organisations also include our details in a number of their own leaflets and in the notes accompanying some of the material they send to their customers. For example, the Inland Revenue refer to us on their tax return forms, assessments, repayment claim forms and coding notices. We find that this is an effective way of publicising our work. But one of the most effective ways for people to find out about our service is for officials in the organisations to tell people about us when they complain.

The media show great interest in my office. I find that, whenever we are mentioned in the press or on television or radio, we receive many new complaints.

We also encourage visitors to the office. We have had visits from a wide range of people and organisations, from Ministers to small community organisations. And our visitors are not just from the United Kingdom. Many other countries are interested in what we do and seek to learn from us. These visits give us an opportunity to encourage and support good complaints handling.

We Try to Make Our Procedures Simple to Understand and Use

If other than the most persistent people are to complain, the mechanism for complaining needs to be simple to understand and use. This is especially so if organisations want to hear about the more minor irritations people have – and these minor irritations may well contain valuable management information as well as being responsible for a general malaise amongst customers and staff.

It is also important to remember that there is likely to be an information gap, and often an education gap as well, between officials in a public sector body and their customers. For an official dealing with a subject every day, it might seem relatively easy to express a complaint about that subject in detail and in writing. Customers may well find this more difficult. They may need help in clarifying the precise terms of their complaint. To many of them there is something frightening about officialdom and its language. And they may find it off-putting if they are asked to put things in writing, or to fill in a form. Research in the United Kingdom for the Citizen's Charter Unit indicates that the majority of people prefer to complain by telephone; yet in the United Kingdom many public sector organisations insist that people put their complaints in writing.

We try to be as friendly and approachable as possible to the public. A lot of our work is done on the telephone.

We Aim to Settle Complaints as Quickly as Possible

The Parliamentary Ombudsman in the United Kingdom has commented that:

> 'Justice delayed is not always justice denied but it may well seem so to an aggrieved complainant. At least it can only aggravate the complainant's sense of grievance.'

What constitutes speedy handling is likely to depend on the nature of the particular complaint. If a person sees their complaint as being straightforward (e.g. 'I have not received a reply to a simple letter I sent 2 months ago') they are unlikely to be impressed if the matter is not sorted out very quickly. But if a complaint is clearly complex (e.g. 'I wish to complain about the way my tax affairs have been investigated over the last 5 years'), most people will accept that a thorough investigation of the complaint is likely to take some time. Surveys carried out by my office have shown that our customers (whose complaints about the Inland Revenue tend to be complex) rate speedy handling of their complaint highly, but not as highly as a thorough investigation.

We Carry Out Full and Fair Investigations

Few, if any, public sector organisations would disagree with the proposition that all complaints should be investigated fully and fairly. And there is evidence to suggest that a full and fair investigation is the top priority of complainants.

However, while there is an apparent symmetry here, it is not always easy to ensure that investigations are in fact full and fair, or, if they are, that they are accepted by complainants as being so.

For the organisation, the initial challenge is to be able to see things from the complainant's point of view, as well as from the organisation's perspective, and then to be able to form a detached and objective judgement. This may not always be easy. Officials are inevitably used to seeing things from the organisation's viewpoint rather than the customer's. What may seem an everyday minor hiccup to an official may feel quite different to a complainant who is unfamiliar with the system. There may also be an understandable tendency for managers to want to support and defend the actions of their staff.

Although an organisation may have carried out a full investigation and reached a fair decision, it may not seem that way to a complainant, particularly if the outcome goes against them. Complainants may be particularly difficult to satisfy if they feel that it is unjust that they have to deal with the organisation anyway.

This is where my office comes into its own. People will often accept my views on their complaint, even when they are not different from those of the organisation concerned. This is because they feel reassured that their complaint has been looked at impartially. This leaves not only a contented complainant but also fulfils a vital function for the organisation.

We Respect People's Confidentiality

People who complain have the right to have their complaint dealt with discreetly and to have no need to fear that they may be victimised or prejudiced in some way in the future. This is an issue linked to fairness. It is vital that organisations in the public sector are sensitive to it. The organisations are often monopoly suppliers. People may be happy to complain about the service provided by a private sector shop, as they may be able to choose which shop to use. They may be less happy complaining about their tax office, which they are likely to have to continue to deal with in the future.

In addition to senior managers making clear to staff that they must not discriminate against complainants, possible ways of dealing with customers' anxieties include making clear in complaints literature that the organisation's policy is not to discriminate, and providing an independent review system for people who feel they are being victimised. We tell people who are worried that we are there to ensure this does not happen. Again we are in the business of providing assurance.

We Ensure an Effective Response and Appropriate Redress

Clearly there is little point in complaining if the outcome is unlikely to be an effective response and appropriate redress. Research for the United Kingdom Citizen's Charter Unit indicates that the reason people most commonly give for not complaining is that they do not think that making a complaint would make any difference.

Redress can take various forms, but there are perhaps three main types:

- an apology;
- putting matters right (for the complainant and for others); and
- compensation.

Apologies. Any mistake is likely to deserve an apology, and for simple mistakes this may be all that the complainant wants. My experience suggests that, to be effective, an apology needs to be given soon after the complaint is made, and needs to be genuine rather than begrudging. Letters which extensively record minor errors on the complainant's part, and only curtly accept major errors on the part of the organisation, cannot be expected to settle a complaint. Our role is to make sure that the remedy is an appropriate one.

We get the organisation to put matters right. Where a complaint is about something that can be put right, it is obviously important that the organisation does so. For example, if an organisation finds that it has neglected to reply to a letter, it should do so without further delay. As with apologies, the speed with which action is taken is likely to be important.

Ideally, organisations should, where appropriate, identify instances where similar mistakes have been made and put matters right without having to be asked. Organisations should also try to prevent similar mistakes happening in the future, perhaps by providing additional training, changing systems, or telling staff more clearly what is required of them.

We ensure that appropriate compensation is paid. Compensation can take various forms. Some organisations make small automatic payments if they do not meet published standards. Others reimburse people for any additional costs or losses they have suffered as a result of an error. This is what the United Kingdom Inland Revenue do if they have made a serious or persistent error. And some organisations recompense people for the trouble or inconvenience they have been put to because of a mistake or problem with the service. These are sometimes called consolatory payments.

An important consideration for organisations is likely to be the cost of paying compensation. If organisations have fixed resources, there is an argument for saying that paying compensation simply diverts resources away from providing and improving services. However, a counter-argument is that compensation schemes help to focus the minds of organisations on the importance of getting things right first time, and so can ultimately lead to cost savings. There is also the subjective matter of what seems a fair outcome in any particular situation.

There is unlikely to be a single approach that is appropriate to all organisations. Each organisation is likely to want to set up its own schemes in the light of its own resources and its own customers' expectations and demands. And all organisations need to ensure that they manage public funds wisely. My concern is that, within proper constraints, the organisations do offer some compensation when things have gone badly wrong.

Is an Adjudicator Too Expensive?

I have mentioned costs briefly in the context of paying compensation. But resource considerations are relevant to the whole issue of complaints handling. If an organisation is to follow the principles I have described, it is likely to have to spend money on things like training, and information technology for logging complaints. It is also likely to have to commit the time of good quality staff to complaints issues.

Balanced against this is the argument that complaints help organisations to identify ways of improving efficiency and of making long-term savings.

The Citizen's Charter Complaints Task Force in the United Kingdom has found some concern amongst public sector organisations about the cost of introducing comprehensive complaints handling systems, given budget constraints. But very few of these organisations seem to have done much work on costing how much they currently spend on complaints handling, how much money it would cost to improve how they handle complaints, and how much money they could save if they were able to identify ways of avoiding mistakes in the first place.

There may be a case for suggesting that organisations do more to estimate the costs and benefits of improved complaints handling. But I am of the view that, if organisations are serious about improving the quality of customer service and the efficiency of their operation, they must accept that complaints handling is an area where they should properly expend resources.

Management Information

If an organisation as a whole is to learn from complaints, rather than just the individual member of staff dealing with the complaint, it is important that information about complaints is brought together within the organisation. In this way, trends can be identified and appropriate improvements put in place for all customers.

A key challenge for organisations is setting up a system which collects sufficient information to allow analysis, without imposing an overly onerous recording burden on staff. My office has developed a computer system to do this.

Adjudication and Ombudsmen schemes can also provide important management information based on their independent reviews of complaints. For instance, in the United Kingdom, my office provides Inland Revenue, Customs and Excise and Contributions Agency operational units with a quarterly report on all complaints that we deal with. I also publish an Annual Report.

Against this background, it seems to me that there are two equally important parts to our work:

- sorting out complaints; and
- feeding back to the organisations our views on what complaints tell us about how they might improve the service they provide their customers.

Sorting Out Complaints

We provide an impartial and accessible service for resolving complaints from the public about the three organisations.

From the date my office opened in May 1993 to the end of September 1997, we had received about 12,300 complaints in total, of which over 10,500 were about the Inland Revenue.

Assistance cases. We do not investigate a complaint until the organisation has had a chance to sort things out first.

People often come to us with a complaint before the organisation has had a chance to resolve the problem. This may be because people are unsure about to whom they should complain, or, sometimes, because they are worried about the possible repercussions if they complain to the organisation itself.

We call these cases *assistance cases*. When we get such a complaint, the staff in our Assistance Team review it quickly and try to understand it; they will clarify things with the complainant if they do not feel a complaint is sufficiently clear. Once they have done this, they refer the complaint to the appropriate office of the organisation.

We always tell complainants that they can come back to us if they are not satisfied with the organisation's response; we tell them that if they do this we will take their complaint up for investigation as long as it within my remit. I see this as facilitating the organisations' internal complaints systems.

Up to the end of September 1997, we had dealt with over 10,000 of these cases, of which around 8,500 were about the Inland Revenue.

This part of our work has proved invaluable. It helps the organisations' complaints system to work and it gets people's problems sorted out. It also keeps the organisations under scrutiny. They try very hard to deal with complaints well because they know that if they fail they will have to face a very thorough investigation by my office.

Investigation cases. We call complaints that we take up for full review investigation cases. Up to the end of September 1997, we had taken up over 2,300 complaints for full investigation. Of these, over 2,000 were about the Inland Revenue.

When we investigate a complaint we try to get to the bottom of what has happened. We ask the organisation for a full report about the complaint and for all their papers. We review this material, together with the information provided by the complainant. Sometimes we find we need to gather more information. Our caseworkers often meet the people involved in a complaint – officials and complainants (or their agents), to get a full picture of the facts.

Sometimes I decide I need to speak to an official or a complainant myself to find out more about a complaint. We call such a meeting a hearing: I want to hear what officials and complainants have to say about the complaint. Because this is the aim, I do not invite people to speak to me through a representative. But if a person wishes to be accompanied, I am happy to agree to this so long as the person concerned has not been involved in the matter under review.

Methods of Settling Investigation Cases

Mediation. Where we think it appropriate, we will try to mediate a settlement of the complaint. In most of these cases we 'broke' an agreement between the organisation and the complainant. But sometimes, after reviewing the complaint thoroughly, my staff explain to the complainant that they believe I will not uphold their complaint. This may be because they believe the organisation has handled the complainant's affairs properly, or, where the organisation has admitted mistakes or other poor service, has offered settlement terms which my staff believe I would consider reasonable. Complainants are very often willing to accept this in settlement of their complaint because they are reassured that the matter has been reviewed independently.

I believe mediation is a very constructive way to settle a complaint. Resolution in this way tends to be quicker, and is therefore cheaper. And where the organisation (and often the complainant) has been willing to reconsider or compromise, this can lead to a better relationship between them for the future.

To date, we have settled close to 40 per cent of investigation cases by mediation, and the trend is upwards. I welcome this and will continue to encourage the organisations in this positive approach. I have seen them develop their creativity and problem-solving capacity through these arrangements.

Recommendation. If settlement by mediation is not possible, I will make a formal recommendation about how I believe a complaint should be settled. We have settled just over 50 per cent of investigation cases in this way. The trend is downwards.

Where I believe that the organisation has given a complainant poor service I can recommend that it takes action to put things right. For example, I might recommend that the Inland Revenue apologises, explains its actions, gives up tax and interest, reviews its procedures, instructions and guidance, carries out a management review and reports back to me, pays compensation for actual costs, and makes a consolatory payment for distress or botheration.

When they pay compensation to people who suffer loss as a result of their mistakes, the organisations have to be conscious of the need to be prudent with public funds. The Inland Revenue have published a Code of Practice which sets out the general circumstances in which they will pay compensation. I think it is right that these polices should be generally known, and I welcome the publication of Codes of Practice in this and other areas.

When I consider a claim for compensation against the Inland Revenue, I try to ensure that they treat all taxpayers fairly and consistently. This means that I look to see whether payment is appropriate within the terms of their Code of Practice. I try to do this by applying common sense to the interpretation of the Code.

In 1996, the Inland Revenue revised their Code of Practice to include rules for paying compensation for such things as the distress and botheration people suffer as a result of Inland Revenue mistakes. The Inland Revenue call these consolatory payments. I am very pleased about this as I had felt for some time that the Inland Revenue should have some mechanism to do this.

In our last full year (1 April 1996 to 31 March 1997), I recommended that the Inland Revenue pay compensation in 136 cases we had investigated, and in 28 a consolatory payment. Compensation for complainants' actual costs amounted to close to £90,000, and the consolatory payments total was a further £7,500.

Of course, in many cases, I feel that the organisation has dealt with a complainant's affairs fairly and reasonably. Up to the end of September 1997, I had not upheld 45 per cent of the complaints about the Inland Revenue we had investigated. In these cases, where I feel that the Inland Revenue have provided a proper service, I will tell the taxpayer as politely as possible that, in my view, the Inland Revenue have acted correctly. I have been pleased to note that many taxpayers, while disappointed when this is my view, find a thorough review draws a line under the matter and provides reassurance.

If someone is still unhappy after I have completed my investigation, they have the right to ask a Member of Parliament to consider referring their complaint to the Ombudsman.

Up to the end of September 1997, we had settled almost 2,000 investigation cases, about 1,700 of which were about the Inland Revenue. We upheld 50 per cent of these complaints overall, and 49 per cent of those about the Inland Revenue, either partly or wholly in favour of the complainant.

The Inland Revenue (and Customs and Excise and the Contributions Agency) have undertaken to accept my recommendations 'in all but exceptional circumstances'. To date, they have accepted all of them.

Providing Feedback

The other important part of our work is to use the experience gained from investigating complaints to enable the organisations to improve the quality of their operation. We supply a view from the 'outside' through the provision of feedback on individual cases and more general management information.

I have regular meetings with Board Members of the Inland Revenue and Customs and Excise, with the Chief Executives of the Contributions Agency and the Valuation Office Agency (which is part of the Inland Revenue), and with the senior managers responsible for the major executive units in these departments. We also spend a lot of time talking to groups of staff from these organisations. And we invite staff to visit the Adjudicator's Office, and provide information to help them with training events.

We prepare quarterly reports for the three organisations. In these reports, we raise issues we think they will find helpful in their work on complaints handling and operational practice. We include summaries of cases which we believe highlight good and bad practice and we provide detailed statistical information about our work. We also publish an Annual Report.

What We Have Seen

I know that the organisations deal effectively with the vast majority of people who tell them things have gone wrong. I see only a small, though important, minority of people who have not been satisfied by the organisations' internal complaints processes.

I have seen improvements in the way the organisations handle complaints and deal with their customers. I am seeing fewer cases where the issues are cut and dried. This improvement suggests that the organisations are sorting out more problems for their customers without people needing to come to the Adjudicator's Office. I very much welcome this.

This probably explains why the proportion of complaints about the Inland Revenue we have investigated and upheld has been decreasing year by year: 62 per cent in 1993-94; 51 per cent in 1994-95; 48 per cent in 1995-96; and 45 per cent in 1996-97. I regard this as some indication of the value of my office.

But I still see many problems. In the complaints we took up for investigation up to the end of September 1997, the main causes of complaint against the Inland Revenue were: mistakes (28 per cent); the way they use (or do not use) discretion (18 per cent); delay (16 per cent); and poor staff attitude (7 per cent). This latter category covers things like arrogance and harassment.

Inland Revenue Investigations

Before the introduction of Self Assessment in April 1997, the Inland Revenue could 'investigate' someone's tax return (including any business or other accounts that formed part of that return) if they were not satisfied that the return was correct.

But under Self Assessment, the Inland Revenue will no longer 'investigate' people's tax returns (although they can, for the moment, still investigate companies' returns because companies have not yet been brought into Self Assessment). They will, instead, make 'enquiries' of people's self-assessment returns. Under this new system, the Inland Revenue may select returns for enquiry at random, or because they feel a return may be incorrect or lacking in explanation. The Inland Revenue have said that they will not give people any reason for starting an enquiry.

The following paragraphs in this section of the chapter look at what I have seen in complaints about the way the Inland Revenue have carried out 'investigations'. At the time of writing (November 1997) I had not taken on any complaints about Inland Revenue 'enquiries' for investigation.

The Inland Revenue is a large and powerful organisation; so officials need to take care in using that power when investigating taxpayers' affairs. Complaints about Inland Revenue investigations have made up a large proportion of the complaints we have received. So this is obviously a sensitive and important area of work for us.

I know that tax inspectors have the difficult task of balancing taxpayers' rights with the need to collect the correct amount of tax. Taxpayers can sometimes cause difficulties, be dishonest or even violent. In the complaints I have seen about investigations, I feel the Inland Revenue have often carried them out well and treated taxpayers under investigation fairly and reasonably.

In many cases I have not upheld complaints about investigations which resulted in no additional profits or liabilities being established, or where there were very small additions. In my view, such an end result does not mean that the investigation was unwarranted. I look at whether the Inspector had good reason for opening the investigation and for continuing it.

The Investigations Code of Practice and the Investigation Handbook. I look at how the Inland Revenue carried out an investigation against their Code of Practice 2, *Investigations*, and Investigation Handbook.

The Code of Practice gives taxpayers some assurance about the way the Inland Revenue will conduct an investigation. This can help make a difficult and worrying situation for people being investigated a bit more comfortable. Where the Inland Revenue fail to observe the Code of Practice, taxpayers may get anxious and frustrated; they may wonder just what is going on. The Investigation Handbook tries to ensure that investigations are handled consistently throughout the country.

I have seen a number of cases where the Inland Revenue have failed to observe the Code of Practice or have ignored their instructions. For example, where I have felt that the Inland Revenue should not have started an investigation on the grounds given by the Inspector to the taxpayer for opening it. I believe that if the Inland Revenue fail to tell the taxpayer the real reason(s) for opening an investigation they deprive that person of their right to deal with the Inspector's concerns. This is contrary to the *Investigations* Code of Practice.

Other problems. It is very easy for the Inland Revenue to forget that to an ordinary taxpayer the Inland Revenue can seem to be a monolithic and frightening bureaucracy. For Inspectors, an investigation is an everyday matter; a normal part of their job. They are well used to how they work and what an investigation can involve; for example, interviews or enquiries into people's personal financial affairs.

But for most taxpayers an investigation is very worrying; for many it is also highly embarrassing. They know it may be highly detrimental to their finances, business and relationships. I have seen that Inspectors sometimes forget how distressing an investigation can be for someone.

Inspectors need to have proper regard to the taxpayer they are dealing with – people are all different and some will need a good deal of care and understanding if the Inspector is to carry out an effective and worthwhile investigation. Some taxpayers can take investigations in their stride; they will do all they can to assist the Inland Revenue with their investigation so that it can be closed as quickly as possible.

But others can react badly; they put up a brick wall against all questions, however reasonable. I have seen some cases where taxpayers have reacted in this way to reasonable Inland Revenue questions and requests.

Opening Investigations. I have seen a range of problems in the way the Inland Revenue open investigations. For example, some cases where they have carried out a poor, or no, preliminary review which has led to an investigation being opened on shaky grounds. In one case, an Inspector opened an investigation of a taxpayer's affairs on information about another taxpayer with a similar name. The Inspector had not examined the information carefully enough.

I have seen the Inland Revenue sending poor opening letters at the start of an investigation. They sometimes do not address the concerns the Inspector has identified and which are evident from information on file; do not explain that the Inspector has opened an investigation; and do not explain what concerns the Inspector has and what information is required from the taxpayer to answer the Inspector's concerns.

Investigations unreasonably prolonged. I have also seen problems in the way Inspectors pursue investigations. For example, where the Inspector has not taken reasonable account of information provided by a taxpayer, or where the Inland Revenue have ineffectively used meetings with taxpayers they are investigating; for example, where the Inspector has not raised all his or her concerns about the taxpayer's affairs or has not raised them properly.

Poor record keeping. When we review a complaint about an Inland Revenue investigation, we want to see in the Inland Revenue's papers a record of what the Inspector did, explanations of their decisions and actions, and details of their dealings with the taxpayer. For example, we would expect to see a full record of the preliminary review which identifies the Inspector's initial concerns about a taxpayer's affairs and which should show why an investigation is considered necessary, and of ongoing review notes. I have seen numbers of cases where these notes are poor - or where there are none at all.

Inspectors do very sensitive work. Because of this it is important that they keep records of their work so that others who may take up the case after them can see exactly what has happened. And of course, managers need to ensure that their people do this so that they can properly audit the work.

Poor investigation review by managers – failure to control and advise. The Inland Revenue's Investigation Handbook says that managers should periodically review investigations. A manager's advice or guidance may help an Inspector deal with an investigation better; for example, they can help avoid any unnecessary work as well as getting a fair result for the Inland Revenue.

Managers' guidance can also help progress complex cases, and help maintain a good relationship between an Inspector and taxpayer. And where things have gone wrong between these two parties, managers can help mend a fractured and difficult relationship.

But I have seen that some managers do not get involved as much as I feel they should when they do these reviews. In the cases I see, there is often a lack of supervision and support; sometimes it seems there have been no reviews at all.

The Inland Revenue are sometimes too easy on taxpayers. In many complaints I have reviewed, I believe the Inland Revenue have conducted investigations reasonably and fairly. But sometimes I feel they have made mistakes and have given the taxpayer a poor service.

Occasionally – in both types of cases – I see cases where the work seems ineffective because the Inspector has been less than rigorous. For instance, by taking too long to carry out an investigation or, from what I have seen on the files, closing an investigation with a surprisingly lenient settlement.

Staff Attitude

I see a number of complaints about the behaviour of Inland Revenue staff: that an official was rude, aggressive or unhelpful to a taxpayer. The introduction of Self Assessment in the United Kingdom is likely to bring more people into Tax Enquiry Centres and maybe increase the number of possible complaints about the way Inland Revenue officials have treated people.

I am concerned that the Inland Revenue do not seem to take these complaints as seriously as they should. I find that these complaints are difficult and time consuming to deal with because we often need to meet the official about whom the complaint has been made, and the complainant, to get their versions of events first hand. And our investigations are often inconclusive because we have two different experiences and accounts but nothing which corroborates either side. This is unsatisfactory for the complainant and the official, as well as for us.

I believe that the Inland Revenue do not handle this type of complaint at all well. There is rarely a meeting about the complaint between the official and the manager responsible. And where there has been a meeting, we often find that there is either no, or an inadequate, note of it. Likewise, they have often not handled the taxpayer well. They have not written a good apology letter or tried to sort things out on the telephone or by a visit.

I believe that the official and his manager should meet in these cases *for the benefit of the official.* Because a complaint has been made about them, I feel they should be given the opportunity to give their side of the story. If they are not, they may remain aggrieved about the matter and this can undermine performance the next time they must deal with a taxpayer.

In my view, managers and complaints handlers are far too defensive and dismissive of complaints about staff attitude or behaviour. Because of this, they can miss opportunities to identify problems which give rise to poor service, or further training needs. They can also miss the chance to coach the official in best practice.

Customs and Excise and the Contributions Agency

In the complaints we have investigated about Customs and Excise and the Contributions Agency we have found similar problems as those in the Inland Revenue cases we review. For example, delays, rudeness and mistakes.

Customs and Excise. About 20 per cent of the complaints we take up for investigation are about the way people feel they have been treated by Customs officers at ports, airports and international train terminals. For example, that they have been improperly stopped and searched by Customs officers because of their country of origin or race; that their baggage or other property has been damaged in a search; or that Customs officers have been rude to them.

Most Customs officers carry out this important work with great care and courtesy but I have found that sometimes they have not acted properly. Sometimes they have not made a proper record of a search, or they have damaged someone's luggage but failed to apologise or offer compensation.

An issue which has caused me particular concern has been the lack of control some Customs and Excise offices have of their civil recovery procedures. I have seen several cases where solicitors, acting on behalf of Customs and Excise, have failed to act on instructions given them by Customs and Excise with the result that people have suffered worry and distress.

For example, in one case, solicitors served a Statutory Demand on a taxpayer although he had agreed with Customs and Excise that they would not do this. The Demand caused the taxpayer great distress. In other cases, this type of problem has arisen because the Customs and Excise office has failed to liaise properly with their hired solicitors; for example, by not following up a discussion over the telephone with specific written instructions.

The Contributions Agency. I am very concerned about the complaints I see about the Contributions Agency. We have upheld over 75 per cent of the complaints we have investigated about the Agency.

One of the most concerning things has been their poor complaints handling. I have seen some very poor apology letters and failures to explain their actions and decisions properly. I have seen some very poor complaints review work: the Contributions Agency often do not review a complaint sufficiently thoroughly and as a result they come to an ill-judged conclusion. For example, in one case they did not review their original papers but relied only on a flawed and incomplete summary from an official. On this basis they did not uphold the complaint. But when we reviewed all their papers we found readily available information, which they had missed, which verified the complainant's view and meant that the complaint should be upheld.

I have also found that the Contributions Agency are, at all levels of the organisation, prone to unreasonable delays. Sometimes they simply do not tell customers how long they will take to deal with a particular matter, or they tell them they will do something by a certain time, and then fail to do so but without an apology or explanation.

Value of a Single Complaints Office

I feel it is helpful for people to have a single office to go to when they are unhappy with the way they have been dealt with by the Inland Revenue, Customs and Excise and the Contributions Agency. We have had some complaints from people who are upset by the service they have received from more than one of these organisations, and, with the permission of all parties, we have investigated these complaints as one. It makes our job very much easier and we feel we are able to provide better customer service by dealing with all aspects of a complaint in one investigation.

I have passed on examples and suggestions of good practice from one organisation to another to help ensure that they all provide a better level of service to the public as a whole.

For example, because I have been impressed by the often quick and effective management action Customs and Excise senior managers have taken in response to my recommendations in individual cases I have told the Inland Revenue and the Contributions Agency that they might learn from this.

And because I have been impressed by the overall breadth and depth of the Inland Revenue's actions to improve their customer service – for example, by devising and implementing a comprehensive Action Plan with specific and detailed targets – I have told Customs and Excise and the Contributions Agency that they have much to learn from the Inland Revenue's example.

Wider Implications

I believe it is vital that public services, especially large, powerful ones such as the Inland Revenue, treat complaints as an integral and important part of their daily business, providing a valuable tool in the drive for efficiency.

Independent adjudicators and ombudsmen can provide an important safety valve where organisations are unable to sort things out to the satisfaction of the complainant. They may also take on the role of a general watchdog of service standards in an organisation.

Several countries have expressed interest in my office, and have sent representatives to visit us to find out more about how we work. We have recently had visits from the Brazilian and Peruvian Revenue authorities, and in May 1995 I was invited to Japan to talk about my experience in dealing with complaints about the United Kingdom Inland Revenue. We have discussed our work with visitors from Russia, Pakistan, South Africa, Chile, France, Canada and the United States.

In their June 1995 report, *Putting Things Right*, the Citizen's Charter Complaints Task Force said they had been 'particularly impressed' by our work in dealing with assistance cases, using conciliation as a means of resolution where possible, and:

'influencing directly the quality of customer care and complaints handling in the Inland Revenue'.

Other countries may wish to follow the example of the United Kingdom in setting up an independent adjudication scheme. We are happy to provide further information.

References and Further Reading

The reader may be interested in the following Adjudicator's Office publications:

How to complain about the Inland Revenue
How to complain about Customs and Excise
How to complain about the Contributions Agency
Annual Reports: 1994; 1995; 1996; 1997.

They are available free of charge from:

The Adjudicator's Office
Haymarket House
28 Haymarket
London
SW1Y 4SP
Tel: 0171-930 2292
Fax: 0171-930 2298

E-mail: adjudicators @ gtnet.gov.uk
Internet http: //www.open.gov.uk/adjoff/aodemo 1.htm

The Departmental Codes of Practice mentioned in this chapter are available free of charge from Inland Revenue Tax Enquiry Centres and other Inland Revenue offices.

CHAPTER 7

TAX COMPLIANCE

Managing the Landscape of Relationships with the Taxpayer

Sean Moriarty*

Introduction

In an ideal world, citizens would voluntarily pay the right taxes at the right times and the role of tax administration would simply amount to facilitating the flow of voluntary payments and accounting for them. Tax law would be the changing formula for calculating the contribution and for setting the rules of administration. All experience of taxpayer behaviour, however, shows that there are varying degrees of departure from the ideal resulting in what has become known as a 'tax gap' – the difference between the ideal and the actual tax outturn achieved in any country. The ultimate performance indicator for tax administration is the extent to which this gap can be narrowed through the influence it brings to bear on taxpayer behaviour.

If the business of tax administration is ultimately about influencing behaviour, then the time may have come to take a fundamental look at how the business is organised and at how it approaches the task. Most modern administrations are in transition from a tax management system which relied heavily on regulation and enforcement to a strategy which contains a delicate balance between this hard edge and an attempt to market compliance through programmes of service, support and education – essentially viewing the taxpayer as a customer or client in much the same way as a service business.

This paper looks at whether there is an emerging more mature environment in which, side by side with a risk-aware regulatory strategy, there is scope for a more consensual approach to the determination of tax liability. It looks particularly at whether there is an emerging political and

*Assistant Secretary, Revenue Commissioners, Ireland.

economic backdrop and a business climate conducive to a different landscape of relationships between tax administration and taxpayer which could support greater consensus. It goes on to examine whether compliance improvement generally can be achieved through specific strategies to communicate with and influence the behaviour of identifiable groupings in the taxpayer base.

It sees the ability of a tax administration to influence taxpayer behaviour as very much linked to its ability to read and feedback overviews of this behaviour and of the changing environment in which it operates.

If new forms of influencing compliance behaviour are to achieve full potential, tax administrations may have to work out how new forms of relationship with its taxpayer base can be built. It may, however, first be necessary for each tax administration to take a fundamental look at its role in the late 1990s and to examine whether its internal organisation and strategies allow for the kind of experience analysis and communication network which are needed to build relationships of this kind as a foundation for influencing.

Rethinking the Role of Tax Administration

The tax administrations which have evolved in the developed world have complex structures and systems which are increasingly being re-evaluated in the 1990s. The forces driving this re-evaluation are the options offered by information technology, the pressure for the simplification of both law and administration, the impact of strategic thinking and the influence of client-centered forms of organisation. In addition, the emphasis on taxpayer responsibility for compliance reflected in the self-assessment approach has influenced the debate.

In practice the emphasis on taxpayer responsibility for calculation and payment of all direct and indirect taxes represented a sea change in relationships between the taxpayer and tax administration.

The entire vista of law governing direct and indirect taxes – corporate and income taxes, value added taxes and excises, employer and social security taxes – is sometimes perceived as a highly complex set of formulae for contributions to government. The primary role of tax administration is to collect these taxes through facilitating and inducing voluntary compliance. Taxpayer service, audit and enforcement programmes must be seen as the means through which this objective is achieved, not ends in themselves.

The Mission Statement of the Irish tax administration, in particular, encapsulates the concept of the core function of tax collection.

'To serve the community by fairly and efficiently collecting taxes.....'

Worldwide tax administration has grown within conventional public administration structures. If the nature of its business is examined, however, it is arguable that the modern tax administration can also find important direction indicators for its future development in areas of the private sector and, in particular, in the financial services area.

Experience in a number of countries in recent years included a re-examination of the business of tax administration, its objectives and the world in which it now operates, aimed at developing a model capable of delivering the outputs demanded by government.

Tax administration must continuously manage a massive funds flow (representing 40.8 per cent of GDP in the European Union in 1995), and in that respect resembles a very large financial organisation. While it tends to create debt by assessment rather than contract, it must nevertheless operate highly professional risk management and account management programmes. Invariably it will be in competition for funds with other creditors.

Like all business in the services area tax administration needs a strong service culture and a high degree of 'market' acceptance from its customer base. Increasingly, it is seen to be in the business of marketing compliance. Tax administration does not, of course, have a profit motive. Nevertheless, effective compliance management is capable of making a substantial quantifiable financial contribution to government from the marginal yield induced by its regulatory programmes and, more importantly, from the indirect yield induced by the impact of these programmes on behaviour in the wider taxpayer base.

To an extent, modern tax administration has many of the characteristics of the commercial world which dictate a strategic approach based on targeted financial outcomes in a customer centred culture. It is nevertheless distinguishable to the extent that it is accountable to government and to the citizen rather than to shareholders. In Ireland and in many other countries it carries a precious tradition of independence from influence and has experienced negligible levels of internal corruption.

One of the major challenges for tax administration may be to achieve optimum results through developing forms of business to business relationships with key elements of its client base while retaining high ethical standards.

If tax collection is the primary objective of tax administration, policy advice and the charting of policy options based on intelligent reading of operational experience, is a by-product of considerable importance which is not always sourced and fed back to policy makers in an effective structured way. The continuous reading of the changing environment to ensure that tax policy and administration respond to commercial realities and the reality of taxpayer behaviour is increasingly seen as essential.

Evolving the Role of Tax Administration in Relation to Tax Policy

How far a tax administration can influence taxpayer compliance behaviour will depend, to an extent, on its ability to influence the internal debate on strategies and to effectively articulate viewpoints on policy and legislative directions in the wider debate on tax policy options – to successfully influence the external customer it must be seen to have a voice in the tax policy debate.

In a modern democracy, various forces come to bear on the shaping of tax policy options ahead of ultimate political decisions and strategies. Ministries of finance will continuously reappraise tax policy options. Lobby groups are increasingly professional and focused in their approach. International commitments resulting from tax treaties or from European Union Directives in the indirect taxes area will also shape domestic tax policy. The role of domestic tax administrations has traditionally been largely and correctly consultative, mainly confined to reactively giving opinions on the administrative feasibility or practicality of tax policy proposals derived elsewhere. Many tax administrations have tended not to initiate a debate, or to see it as their role to proactively present tax policy options, so as to avoid being perceived as straying into the political arena.

The operational wings of tax administration, in both the taxpayer services and regulatory areas, are potentially the eyes and ears of the policy maker in relation to the impact of the tax system on the ground and to the behaviour of taxpayers generally in relation to various aspects of tax law and its implementation. Where quality feedback is sourced and channelled, tax policy makers will have access to continuous overviews of emerging experience in relation to various dimensions of tax policy and its implementation. Equally importantly, the feedback can provide a flow of ideas for administrative, legislative and policy solutions and for simplification of law and administration.

The linkage between operational experience and tax policy has been traditionally very strong in Ireland. Since 1993, the role of the tax administration in this area has been implicitly recognised in its representation on a Tax Strategy Group, set up by government, consisting of political representatives, representatives of the Ministry of Finance, of other government departments and of the tax administration. In this forum, all tax policy proposals are considered, debated and teased out ahead of final proposals to the Minister for Finance. This direct involvement has allowed the tax administration to participate at an early stage in the debate.

The sourcing of tax policy proposals from operational experience is not something that happens automatically simply because proposals are requested from operational areas. Experience in Ireland suggests that the feedback and proposals can best be derived through a structured process which recognises the feedback as an important output or product from operational activity.

Operational staff need to see the feedback output as the raw material for strategic thinking in relation to directions in both tax policy and tax administration. Tax policy makers, on the other hand, need to understand that tax policy formulation cannot be disembodied from ongoing operational experience. In Ireland, the emphasis on the sourcing of tax policy advice has led to the inclusion on the planning and operational review agendas of the tax policy role and to its inclusion as both an output and a performance indicator in the returns of district and regional performance.

One of the most important readings which tax administrators can bring to the debate on strategy and tax policy is an overview of the perspective of the taxpayer on both taxation and its administration.

Understanding the Perspective of the Taxpayer

Compliance behaviour can be most effectively influenced where the reasons for behaviour are understood. In this context some understanding of taxpayers' differing perceptions of taxation itself is important.

First a look at the employed sector which accounts for a very high percentage of taxpayers. In virtually all tax administrations withholding tax and PAYE systems exist to deduct their contributions at source. While employees will have a strong sense of contribution which must be underpinned by tax administration, there is nevertheless an increasing focus on the significance of take-home pay after tax and social security contributions in wage/salary negotiations at firm and industry level. In Ireland the impact of budgetary changes tends to be examined by media analysts in the context of take-home pay. The significance of take-home pay is also highlighted in Irish national level pay agreements, through the linking of pay provisions with government commitments on personal tax and social security contributions.

Employer attitudes may also be influenced by pressure from the shop floor for tax-effective methods of influencing take-home pay such as tax-free expenses and untaxed payments. The pressure can be particularly strong in situations of skills scarcity.

The attitude of employees to taxation can also be influenced by the extent to which they perceive the self-employed shadow economy to be significant. This debate about relative equity has rumbled in Ireland for many years and has remained continuously on the agenda of discussions between government and trade union and business.

The behaviour of the business taxpayer, on the other hand, frequently suggests that tax is perceived as a cost. This can be partly seen in the behaviour of internationally mobile investment seeking to locate elements of worldwide activity in areas of low tax exposure. Similarly, international business appears to consider employment and social security taxes as part of the local cost environment.

This sense of tax as a cost is particularly strong in owner/managed small to medium sized businesses. As employers, there can be a tendency to regard withholding or PAYE taxes and the associated social security taxes as part of the burden of the employer over and above the take-home pay which market conditions and industrial relations agreements will require to be paid to an employee. The smaller business also sometimes finds it difficult to see value added tax as an amount added on to a selling price but rather as a share for government from the prices dictated by market forces. Equally, direct taxes can be seen as a drain on the amount of resource available for distribution or reinvestment.

In essence, resources transmitted to the state in the form of taxation are seen as an ongoing charge which must be funded and paid. The tax office is frequently the biggest creditor of a business and the one with the greatest capacity to threaten its survival.

Unless the perceived incidence of tax is fully understood, there will be a difficulty in attempting to influence behaviour driven by these perceptions.

The Changing Nature of Relationships between Tax Administration and Taxpayer

At the same time as the role and objectives of tax administration were being re-examined in the past decade new influences were coming to bear on the relationship between tax administration and taxpayer.

The overall debate about more open relationships between government and citizen was underway, leading to the introduction of freedom of information and data protection legislation in many countries. This involved fundamental examination of the relationship between government, its administration and the citizen and, inevitably, included a focus on taxpayer/tax administration relationships to the extent that this was and remains a major area of government/citizen contact.

The debate also coincided with a strong emphasis on deregulation through the late 1980s. This led to considerable analysis of the overall interaction between state agencies involved in regulation and the business sector. The burden of compliance posed by regulation became a major issue and, in particular, the burden of tax compliance in terms of both direct cost and of the diversion of management time. There was a renewed emphasis on the critical role of business as the engine room of economic growth and employment creation. The traditional relationship between tax administration and business had been characterised by a significant level of mutual distrust. Business frequently regarded the administration as hostile and lacking in understanding of the realities of business and of the enterprise culture which was necessary for economic growth and employment growth. Tax administrators, on the other hand, because of continuing detection of patterns of tax evasion and avoidance, tended to have a view of business overall which was rooted in their perception of the deviant taxpayer.

In Ireland and in many other countries tax administration had traditionally been heavily driven by a regulatory culture with a limited sense of support and service roles. In recent times, the regulatory culture has increasingly been balanced by a growing awareness of taxpayers as clients or customers, responsible, in a self-assessment environment, for their own destinies. The consequent changing of attitudes led towards a delicate balance between service and regulation. In practice, a new realisation has dawned that tax compliance behaviour could be influenced by apparently contradictory soft and hard edged strategies – the interaction of a programme of taxpayer service and education and a targeted, risk-based, intervention system based on tax audits and enforcement which could sustain a strong perception of the risk and the cost of detection of non-compliance.

The gradual move towards a service culture and towards openness in government administration has, particularly in the last decade, significantly improved the climate for debate between tax administration and business and has opened up the possibility of movement towards more positive forms of relationship and towards a more consensual approach to the determination of tax liabilities.

The Irish experience in the past ten years is interesting. A Report by the Commission on Taxation on tax administration in 1985 raised fundamental issues about future directions in tax administration. In 1987 the Irish Government commissioned an IMF report which analysed aspects of both tax policy and tax administration. The government adopted and implemented a specific recommendation that a self-assessment approach should be adopted to direct taxes. In practice, with the advent of self-assessment for direct taxes, business taxpayers would now see themselves as taking responsibility for the calculation, collection and payment of direct and indirect taxes. Self-assessment was successfully introduced and proved to be the catalyst for a significant change in both the culture of the tax administration and in the attitudes which had previously dominated the tax administration/taxpayer relationship in Ireland. The consultative process with stakeholders in the Irish taxation system entered a new phase.

The other force on the political horizon which influenced government administration generally towards a culture of dialogue and openness was the consensus approach to economic management between government and bodies which became known as the social partners – the Irish Congress of Trade Unions and business, industrial and farming representative groups. This led to a series of national plans from 1988 onwards which represented the consensus of the social partners on specific strategies in relation to the economic and social agenda for three year periods. These plans included commitments on tax policy and tax reform and specifically on tax administration. The plans recognised the consultative role of the social partners in relation to tax administration. For example, the 1987 Programme for National Recovery led to the setting up of a body known as the Black Economy Monitoring Group which was to include representatives of the tax administration, the department of social welfare and of each of the social partners. Within this Group, the progress of programmes for countering tax evasion and welfare fraud were monitored. Reports on specific problem areas were researched and the Group, as a body, made specific recommendations for both legislative and administrative changes. Most importantly, however, the national agreements endorsed the moves towards new forms of communication and relationship between the tax administration and its stakeholders – the consultative role of the social partners in monitoring the effectiveness of tax administration programmes represented a new departure.

The influences coming from the introduction of self-assessment and the consensus approach to economic management were complemented by a simultaneous drive towards a taxpayer services culture in the Irish tax administration and overall, led to a very significant improvement in the relationship between the tax administration and both personal and business taxpayers.

Another permanent consultative forum was that formed to debate and facilitate the introduction of self-assessment (the Tax Administration Liaison Committee), which included representatives of the tax administration, the various accountancy bodies, the Institute of Taxation in Ireland and the Irish Law Society. This body has continued since and has gone on to become an important forum for dialogue in relation to all aspects of tax administration.

Bilateral contacts were subsequently established with a wide range of trade and business representative groups which allowed tax compliance patterns in business generally and in specific sectors to be discussed between the tax administration and business representative groups. For example, patterns of tax evasion detected in the public house and pharmacy businesses were discussed centrally with their representative bodies to enlist their support for a general voluntary disclosure of under-reported tax liabilities by the minority of their member firms who had participated in the evasion schemes detected.

The changing nature of relationships and the gradual improvement in the climate of trust through dialogue allowed a fundamental look to be taken at how voluntary compliance might be further influenced in this environment.

The Primary Centres of Influence?

How does a tax administration set about influencing taxpayer behaviour? Because of the sheer scale of taxpayer numbers, this cannot be achieved by one to one relationships. The potential for success depends instead on finding critical centres of influence in its relationships with both society and the taxpayer base and on segmenting that taxpayer base.

The influencing process must, however, be two way – a tax administration seeking to influence behaviour must be seen to be a listening and learning organisation which is sensitive to external viewpoints.

There are essentially three broad centres of influence which have the potential to respond or not to respond to the overtures from a tax administration. These are the citizen, business in its broadest form (including institutions etc.) and the tax practitioner.

The citizen, of course, includes both business and tax advisers. Nevertheless, in the context of tax administration, the significance of business, and in particular of its top tier, as the channel for a very high percentage of tax contribution and the role of the tax practitioner, as a key influential intermediary between the taxpayer and tax administration, makes it important to consider them separately.

The primary constituency to be influenced is the citizen. Although including all taxpayers, the citizen has an identity in relation to the state and its institutions which is distinct from the role of tax contributor. A high percentage of taxpayers pay through the withholding tax or PAYE system and tend to regard themselves as a captive market with limited ability to influence their individual tax positions and consequently are more inclined to view taxation from the perspective of the citizen.

The attitude of the citizen to tax and to tax administration is extremely important. The fundamental learning experience of modern democracies is that, just as government is conducted with the consent of the governed, tax administration is ultimately conducted with the consent of the taxpayer and the citizen. The extent to which taxpayers and citizens generally have confidence in the professionalism, consistency and ethical standards of a tax administration will be a factor determining the level of acceptance of tax and of its administration and is therefore extremely important. The level of citizen support can be particularly important in influencing the degree to which parliament in any country is prepared to grant significant legislative powers to tax administration.

In Ireland, since 1988, considerable effort has been put into building a taxpayer services culture and into building bridges to taxpayers generally. This has resulted in a significant change in the tax administration/taxpayer relationship. Perhaps the most important factor was the adaptation of attitudes within the administration to a view of the taxpayer as a customer. There was a major investment in taxpayer information and education and in training for service delivery. Tax officials became more visible and more open, and set up lines of communication. Media interest in taxation was seen more as an opportunity for communication than as a threat. A well publicised 1989 Charter of Rights for taxpayers was effectively embedded in tax management programmes.

The improved relationship was reflected in two independently conducted customer service surveys of taxpayers in 1995 and 1996 which reflected substantial confidence in tax administration. The general level of confidence in tax administration would have been a contributory factor to the climate in which government moved to strengthen legislative powers to deal with tax evasion and criminal activity in 1992 and 1996.

In practice, the tax administration deliberately set out to win the confidence of the citizen.

In terms of exercising the maximum degree of influence on compliance patterns, the business taxpayer is the critical centre of influence representing the channel through which a very high percentage of both direct and indirect taxes reach government. It is increasingly recognised that the capacity to understand business in its various forms and the environment in which it operates both domestically and internationally is central to the capacity of a tax administration to influence the compliance behaviour of the business taxpayer. For this reason, in Ireland, the tax administration made a major attempt to improve its linkages with business.

Businesses of any reasonable size will engage the services of independent tax practitioners, some of whom may also fulfil the role of statutory auditor. The larger the business the more distanced the owners and management will be from tax decisions and the more important the tax practitioner will figure in the relationship between the tax administration and the business entity. This is because the tax advisers in conjunction with other financial advisers will be centrally involved in reviewing the tax exposure of the business and in planning, forecasting and arranging funding for tax commitments.

In practical terms the adviser is in a unique position to be a significant influence on the compliance behaviour of clients and, as such, is an important focus of influence for the tax administration. The adviser's influence has the potential to be positive, where clients are directed towards acceptable compliance norms, or to be negative in the case of the minority of tax advisers who devote energies towards unacceptable forms of tax minimisation.

To the extent that tax is viewed as a cost and that the adviser is seen as an expert by the business client, the adviser will frequently be under pressure to minimise tax exposure. Tax advisers operate in a competitive environment. Support for those operating to high professional and ethical standards and confrontation of advisers operating outside these parameters are important strategies in winning the considerable influence of tax advisers on compliance behaviour.

In Ireland, the consultative process with tax advisory bodies was institutionalised in the Tax Administration Liaison Committee from 1988 onwards and this Committee is seen as an important channel of communication to and from tax advisers and indirectly to and from the business community. Sub-committees of the Liaison Committee continuously look at a range of issues including compliance costs, tax audit programmes and their impact, technical tax issues and definition of practice. Consultation at this level facilitated the introduction of self-assessment and the introduction of the new regime resulting from the European Single Market in 1992. It has also allowed the tax practitioner bodies to act as a filter for business viewpoints on the tax system. Its strength has been the facilitation of two-way communication despite strong contrary viewpoints on a number of issues.

The growth of communication and consultative structures with centres of influence has had varying degrees of success in western democracies. It has, however, proven to be considerably more difficult in countries in the early years of transition to market economies. Attitudes to tax and its administrators are influenced to varying degrees by ingrained cultural attitudes to the state and its institutions which grew in a different political climate.

In addition, the absence of an institutional framework for consultation and discussion and the lack of a culture of dialogue between state and citizen will, in some transition countries, for some time to come, inhibit the emergence of consultative structures along the lines of those which have evolved in many western countries.

The success potential of tax administrations in economies in transition is likely to depend partly on the degree to which they are prepared to recognise the critical importance of the consultative and influencing process in approaches to improving tax compliance. In an environment where a consultative culture and consultative structures may not be strong, tax administrations, because of the frequency and sensitivity of their interface with the citizen, may simply have to be one of the catalysts for the emergence of these structures.

The alternative is likely to be an overwhelming emphasis on tax compliance management by regulation and enforcement which is in fact emerging in many of these countries and which, based on the experience of western countries, is unlikely, on its own, to yield longer term behavioural changes.

Segmenting the Taxpayer Base

Any attempt to build a strategy based on influencing taxpayer behaviour presumes that the overall taxpayer base can somehow be divided into manageable groupings or segments which represent specific targets for identifiable improvements in compliance – the exercise should bring into focus the points at which wealth is created, held and distributed nationally. It also presumes that somewhere there is a manager or team which can pull together all of the strings that influence taxpayer behaviour in a particular segment.

What has gradually emerged in a number of countries is a client or customer-centered form of organisation in tax administration built around particular taxpayer groupings with the specific objective of both facilitating and influencing compliance behaviour in each group.

In this form of organisation the segments chosen essentially define the business lines of the organisation around which all points of taxpayer contact will be brought together – including taxpayer services, audit and debt management and research and technical support. Very importantly, the communication network with the taxpayer group operates directly out of this centre of expertise and experience. The resultant deep knowledge of the taxpayer category allows for highly focused contributions to the design and review of policy options. The deep knowledge is, in addition, the foundation for a proactive influencing strategy.

The broad segments identified in Australia, Canada and New Zealand are large business (of which high net worth individuals are a sub-set) small to medium business, and non-business individuals (largely the employed sector).

Ultimately, however, the business lines can only be chosen based on a realistic appraisal of the wealth creating forces which exist in any country. For example, certain economies in transition may need specific strategies to deal with state enterprises, with the penetration of organised crime into legitimate business and with the multiplicity of difficult-to-detect small businesses which mushroom in the early stages of transition to the market economy.

In every country, however, business in all its forms is a tax administration's primary constituency.

Large business is understandably a primary focus in most countries. The potential for influence on compliance behaviour is particularly marked in relation to large business because of its relative significance in terms of volumes of tax. (The top 500 taxpayers in Ireland pay approximately 64 per cent of the total tax yield.) In the developed world, because of the sophistication of its organisation and the degree of its continuous interaction with government on many issues, large business offers a particular focal point for any strategy to build a more consensual approach to tax compliance.

Large business is increasingly in the market for certainty as to the tax consequences of investment decisions. It will also seek a guarantee of consistency of tax treatment across its own industry to avoid the emergence of unfair tax-based competitive advantage – the pressure on tax compliant business to move downwards to a 'lower cost' form of tax compliance will be enormous if its market share is threatened by poor tax compliance among competitors. Better communication with large business can create a climate which will allow agreed compliance frameworks to be established. It is essential that this communication is structured and transparent to avoid any perception of a disproportionate influence by big business on tax policy and administration.

This is not to understate the difficulty of attempting to influence businesses operating global strategies or to understate the need for a parallel strong default confrontation strategy. It simply identifies mutual needs in business and tax administrations which may be negotiable towards a measure of agreement on compliance frameworks – it is in this area that the greatest potential dividend may exist for building some measure of consensus.

The small to medium business can be classified as a specific segment or business line even though it is more fragmented and, for this reason, less amenable to direct influencing or compliance marketing. In practice, government will also frequently require a specific strategy for small to medium business to ensure that tax administration can be conducted in a climate of minimum regulation and low compliance costs.

The vast majority of enterprises in this classification will be privately owned and frequently owner managed. Experience has shown that the most common behavioural characteristic demonstrated by non-compliant business in this category is the tendency to simply divert business receipts and consequently under-report tax liabilities. Since under-reporting of business receipts can have simultaneous consequences for direct taxes, value added taxes and excises (and sometimes for employment taxes if the unreported takings are used as employee remuneration) – the case for consolidated management of these taxes is very strong.

Again, the influencing of compliance levels is partly about building communication structures and promoting and establishing compliance norms. In Ireland, considerable efforts have been put into communication with small business representative groups and into improving the information flow to business. Again, understanding the business type has been the key to influence and for this reason there has been a significant resource investment in profiling business types.

The potential to influence compliance levels in this sector is at its greatest where there is a strong perception among potential tax evaders of the risk and cost of detection of under-reporting of tax liabilities. The strength of this perception is critical to the behaviour of the potential non-complier in small to medium business. This perception can be influenced through the reality of risk-based control techniques, through an established communication network with business and through a media policy. Managing tax compliance and controlling the black economy is partly about creating and sustaining perceptions of the risk and cost of detection.

The facility for communication with business at all levels is considerably enhanced where it can be sub-divided into its constituent economic sectors which are frequently highly organised in the interest of member firms. This sub-division into economic sectors allows for the building of business to business relationships between the tax administration and particular industries or business sectors through industry representative groups. It allows a tax administration to think in terms of managing the tax performance of an industry from deep knowledge of that industry. This will include an understanding of the industry or business sector including its current performance and prospects, employment trends, national and global strategies and industry-specific patterns of tax planning.

Knowledge of a business or industrial sector also allows a climate to be created for influencing compliance levels through highly targeted, risk-driven, compliance management programmes. It allows for the building of current knowledge-based programmes involving 'real time' auditing and debt management based on current rather than historic business activity and using current overviews of tax funding capacity.

In Ireland the tax audit programme is based on a sectoral analysis of the Irish economy – construction and natural resources, food production, financial services, manufacturing and large service business. The possibility of managing, for example, the construction industry as a single national project, covering large and small enterprises, is being examined. The compliance management programme in this industry may, in future, shadow the major construction contracts actually in progress and follow the flow of funds through land owners, developers, contractors and employees. Again, an attempt to agree and sell compliance norms would be expected to play a central role.

The relatively small number of individuals of high net worth who directly or indirectly control significant wealth in all countries may merit separate attention in examining potential influence on tax compliance patterns. This is because their decisions in relation to the management of their personal income and wealth and in relation to their residence for tax purposes can have significant implications for tax yield. This group is also important to the extent that they may also include many of the key decision makers in the business arena generally.

The scale of income and investment will not always be obvious and may surface sometimes only through a maze of controlled companies or trusts in various jurisdictions including tax havens. Their behaviour will frequently be characterised by a search for shelter from the full impact of domestic exposure to income, gains and inheritance taxes – succession planning will have a high priority – and by a willingness to pay significant fees for professional tax planning. In Ireland the tax audit programme has identified this group as a specific focus.

In many ways this is perhaps the most difficult group to influence since it is not cohesive and is both mobile and tax-sensitive. By taking a specialist view, however, a tax administration can put itself in a position to build specialised approaches to the gathering of business intelligence and to the tax and residence issues involved. Again there is no substitute for specialist knowledge and for some understanding of the motivation for behaviour. As with other categories some degree of influence on behaviour can be obtained by identifying the key players and clarifying the rules through Statements of Practice and equally importantly by establishing clearly that the administration has the capacity and expertise to track and confront tax avoidance and evasion by high net worth individuals. The perception of the effectiveness of exchange of information arrangements between tax administrations will be important to this group's view of the risk or detection.

Ensuring tax compliance by wealthy individuals is particularly important in economies in transition because the perception of the capacity of government to distribute the benefits of a market economy can be harmed if a high spending new elite appear to escape the impact of taxation, either because of weak legislation or poor compliance management.

The problem of unidentified business activity is particularly acute in countries in the early stages of transition to market economies and may have to be considered as a specific business line. This is because these countries have seen the mushrooming of new small enterprises in distribution, retailing, manufacturing and services, whose proprietors are difficult to identify. In the absence of the kind of loan finance that comes with a developed banking system, savings are the main form of investment capital and taxation is, of course, a threat to the capacity to save and grow the business.

The public perception of a tax administration's capacity to deliver equity in taxation is partly linked to the extent to which it can be seen to be in control of this shadow economy. Even relatively small non-compliant businesses, if well organised, can pose a competitive threat to tax compliant larger business. People in employment paying withholding and social security taxes resent the shadow economy whose operators may also be a burden on state finances to the extent that they illegally claim social security, health and employment benefits etc.

For these reasons, it is important for tax administrations to have a clear policy and strategy in relation to countering this aspect of business activity. Management of the business line represented by the undetected shadow economy requires central research closely interacting with the operational programmes. As in the other categories, compliance improvements can be obtained in this segment through an integrated programme bringing together the intelligence and confrontation dimensions with publicity, education and research programmes. In this way, accountability can be centralised for the influencing of behaviour towards payment of tax contributions.

In attempting to identify the broad segments of wealth creation in society, one of the most difficult issues for tax administrations is to define their role in relation to profits from criminal activity. The significance of criminal activity will depend on the level of penetration into legitimate business activity by the criminal world. This will vary from relatively effective control by the institutions of state to very significant degrees of involvement in economic activity by organised crime. At its most extreme, in certain economies in transition, criminal forces operate an almost parallel economy, have a significant corrupting influence and probably pose the single biggest threat to emerging democratic structures.

The influence of criminal activity will not be confined to the profits from illegal activities but will also involve the laundering of the proceeds of crime into the domestic or foreign financial system and also, by various means, into apparently legitimate business activity.

Criminal activity creates a dilemma for tax administrations. On the one hand, the tracking of the activity and the confiscation of the proceeds of crime, where permitted in the criminal code, will be regarded primarily as police work. On the other hand, tax administrations will sometimes be first to detect unexplained accumulation of wealth which may represent the proceeds of crime and will unavoidably come face to face with criminal elements where criminal funds are invested in apparently legitimate business activities. Nevertheless if a tax administration regards the wealth creation of criminal activity as outside its remit it runs the risk of losing the confidence of both the citizen and the other groupings of taxpayers which it is attempting to influence towards tax compliance. Unchallenged criminal activity either in illegal activities or in quasi-legal business is a source of serious concern in society. The scale of the involvement of organised crime in some of the economies in transition makes it extremely difficult for tax administrations to inspire in the taxpayer population the kind of confidence in tax administration which could allow linkages and influencing to take place.

Therefore, because of the frequently blurred boundaries between legitimate and illegal activities and because the tracking of wealth creation is a fundamental technique of tax investigation, tax administrations generally cannot avoid, at the very least, participating in the overall strategy to confront criminal activity. Many countries, including Ireland, the United Kingdom and United States have enacted legislation which allows unexplained asset accumulation to be deemed to have arisen from taxable profits and which allows these profits to be subjected to income tax. Exposing the profits of criminal activity to taxation is obviously much less satisfactory than the securing of convictions in respect of the activity leading to confiscation of the assets acquired through crime. Nevertheless, in countries whose tax law places the onus of proof on the alleged owner of the assets, rather than on the tax administration, attaching a tax charge to the assets may be acceptable as a fallback position in the event of failure to obtain a criminal conviction for the illegal activity itself.

In Ireland, legislation was introduced in 1996 to set up a body known as the Criminal Assets Bureau which is led by a senior Garda (police) officer and which includes representatives of the tax administration, the Customs and Excise service, the department of social welfare and the Gardai (police). The Bureau targets the assets of criminals by using any of the powers contained in either tax law, social welfare law or to use the criminal law. This gives them the option to use either the tax law, which deems unexplained asset accumulations to be subject to taxation, or criminal law which allows the confiscation of criminal assets in certain circumstances. The unity of purpose of the Bureau is underpinned by legislation which allows a structured and strictly controlled sharing of information in relation to criminal figures between the agencies involved in the Bureau.

The setting up of the Bureau represents one country's response to the emergence of wealth controlled by criminal elements to ensure that this wealth is not ignored in the overall analysis.

Conclusion

A better understanding of the taxpayer's view of the world has been and continues to be an important determinant of directions in tax administration.

This, in turn, has allowed much greater insights into taxpayers' behaviour and has led tax administrations to look for more imaginative ways to influence this behaviour towards higher levels of voluntary compliance. Experience so far suggests that the key to influence is sophisticated and focused communication channels to the various elements of the taxpayer base – something which many tax administrations found themselves ill-equipped to build.

In practice, tax administrations looking at their own forms of organisation were independently coming to the conclusion that the customer-centred form of organisation, which was the key to influencing quality of product, customer loyalty etc. in the commercial world was also the key to influencing voluntary tax compliance. The fact that the marketing dimension of tax compliance had to be balanced with a strong regulatory dimension was no longer seen to be in conflict with a customer-centred strategy.

Gradually many tax administrations are beginning to re-invent themselves around segments of their taxpayer base and to take a new look at the kind of skills and competencies which may be needed to influence voluntary compliance in the environment which is emerging.

At the end of the day the potential for success will very much depend on the extent to which the landscape of relationships with the business taxpayer can be developed to allow a more consensual approach to the determination of tax liabilities.

References and Further Reading

Australian Tax Office, *Annual Report 1995-96*, AGPS, Canberra, 1996.

Commission on Taxation, Fifth Report, *Tax Administration*, Stationery Office, Dublin, 1985.

Criminal Assets Bureau Act, 1996 (Ireland), Stationery Office, Dublin, 1996.

Government and Social Partners, *Programme for National Recovery*, Stationery Office, Dublin, 1987.

Government and Social Partners, *Programme for Economic and Social Progress*, Stationery Office, Dublin, 1991.

Government and Social Partners, *Programme for Competitiveness and Work*, Stationery Office, Dublin, 1994.

Minister for Finance (Ireland), *Self-Assessment for Income Tax and Corporation Tax*, Stationery Office, Dublin, 1987.

New Zealand Inland Revenue, *Profile for Change*, 1995.

OECD, *Revenue Statistics 1990 -1995*, OECD, Paris, 1996.

Revenue Commissioners, (Ireland) Annual Report, *Customer Service Satisfaction Survey*, Stationery Office, Dublin, 1994.

Revenue Commissioners (Ireland) Annual Report, *Customer Service Satisfaction Survey – A Survey of the Business Community*, Stationery Office, Dublin, 1995.

Taylor, G., *A Giant Learning to Dance – Restructuring Revenue Canada*, Canadian Centre for Management Development, Ottawa, 1995.

FURTHER
KEY ISSUES IN TAX REFORM

PART III
TAX REFORM – SOME WIDER ISSUES

CHAPTER 8

THE ROLE OF TAX INCENTIVES: THE IRISH EXPERIENCE

Donal de Buitleir*

Introduction

This chapter considers the experience in Ireland of the use of tax incentives. Ireland has made very extensive use of tax incentives for a whole range of activity from industrial development to urban renewal to encouraging individuals to take out health insurance and buy houses. It concludes that, while tax incentives may often be an uneconomic use of resources, provided other policies are appropriate, tax incentives, used with care, can be effective in promoting certain economic and social objectives.

A tax incentive may be defined as a provision in the tax code which is designed to promote a particular activity. It is a departure from tax neutrality which gives rise to a tax expenditure which is a subsidy, relief or concession in the tax system which reduces tax liability and has an effect on the government's budget similar to direct expenditures.

Extent of Incentives in Ireland

Tax incentives are used to a very great extent in Ireland. The 1995 Annual Report of the Revenue Commissioners gives the cost of reliefs from income tax and corporation tax for 1993-94. The most important reliefs are set out in Table 8.1.

The cost of these reliefs is substantial, amounting to almost 10 per cent of GNP in 1994 (Central Bank figure of £30,614m). This compares with a total tax burden of 42.6 per cent of GNP. The cost of these incentives could be greater if account were taken of the fact that marginal

---

*Currently a General Manager with Allied Irish Banks; formerly Secretary to the Irish Commission on Taxation.

income sheltered by incentives is likely to bear higher rates of tax than the average. However, one could also argue that the cost may be overstated in that at least some of the activity would not take place if the incentive did not exist. What is clear is that incentives are an important feature of the Irish tax system.

Table 8.1 Cost of Main Tax Incentives in Ireland 1993-94

Incentive	Cost (£m)
Manufacturing relief (Reduced corporation tax rate of 10 per cent)	1,079
Capital allowances	816
Superannuation contributions & funds	445
Interest relief (mainly mortgage relief)	191
Exemption of social welfare payments	103
Medical insurance and health expenses relief	72
Retirement annuities	43
"Section 84" loans [1]	43
National savings schemes	31
Income of charities	25
Urban renewal relief	20
Investment in films	19
Redundancy payments and compensation for loss of office	18
Business Expansion Scheme	12
Profit sharing and share options	9
Total	**2,926**

Source : Annual Report of the Revenue Commissioners

[1] Section 84 of the Corporation Tax Act, 1976 was intoduced as an anti-avoidance measure. Section 84 loans are constructed in such a way that the interest on the loans is treated as a distribution and is tax free in the hands of the company and is not allowable as a deduction to the paying company. This form of lending is attractive for companies which are liable at low rates of tax.

Some Theoretical Considerations

Before incentives are introduced, a number of theoretical considerations should be borne in mind.

Market Imperfections

Taxation should not interfere with the allocation brought about by the market except in instances in which the market fails. There are many imperfections in the market. Lack of information about market conditions or inaccurate expectations about future conditions may lead to waste. The existence of economies of large-scale production may mean that small changes are unattractive and that highly organised large-scale structural changes are necessary to improve efficiency. Monopolistic restrictions by large productive concerns or by groups of workers may impede change. Certain social costs (or benefits) resulting from an economic activity may not be taken into account by private individuals. Due to inertia individuals may fail to respond to market pressures.

In a number of these cases, the best form of corrective action lies in measures other than fiscal incentives, for example, through retraining, state enterprise, wage or price regulation and control of monopoly powers. However, in some cases, fiscal incentives or disincentives may be appropriate to counteract the effect of market imperfections.

Incidence of Tax Incentives

The formal incidence of taxation is the point at which a tax is legally assessed. This may differ from its effective incidence, which reflects who ultimately pays the tax, following changes in economic behaviour which occur after the tax is imposed. Similarly, it is important to distinguish between the formal and effective incidence of a tax incentive. For example, the formal incidence of tax relief on company profits is an increase in post-tax profits attributable to shareholders : the benefit of tax relief could accrue to employees in increased pay, to shareholders in higher returns, to customers in lower prices or to suppliers in the form of higher prices.

Tax Capitalisation

In addition to being shifted forwards or backwards, tax incentives may be capitalised through their effect on the capital values of the assets which qualify for tax relief. For example, incentives to encourage owner-occupation of housing may lead to an increase in the price of houses.

Views of Commissions

The use of tax incentives in Ireland has been reviewed by a number of Commissions. The first was the Commission on Taxation which examined the Irish tax system and published 5 comprehensive reports between 1982 and 1985. The second was the Culliton Committee which reported on the question of industrial policy in 1992.

Commission on Taxation

The Commission on Taxation (Second Report) concluded that incentives were justified only on very limited grounds. These were:

- where the market clearly fails to bring about the desired allocation of resources;
- to accelerate the growth in national income, incentives may be required to match those offered in competing countries in order to attract internationally mobile capital investment;
- finally, incentives may be required to offset shortcomings in other policy areas. This was recognised to be a second best solution.

The Culliton Committee in its review of industrial policy argued for a drastic simplification of the tax system with a programme of phased removal of special reliefs on a consistent basis. The tax reform philosophy to which the Committee subscribed had two main tenets.

First, if tax is collected on a sufficiently broad base and, provided government spending is kept under adequate control, rates can be reduced to sufficiently low levels so that the need for special reliefs, exemptions or allowances to promote activities perceived as necessary for economic development is drastically reduced.

Second, the response of taxpayers to reliefs designed to achieve particular objectives is invariably ingenious and unpredicted so that the result is frequently different from what was intended. Tax reliefs represent a blunt instrument of policy.

While the Culliton Report was very well received, its specific recommendations on taxation were not acted on.

Neither report has deterred government enthusiasm for tax incentives. Since they were published governments have continued to introduce incentives for a wide range of different activities.

Background to Incentives in Ireland

Since the mid 1950s, Ireland has relied to a considerable extent on the use of the tax system to encourage economic development. A basic objective of the State since its foundation in 1922 has been to set in motion and sustain a pace of economic development which would reverse the decline in population and achieve a rate of employment creation leading to the elimination of involuntary emigration and the reduction of unemployment. It was clear that in the circumstances in which the Irish economy was placed these aims could only be achieved through industrialisation. Incentives and inducements to stimulate interest and investment in the industrial sector were therefore required. Industrialisation was fostered initially by a policy of production for the home market. This policy led to a considerable increase in industrial employment, but, by the middle of the 1950s, it had become clear that it offered little scope for further expansion.

A change was called for and this led to the adoption of a policy of export-oriented growth in industry. In the tax field reliefs were provided for new investment in plant, machinery, industrial buildings and hotels and measures were introduced to exempt from tax the profits earned on exports of manufactured and processed goods (export sales relief).

Tax relief for profits from exports was introduced in 1956. The effect of the relief originally was that for a five year period the tax on profits from new exports sales of manufactured goods would be reduced by 50 per cent. In 1957 the rate of relief was increased to 100 per cent and in 1958 the number of years for which the relief could be claimed was increased from five to ten and the period for which the relief was available was extended to 1970. Further improvements were made in subsequent years until the the profits of a company from export sales were fully relieved for a period of fifteen years and were partially relieved for a further period of five years until the relief expired in April 1990.

At that time, due to pressure from the EEC Commision which regarded export sales relief as contrary to the Treaty of Rome, the relief was abandoned and replaced by a 10 per cent rate of tax on manufacturing profits until the year 2000, which was extended subsequently to 2010.

In May 1997, the Government announced proposals to remove uncertainty about the tax regime following the expiry of the existing incentive reliefs 'in order to ensure continuity in the continued flow of investment and jobs – and to remove an increasingly anachronistic distinction between manufacturing and services'. It is now proposed to introduce a new corporate tax regime involving a single rate of 12.5 per cent on profits arising from trading activity and a higher rate of 25 per cent on profits from non-trading activity (yet to be defined). This new regime will become effective from the beginning of the year 2011 for companies availing of the 10 per cent manufacturing rate of corporation tax and from the year 2006 for other companies.

In association with this change the Government is committed to introducing new and strengthened anti-abuse measures coupled with compensating revenue-raising measures. These latter measures will include :

- a change to a classical system of corporation tax from the present partial imputation system, so that dividend income will be subject to full personal tax rates;
- the extension of an existing surcharge on undistributed income of closely held companies to ensure that profits are not sheltered from income tax;
- a withholding tax on dividends to resident shareholders;
- a significant curtailment of the various business reliefs including the Business Expansion Scheme and other investment incentive tax reliefs;
- new targeted revenue-raising measures aimed at maintaining the existing revenue yield from those sectors benefitting most from this change. (This refers to retail, distribution and domestic financial services.)

Ireland has been a world leader in the use of preferential corporation tax rates, which have been designed to promote the growth of employment in the manufacturing sector. For over twenty-five years firms establishing in the manufacturing sector in Ireland enjoyed a tax holiday on profits attributable to increased export sales. This incentive was very generous and only ended for some firms in 1990, when these firms moved to the preferential rate of corporation tax of 10 per cent. Ruane (1996) concludes that the true cost of this incentive only became apparent with the growth in tax revenues from the manufacturing sector. Clearly the incentive was very successful in the 1960s and 1970s in promoting investment in Ireland particularly in the later period when, following Irish entry to the EEC in 1973, access to the large European market was guaranteed, a factor that proved to be very attractive to the significant number of United States firms which located manufacturing plants in Ireland.

An important factor in the efficacy of manufacturing tax incentives has been the existence of a significant network of international double taxation agreements. A very interesting aspect of work by McCutcheon (1995) has been to draw attention to the role of excess tax credits for United States multinationals. If a United States-owned multinational has paid tax at a higher than United States rate on profits earned in a high tax jurisdiction, then by use of an averaging provision in United States tax law, the lightly taxed Irish profits can be used to get full value from what would otherwise be excess (or useless) credits. After tax the Irish profits are actually worth more than before tax; in other words the effective rate of tax may be negative.

This highlights a very important aspect of tax incentive policy. Tax incentives aimed at attracting investment by non-residents must not put at risk the normal international double taxation treatment of cross-border flows of income and profits. If an incentive is perceived by other countries to be abusive, it may attract retaliatory measures which negate the effect of the incentive in the first instance. It is vital that countries do not get classified on gray or black lists of tax havens by those countries which are the major sources of internationally mobile capital investment.

Industrial Policy Implications

The Culliton Report argued that the 10 per cent regime has been the single most effective tool in inducing inward foreign investment. However, a number of disadvantages of the incentive were identified:

- it discouraged the location of cost centres in Ireland such as high-level management and support functions;
- it tended to encourage unnecessarily capital intensive production;
- it led to complex tax avoidance schemes;
- it was far more valuable to foreign-based than to Irish-owned industry.

Performance of the Irish Economy

In recent years the Irish economy has recorded a growth rate far above the average performance of its main trading partners. This represents a significant improvement from the prolonged recession of the early and mid-eighties (Sandford, 1993 p.179). The figures are in Table 8.2.

Table 8.2 Ireland's Relative Economic Performance 1981-95 Annual Average GDP Growth Rate

Period	Ireland	EU
1981-86	1.8	1.7
1987-91	4.7	3.0
1992-95	5.1	1.5

Source: *Shaping our Future*, Table 1.8, 1996

An influential report (ESRI, 1997) concludes that the underlying causes of recent strong growth are complex. No single cause provides the full explanation, which is better provided by the mutually reinforcing effect of different domestic and external forces operating over different time-scales.

Over the long-run, there was a gradual accumulation of human capital (arising from investment in education) and the effects of demographic change on the supply of labour, the progressive opening up of the economy over a period of 30 years culminating in the European Single Market in 1992 and the success of industrial policy in attracting multinational investment. In the medium-term there was an institutional shake-out caused by the recession of the early 1980s, the contribution of EU structural funds to growth and to the investment planning process of the early 1990s and the confidence restoring correction to the public finances in the late 1980s. The positive trends in Irish wage competitiveness have been sustained by successive pay agreements and social partnership arrangements.

The key conclusion from this analysis regarding the provision of tax incentives is that they have a role to play but are not a substitute for the right policies in other areas. Tax incentives are best used to reinforce and support good policy in other key economic and social areas. They cannot substitute for poor or inappropriate policy in these areas.

Urban Renewal Incentives

In 1986 major incentives were introduced for developers and occupiers of buildings in designated areas. For example, up to 100 per cent of building, reconstruction or improvement expenditure was made allowable against income tax or corporation tax.

These incentives generated very significant volumes of investment. A study by Convery and Blackwell (1991) indicated that about one-half of the investment would have gone ahead anyway, but two-thirds of that would have been located outside the designated areas had it not been for the incentives. Thus about 16 per cent of the total was pure deadweight and a further 30 per cent represented displacement. The methodology did not allow for any assessment of displacement or spin-off effects, positive or negative, outside the construction sector.

Although clearly enthusiastic about the need for an activist policy for urban renewal, Convery and Blackwell stressed the need for complementary policy instruments, and the key role of local initiative and of pioneer developers that remains even in the presence of such generous tax incentives. They also noted that use of tax incentives was unlikely to be redistributive, and that the incentives chosen had not been effective in maximising conservation of existing buildings in the inner cities. Honohan (1996) suggests that the incentives were 'a blunt instrument used in a good cause'. Since Convery and Blackwell wrote, and despite their warning that diminishing returns would set in, there have been extensions of this type of incentive.

A major report (Department of Environment, 1996) on urban renewal schemes concluded that the tax incentives which were introduced 'were successful when measured against the original objectives they were designed to achieve. Significant private sector investment was generated, residential development occurred in inner city areas and much dereliction and dilapidation has been addressed. Tax based incentives, on the other hand, have failed to effect urban renewal in the broader sense. Urban renewal cannot be achieved by tax incentives in isolation, nor should urban renewal initiatives be led by tax incentives.'

Business Expansion Scheme

Adopted in 1984 in imitation of a similar United Kingdom initiative, the Irish Business Expansion Scheme (BES) was designed to encourage risk-taking and as an alternative source of finance to grant aid. Stewart (1992) in a highly critical evaluation of the scheme shows that it tended to increase the Exchequer cost per job by about one-half. In 1987 the scheme was extended, among other economic activities, to tourism and ship purchase with very visible consequences for economic activity in these sectors.

It generated very significant tax avoidance activity. Because of the ingenuity of financial engineers and because of the large tax concessions involved, schemes were constructed in such a way that the providers of funds received very large guaranteed returns up to 19 per cent per annum – a perversion of the original concept of stimulating risk investment. Other schemes benefitted from bank guarantees that loan finance would be provided to the borrowing company on maturity of the BES fund. Intermediary fees were large, averaging over 10 per cent of funds raised in a dozen cases studied by Stewart.

Irish Lessons

Tax incentives are pervasive in Ireland, amounting to almost 10 per cent of GNP. One implication is that if all incentives were removed tax rates could be reduced significantly.

The Irish experience shows that tax incentives can be very effective instruments of public policy if other conditions are right. Entry to the EEC in 1973 provided a great opportunity to attract foreign investment. Ruane and Georg have shown that in the period 1973 to 1995 the significance of foreign companies in Irish manufacturing industry has increased considerably. While employment in Irish-owned firms decreased by around 23 per cent (which is slightly less than the EU-wide decline of 25 per cent in manufacturing employment for the corresponding period), employment in foreign-owned firms rose by almost 25 per cent during the same period. This period also saw a strong decline in the significance of companies from the United Kingdom, which was traditionally the strongest investing country in Ireland and a steady increase in United States investment in Ireland, leaving the United States by far the most important investing country in Ireland in the 1990s. This latter development has no doubt been assisted by factors other than an attractive tax regime, most notably by guaranteed access to the EU market and an abundant supply of skilled and English-speaking labour.

The Culliton Report (1992) drew attention to the proliferation of tax incentives in trenchant terms: 'In the attempt to boost economic performance over the years, the proliferation of tax breaks and grant assistance has had some unintended negative side-effects, on the structure of industry, on the level of government borrowing and on the self-reliance of Irish entrepreneurs. In particular, the competitive edge of Irish industry has been blunted as effort and energy has been distracted from the proper emphasis on serving the market and on achieving high productivity, into maximising the grant or tax benefit. Tax avoidance and grant maximisation are the directly unproductive activities (or 'rent-seeking' in the economists's jargon) *par excellence.*' (Culliton Report p.22).

Olson (1965) shows the incentive that organised groups have to direct their efforts to lobbying rather than increasing output. Take a group whose share of national income is one per cent. If such a group uses its resources to try to make the country more prosperous, its members will, on average, get only one per cent of the extra national income generated even though that group will have borne the whole cost of that effort. Normally the best thing for a collective group to do is to try to get a larger share of national income, such as by lobbying for tax reliefs and incentives or subsidies, which will give them a larger share of national output. The larger the role of the state in the economy, the greater is the incentive for lobbying as opposed to productive effort.

An unfortunate side effect of the introduction of tax incentives is the tendency for increased tax rates to have to be applied to the non-favoured activities. This sets in motion pressures to get one's area of endeavour reclassified from the non-favoured area to the favoured. Notorious examples were the results of court decisions which held that banana ripening and coal bagging were manufacturing processes and hence qualified for the favourable tax regime. When the difference in the corporation tax rate applied to different sectors is as high as 58 per cent, as it was at one stage, it is clear that the returns to skilful tax lawyers arguing technical points of tax law are far in excess of any that might apply to money, time and effort invested in attempting to grow a business.

It is also clear that tax avoidance thrives in an environment in which there is a significant difference in the tax rates that apply to different areas of economic activity. A brief perusal of the Irish Finance Acts and Budget speeches over the last twenty years shows many references to the unacceptability of tax avoidance and reveals a plethora of measures designed to combat it. This culminated in the introduction of a general anti-avoidance provision in 1989 (Section 86 Finance Act, 1989).

It is important to avoid the introduction of incentives in cases in which the value of the incentive is likely to result in a windfall gain to owners of certain assets. Where such tax capitalisation is likely, the deadweight loss, which results from the increase in tax rates on other activities which is implicit in the introduction of any incentive, has no compensating offset. Irish experience suggests that this is likely to occur where tax designation applies to certain classes of property.

The Irish experience also suggests that once introduced tax incentives are extremely difficult to dispense with. The experience of Lord (Nigel) Lawson (former United Kingdom Chancellor of the Exchequer June 1983- October 1989) reflects the Irish one. Sandford writing about Lawson's attitude to tax reform concludes that Lawson's 'lack of openness was deliberate. It was a way of dealing with, or circumventing, the lobbies. After the extension of the VAT base in his first Budget, more moves to broaden the VAT base were anticipated and campaigns took place against the possible standard rating of books and newspapers. But as Lawson put it , "The campaigns against VAT extension were as nothing compared to the barrage that emanated from the beneficiaries of occupational pensions and the industry that catered for them." Following the abolition of the tax relief on new life insurance premiums in the 1984 Budget, it was guessed that the tax free treatment of lump sum payments might come next. "There followed the most astonishing lobbying campaign of my entire political career, devoted both to the preservation of the lump sum relief and to pension fund privileges in general." His conclusion was that "reform would be more likely to be achieved by a well-directed side offensive with no prior warning." Secrecy, subtlety and speed thus became his watchwords.' (Sandford, 1993, p.38).

It is clear that incentives lead to a greater expansion in an area of activity than would otherwise be the case and that level of activity would be put at risk if the incentive were withdrawn. Hence their abolition is resisted tenaciously by lobby groups. In other cases where incentives are capitalised in asset prices and their withdrawal would lead to a decline in such prices, similar resistance applies.

However, Irish Governments have had some success in removing certain tax incentives; an important example has been mortgage interest relief which has been substantially restricted since 1974 through a combination of small incremental restrictions and allowing inflation to erode the real value of nominal thresholds. From a situation in which, in 1974, there was unrestricted allowance of all interest the situation now is that mortgage interest is allowed only at the standard rate of income tax (26 per cent) up to a limit of £2,500 for single persons and £5,000 for a married couple. [1]

Similar small incremental restrictions have succeeded in abolishing relief in respect of life assurance premiums and reducing the relief on private medical insurance which is very important in Ireland, to relief at

---

[1] For mortgages taken out before April, 1992 these limits are £1,900 and £3,800 respectively.

the standard rate of income tax only. Given that about one-third of all income taxpayers are liable at the higher rate of income tax (now 48 per cent), this is a significant restriction. In reducing the mortgage interest relief from the marginal rate to the standard rate only, a four year phasing period was enacted and legislated in year one (1994). A similar policy was followed in relation to medical insurance relief. This enabled quite sensitive reliefs to be restricted significantly without major political controversy.

This incremental approach may be constrasted with the very successful 'big bang' approach adopted in New Zealand during the Douglas reforms in the mid-eighties (Sandford, 1993). Douglas's approach was, to use his own words, 'Do not try to advance a step at a time. Define your objectives clearly and move towards them by quantum leaps. Otherwise the interest groups will have time to mobilise and drag you down' (Douglas,1990).

Conclusions

Based on the Irish experience, the following conclusions may be drawn about the use of tax incentives. First, tax incentives are not a substitute for good policy in other areas. Once this is in place well designed and targeted incentives can support the achievement of desirable economic and social objectives. They should be reserved for key priority areas, as the proliferation of incentives drives up tax rates. In addition, each additional incentive dilutes the effect of all existing measures. In general, tax bases should be widened as far as possible to keep tax rates low. Incentives should be avoided in cases in which the value of the incentive is likely to be capitalised in asset prices. If it is desired to remove an incentive which is already in place, the Irish experience suggests that this is more likely to be successful if the removal is phased in over a period of years.

References and Further Reading

Commission on Taxation, Five Reports, Stationery Office, Dublin, 1982-85.

Convery, F. and J. Blackwell, 'The Impact of Urban Incentives in Ireland' in ed. F. Ruane, *The Role of Fiscal Policy in Urban Renewal*, Proceedings of the Sixth Annual Conference of the Foundation for Fiscal Studies, Dublin, 1991.

Department of the Environment, *Study on Urban Renewal Schemes*, Study prepared by KPMG in association with Murray O'Laoire Associates, Architects and Urban Designers and Northern Ireland Economic Research Council, Stationery Office, Dublin, 1996.

Department of Finance, *Ireland – Convergence Programme 1997 to 1999*, Stationery Office, Dublin, 1997.

Douglas, R., 'The Politics of Successful Structural Reform', *Administration,* Vol. 38, No. 2, 1990.

Duffy, D., J. Fitzgerald, I. Kearney and F. Shortall eds. *The Medium-Term Review: 1997-2003* , ESRI, Dublin, 1997.

Forfas, *Shaping Our Future: A Strategy for Enterprise in Ireland in the 21st Century*, Dublin,1996.

Honohan, P., *Assisting the Process of Tax Reform: A Review of FFS Research*, Foundation for Fiscal Studies, Dublin, 1996.

McCutcheon, M., 'The Tax Incentives Applying to United States Corporate Investment in Ireland', *Economic and Social Review*, Vol. 26, pp.149-172, 1995.

Olsen, M., *The Logic of Collective Action*, Harvard University Press, Cambridge, 1965.

Report of the Industrial Policy Review Group (The Culliton Report), *A Time for Change: Industrial Policy for the 1990s*, Stationery Office, Dublin, 1992.

Revenue Commissioners, *Annual Report*, Stationery Office, Dublin, 1995.

Ruane, F. and H. Goerg, *Aspects of Foreign Direct Investment in Irish Manufacturing since 1973: Policy and Performance*, Paper to Statistical and Social Inquiry Society of Ireland, November, 1996.

Sandford, C. T., *Successful Tax Reform: Lessons from an Analysis of Tax Reform in Six Countries*, Fiscal Publications, Bath, 1993.

White Paper, *Growing Our Employment – Sharing Our Growth: A Comprehensive Policy for Enterprise and Jobs*, Stationery Office, Dublin, 1997.

CHAPTER 9

MINIMISING THE TAX EFFECTS OF INFLATION

Leif Mutén[*]

Introduction

Inflation affects taxation basically in four ways. One effect has to do with the timing of the collection of tax in relation to the taxable event. The higher the rate of inflation, the greater the loss to the fisc involved in any deferral of the tax payment.

The second effect comes to the fore with respect to taxes on goods and services, to the extent they are fixed in specific terms, in other words when the tax is set in nominal terms on a specific (per unit) basis rather than *ad valorem*.

The third effect is that tax rate tables and personal allowances fixed in nominal terms will be reduced in value, as an effect of inflation.

The fourth effect, and the one most difficult to deal with, is the distortion of the tax base, particularly noticeable in connection with the income tax. The cost basis of items that when sold give rise to taxable profit or capital gain, will differ in real terms depending on when the acquisition was made. The same will apply to depreciation allowances. Moreover, the yield of an investment measured in terms of nominal interest will, with inflation, tell little about the yield in real terms, if the capital has a fixed nominal value.

Tax legislators in many countries have tried to cope with these problems. It is fair to say, however, that many governments and parliaments have chosen to ignore them, hoping to be able to cure inflation and thus to render an inflation-adjusted tax system unnecessary. Adjusting the tax system to inflation may also have been seen as having a negative announcement effect: if government and parliament feel that such adjustment is necessary, the public will quickly draw the conclusion that

---

[*]Professor of International Tax Law, Stockholm School of Economics.

inflation has come to stay. If inflation is ignored, the public, if sufficiently sanguine, may take it as evidence for its forthcoming disappearance.

Much has been written about this subject. An excellent presentation of the issues with numerous source references is found in Victor Thuronyi's Chapter 13 (Thuronyi, 1996). This chapter adds little to Thuronyi's contribution. Mention should also be made of the treatment of the subject at the 1977 International Fiscal Association (IFA) congress, Prof. H. G. Ruppe general reporter, where no resolution was adopted but the resumé very much corresponds to the line taken here. IFA's work on inflation was continued at a seminar in Buenos Aires, 1984, entitled *Adjustments for Tax Purposes in Highly Inflationary Economies*, where Milka Casanegra de Jantscher's contribution on Chile is particularly noteworthy (see also on inflation and tax administration Casanegra de Jantscher, 1992).

Speeding Up Collection

The effect of inflation that is easiest to do something about is the loss on late tax payments. This effect seems to have been pointed out first by a tax reform committee in Chile (Piedrabuena 1960, p.45 *et passim*), and later in Hirao and Aguirre (1970). After Tanzi (1977) it has been commonly referred to as the Tanzi effect.

Already for other reasons, withholding taxes are enjoying growing popularity. They are particularly useful in inflationary times, in as much as they connect the tax payment with the taxable event, thus avoiding tax deferral.

Withholding taxes cannot solve the deferral problem, however, unless the tax withheld is duly paid in to the tax authority. The more severe the inflation, the more costly are the delays between the moment when the tax is paid by the original taxpayer and the moment it is paid to the account of the tax authority.

The swift collection of turnover taxes, VAT, etc. is in the same category. Yet, it is a peculiar problem in this context that the taxpayer, who plays the part of the tax collector *vis-à-vis* his customer, will not necessarily receive the money at the same time that he is under an obligation to declare it. If an accrual principle rather than a cash principle applies, the liability to pay tax will arise at the moment the invoice is or should be issued, whereas the cash payment by the customer may take time, perhaps a few weeks, perhaps even longer. Inflation will erode the value of the payment to the tax office, if collection is postponed to accommodate cases of late payment of the tax to the registered VAT payer.

On the other hand, VAT payers may be hard put to deliver tax payments, if their own customers let them wait for the money beyond the day when the money is due at the tax authority. Then, the inflation loss will hit the VAT payer and his customer will be correspondingly better off. For this reason, I am not sure that Thuronyi's idea (Thuronyi, 1996, p.440) to adjust VAT liability for inflation between the occurrence of the taxable event and the payment of tax is always an improvement, if the taxable event is a credit sale.

Tax payments may sometimes be required both by withholding and by individual payment. The individual tax return, particularly if the tax is progressive, may show a liability to tax in an amount either lower or higher than was collected by withholding. In the case of inflation, it will be particularly important to ensure prompt payment of any supplementary tax due. This may be done either by a short deadline for filing the tax return and a requirement that the supplementary tax be paid when the return is filed, or possibly by an early date for the main supplementary tax payment, if significant, with the payment of the small rest possibly postponed until the date the tax return is due. Again, the fundamental problem is that a delayed payment is a reduced payment, if the inflation rate is higher than the penalty interest rate.

The last statement indicates that the alternative to quick payment is payment of the tax plus interest and penalty. The interest rate has to be high enough to represent a realistic real interest rate. If the interest rate on delayed tax payments is lower than the inflation rate, taxpayers will tend to use whatever opportunity there is to keep their regular tax payments low, their supplementary payments correspondingly high. If, on the other hand, there is a penalty rate, either on top of the interest rate or in lieu of it, that compensates the Treasury both for inflation and the time value of the money, the need to speed up collection by measures such as provisional assessments and tight deadlines for filing returns may be less pronounced.

Ad valorem Versus Specific Rates

Another effect is the inflationary erosion of specific duties, i.e. duties fixed at a stated amount per physical unit. It is an often heard argument that all taxes should be *ad valorem*, so as better to avoid the erosion that affects a duty of the specific kind in the case of inflation. Provided the development of the actual price can be duly reflected in the tax payments – not always easy, if a tax is collected at the production stage but an *ad valorem* rate applied on the retail price – this approach is obviously better than that of a fixed specific duty per manufactured unit.

Nevertheless, it is conceivable that a specific duty, if regularly adjusted to follow suit with inflation, might raise less practical problems than an *ad valorem* duty based on a retail price that is difficult to establish.

Moreover, the use of an exclusively *ad valorem* duty on a product such as liquor may be counter-productive for other reasons than inflation. There is a considerable risk that an *ad valorem* duty high enough to price quality beverages out of the market, may still be totally insufficient to deter addicted consumers from overusing the cheap booze.

Adjusting Bracket Limits and Allowances

It is a rather common form of adjusting the tax system to inflation that allowances, particularly the personal allowances and allowances for dependents, are inflation-adjusted. It is, however, not an unproblematic road to take.

Of course, the basic argument for indexation in this case is obvious. If the legislating body has once regarded a certain amount as fair for the allowance in question, or if it has regarded as appropriate the bracket limit, surtax exemption, or whatever it is called, that defines a higher income suitably subject to progressive taxation, then fairness seems to require that the amount of the allowance or the limit is fixed in real terms.

Yet, there are several arguments even against this seemingly simple inflation adjustment measure. One is that indexation of allowances and bracket limits reduces the built-in flexibility of the tax. By another name, this flexibility is denounced as 'bracket creep', but there are those who feel that the bracket creep is a good thing, something that automatically pulls the emergency brake in times of overheating. Moreover, the general tax effort of a country might be on the low side, and urgent governmental responsibilities may require a higher overall tax ratio; to achieve this, bracket creep may be a politically more palatable way than discretionary measures to bring the effective tax rate up to a more satisfactory level.

More often, government may well feel that it is reasonable to reduce the tax rates, or increase the allowances and bracket limits, to cope with the inflationary pressure, and to prevent taxpayers from automatically being hit by progressive rates that were originally not conceived of as suitable for taxpayers with real incomes that have come into the present bracket only because inflation has eroded the value of the allowances and bracket limits. Of course, this may be achieved either by automatic inflation adjustment or by discretionary measures. Faced with this choice, a minister of finance keen on his popularity among the voters might well find that it is in his interest to make the tax reduction discretionary rather than automatic. With such an approach, the nominal tax burden can be reduced by increased allowances and bracket limits, touted in the media, whereas the outcome in real terms may still be an increase of the effective tax burden, the discretionary changes made being insufficient to make up for the full inflation effect.

Another argument has to do with timing. If allowances and rate brackets are adjusted before the beginning of a tax year, the inflation rate used as the basis for adjustment must be the inflation rate actually measured in the year before. In the case of a government successfully fighting inflation, an adjustment that takes effect in a year when inflation is zero will reduce the tax burden in real terms and thus may run counter to a prudent fiscal policy. Needless to say, this argument can be turned around in the case when inflation turns worse in the tax year. Then, an inflation adjustment adapted to the inflation rate of the previous year may be quite insufficient to prevent bracket creep.

It is obvious that the choices here are political and that those making them will be guided by conflicting principles. It is easy to envisage how the attitude to indexation will differ between a politician whose inclination it is to increase the public sector and one who feels that the role of the public sector should be reduced. It is also obvious that if a government wants to convey the message that its anti-inflation policies will be firm and successful, the abolition of indexation rules may be an element of such a policy, rational both as a means of convincing and as a means of avoiding an inopportune weakening of the government finances as a result of a delayed effect of the indexation rules.

Simple Alternatives to Global Adjustment of the Tax Base

General

The issue that raises the most interesting and complicated problems with respect to the subject inflation and taxation is the inflation adjustment of the tax base.

It is a general experience that inflation adjustment of the tax base is seen as an undesirable complication of the tax system, resorted to only in the case of rampant inflation. The choice is normally between crude and simple measures, aimed at reducing the effects of inflation on the tax base, and a sophisticated system of global adjustment for inflation. Thuronyi, (1996, p. 443), uses 'ad hoc adjustment', as opposed to 'partial' and 'global' adjustment.

It is arguable that *ad hoc* measures and partial adjustment have the same practical advantages and theoretical shortcomings in comparison with a global adjustment. The patterns for the latter are not to be found among the economic heavy-weights in the OECD, but rather in countries with traditionally high inflation such as Argentina, Brazil, Chile, and Israel. Just as was pointed out with respect to inflation adjustment of allowances and bracket rates, the countries applying sophisticated inflation-adjustment systems have normally been keen on getting rid of them, to the extent that they have been able to reduce the inflation rate. Even countries that have experienced rather high inflation rates at times, have usually found it better to make partial or *ad hoc* adjustments than to announce – by adopting a global adjustment system – that inflation has come to stay.

In this context, it is worth mentioning the type of measures taken in countries hit by what might be called complete state bankruptcy. For instance, at the time, June 1948, when Germany liquidated the defunct Reichsmark system in favour of the later so successful Deutsche Mark, a new start was made by establishing, for all business firms, an 'opening balance' in the new currency (DM-Eroffnungsbilanz). Here, break in the continuity of the books was legislated on under the (correct) assumption that the erosion of the old currency would not be repeated in the future. Thus, the adjustment to the past inflation could be given the form of a once and for all adjustment. Similar measures, particularly revaluations of assets, have been undertaken in many countries, albeit not always with the same accuracy with respect to future needs of inflation adjustment.

Capital Gains

If inflation distorts the tax base, the simplest way out is not to tax at all. There is a rich experience of capital gains taxation being avoided, when capital gains are expected to be nominal rather than real in most cases. One way of doing this is to abstain from capital gains tax altogether, another to modify the D-day provisions with the effect of excluding some or all of the gains on assets held for a long time. On the other hand, just with respect to capital gains taxation, a simple form of indexation may be used. The method is simply an adjustment to the cost base, multiplying the investment by an index factor for the respective year.

Regrettably, neither method is really satisfactory. Eschewing capital gains tax in general opens the avenue for tax arbitrage. Moreover, to the extent gains are real, there is both an equity argument and a revenue argument for imposing a capital gains tax on the real element.

Indexation of the base, in turn, does not solve the problem of how to deal with the real gain made if corresponding debts are in nominal terms and the interest deductible. If a taxpayer has bought a house for 100, and borrowed every penny of the purchase sum, he has *prima facie* made a real gain, if after 100 per cent inflation he can sell the house for 200, while his loan is still 100. But things are more complicated than that: if the interest rate on the loan is such as to compensate for the lender's inflation loss, the house-owner may have paid dearly for the half of the house representing his equity at the time of the sale. If the interest relief he enjoyed during the time of his ownership was less than complete, or if the interest rate was more than adequate to compensate the lender, these circumstances must likewise be weighed in.

Finally, if the house-owner, repelled by the high domestic interest rate, sought financing in the international market, the value in domestic currency terms of his debt might have moved up with inflation so as to imply no equity gain at all. In that case, it would be fair to say that there was no real gain on the house worth taxing, but a similar real approach to the loss on the currency debt would dictate a finding that there was no real loss on that count, either.

Depreciation

Depreciation allowances computed on the basis of original costs pose a problem if the inflation rate is high. A real approach to income taxation rather than a nominal one presupposes an adjustment of the depreciation rules, implying a continuous indexation of the depreciation base. Needless to say, this procedure must be complicated, and tax legislators have normally been loath to allow it, let alone make it mandatory.

Instead, as mentioned above, what many countries have done has been one-time adjustments of the depreciation base, a measure that might be reasonably adequate, provided inflation is put a stop to, but less than adequate if inflation goes on. In some countries, the adjustment of the depreciation base has been optional, and sometimes there has even been some tax on the adjustment. In the latter case, if the tax is equal or close to the normal tax rate, the adjustment has been of no use to the taxpayers, possibly even speeding up the realisation for tax purposes of profits not yet realised in the market.

Alternatively, resort has been had to accelerated depreciation, in the hope that by such a measure, the same objective can be achieved without undue complication. It is a telling example that when Sweden modified its corporate income tax in 1938 by introducing free depreciation for other tangible assets than real property, an *ex post* analysis by Professor Västhagen (1953) showed that the actual outcome of this experiment (it was terminated in 1951) implied an actual depreciation rate on a level with what would have been applicable, if depreciation had been granted on a real basis. In other words, the interest gain on the accelerated depreciation was sufficient to make up for the real value loss on the amounts of depreciation proper.

It is only fair to say that legislation in most countries shows a certain degree of legerdemain on this point. The explanation is very simple – if depreciation is granted more generously than would have been dictated by a precise computation of the declining nominal value over the useful life period of an asset, this can always be defended as a rough and ready adjustment to the inflationary situation. On the other hand, if a purely nominal approach has been chosen with respect to other assets, it might be difficult to defend too generous depreciation rules, when the value of the depreciating assets, measured in nominal terms, is rising rather than declining.

Again, just as with capital gains, the problem arises whether it is acceptable to make an open or implicit inflation adjustment on the asset side only, without making a corresponding adjustment on the liability side. It gives food for thought to notice that in a number of industrial countries, business lobbyists have pushed hard for liberalised depreciation, indexation of cost bases, reduced capital gains taxation and the like, whereas their interest in a consistent global adjustment of the income tax system as a whole, including adjustments on the liabilities side, has been cool. The explanation has often been that changing the tax system from a nominal basis to a real one would not imply any great improvement – partial measures on the asset side already having been taken in one form or another – whereas the reform would bring unwelcome changes in the treatment of the liabilities.

In the same vein, it is relatively easy to gain business support for a cash-flow corporate tax system, implying immediate write-off of investments and inventories, but a clear tendency for such support to fade out, when the corollary is described in the form of no tax relief for debt interest.

Inventory Valuation

Again, with respect to inventories, the choice of the legislative bodies is between a pure real base system and simpler but less exact solutions. The solutions may include a cash-flow system, under which inventories are written down to zero on acquisition. Another approach, less obviously deviating from traditional accounting principles, is the last in, first out (LIFO) rule. Under that rule, the inflationary gain on the amount of inventories that is always kept will not be realised and taxed until the firm is liquidated. A similar technique, better for those firms whose inventories fluctuate over the years, is the normal inventory method, under which a fixed historical cost value is applied to a given physical amount of inventories, regardless of whether they are present on the final day of the accounting year or not. Inventories above that amount are valued at cost or market, whichever is the lower, whereas a shortage of inventories gives rise to a debt item, representing the difference between the historical cost value and the (higher) market value on the lacking amount. A still simpler method is one that combines the first in first out (FIFO) rule with a generous inventory reserve provision. As long as the physical inventory is large enough, such a provision may fulfill the same purpose as a FIFO valuation rule.

Roll-over Provisions

To the extent that income tax is levied applying a realisation criterion, the tax on profits and gains may be postponed by avoiding realisation. This simple fact takes on particular importance in the context of inflationary gains. If the system is based on nominal values, the locking-in effect of the tax on gains and profits must be more important, the greater the rate of inflation.

If a system of taxation representing a real rather than a nominal approach seems too complicated, there are ways of mitigating this lock-in effect by applying roll-over provisions. One example is the capital gains tax on homes. A taxpayer, whose residence has increased in nominal value through inflation, will be unwilling to move, if selling his home implies that the inflationary gain on his home is subject to taxation. Needless to say, the same effect may occur as a result of a real price increase of the home, but the greater the inflation, the more important will be the nominal part of the gain.

This tax, sometimes called a tax on moving, will not be conducive to mobility of labour, nor to the rational function of the housing market.

Already a long time ago, the United States Internal Revenue Code, being ahead of most other tax laws in its dealing with capital gains, contained a provision, now Sec. 1034, allowing a roll-over of the gain for a taxpayer who invested the same amount or more in a new home than he realised for the old one. This provision has been emulated elsewhere.

Similar provisions may apply to cases when an asset has been damaged by fire or accident, and the insurance payment is used to purchase a similar asset. This is for all practical purposes something less than a realisation, and a roll-over provision is easily defended.

It is a bit more tricky to decide whether a similar roll-over provision should apply to all assets. Obviously, the use of a nominal method to compute profits and gains will be seen as less disturbing, if the nominal gains realised on the alienation of machinery and plant can be rolled over by an immediate write-down of the replacement asset. If for each category (the number of categories should be held very low for simplicity's sake) each year's net investment is brought forward as depreciation base, only a negative net investment exceeding the cumulated rest value being taxed as realised gain, the application will be extremely simple, and the disturbing effects of the nominal principle will be minimised.

Such a system will, of course, be very similar to a cash-flow system, and like that raises the issue of how to deal with debt interest. Moreover, it is a general problem with all roll-over provisions, whether it is really in the best interest of the economy that investors are influenced by the tax system to hold on to their investments, or to investments of the same kind. It is easy to see why unsuccessful investors and businessmen should be encouraged to abandon the field of investment or business where they have been less than successful and leave the investments or the running of the business to other, more skilful actors. If the tax system is nominal, even a very unsuccessful investment might well have resulted in nominal gains that would be taxable on liquidation, while taxation is deferred to the extent gains may be rolled-over. There is, accordingly, no contradiction in the statement that an unsuccessful investment or a losing business may still carry a potential tax debt motivated by inflationary price movements.

Global Adjustment Systems
General

It is only what could be expected that the development of global adjustment, i.e. full indexation systems, in practice has been restricted to a few superinflation countries. Proposals for a full indexation have, of course, been made even elsewhere. In Sweden, Professor Gustaf

Lindencrona prepared a noteworthy report in 1982 (Lindencrona 1982), and he also co-operated in a later report (von Bahr et al. 1989). Neither report led to legislation, however. The technical arguments were in the foreground, but a suspicion lingers that the system of *ad hoc* adjustments was preferred. The reason they have not been accepted can only be speculated about. One reason, often mentioned, may be their complication. Tax systems, even nominal ones, are complicated enough without being further burdened by indexation rules that may seem difficult to understand, more so, the more detailed and precise they are.

Another reason is that the indexation of the tax system may be interpreted as an outflow of defeatism in the government's defence of the value of the money. If a government is eager to pursue an anti-inflationary policy, the introduction or even the maintaining of an indexation system in the tax field may be at cross-purposes with the official policy. A government may look far more resolute in its purpose, if it refuses to adapt the tax system to inflation, referring to past inflationary gains as an unfortunate aberration and promising that the future will be one of a stable currency implying no difference between a nominal system and a real one.

The real reason may, however, be a different one, to the extent the nominal system already includes provisions, what Thuronyi calls *ad hoc* or partial adjustments, that compensate for inflation in a simpler form. In particular in those cases, where inflation is overcompensated for, resistance may be strong among taxpayers against an indexation system that will only bring new burdens, adding nothing to the already existing reliefs.

It is difficult to say where the breaking-point lies, when inflation is so high as to render a full indexation system necessary at the risk of total break-down of the nominal system. Thuronyi (1996, p. 465) mentions 30 per cent as a dividing line, where global adjustment is appropriate. Obviously, the crucial number here is less the historical inflation rate, more the rate of inflation anticipated for the future. A great number of OECD countries have gone through periods of rather strong inflation, yet managed to keep up hopes for the future strong enough to make the preservation of a nominal system politically acceptable.

Perhaps there is a dividing line between those countries where inflationary developments are seen as aberrations and those, where the public expects nothing by way of stability of the currency. In the latter countries, indexation or currency clauses in civil law contracts will be the order of the day. Accordingly, the public grows used to indexation clauses, and to the extent that this has happened, the acceptance of indexation clauses in the tax system may be easier to achieve.

Methods for Global Adjustment

This is not the place to enter into all the details of how to make a global adjustment on an income tax system. Thuronyi (1996), offers some detail. The discouraging Israeli experience is described by Pick (1983) and Lapidoth (1986). The general principle is simple. We may first assume that we use a balance-sheet method to compute the profit, i.e. the profit is the difference between the equity at the end of the year and the equity at the beginning of the year, with an addition for what has been taken out of the business and a deduction for contributions to the business. Indexation in this context means that the value of the opening balance is adjusted by the index factor, in other words the relation between the index figure at the end of the period and the same figure at the beginning of the period (possibly the cost-of-living index, but other methods exist), and that the same type of adjustment is given to the additions and deductions for money taken out or invested in the business. Depending on the pace of inflation, these adjustments may be based on monthly, weekly, or even daily index figures.

In a country where balance-sheet comparison is not the traditional approach, it is, however, possible, although a bit more complicated, to take the profit-and-loss account as the point of departure.

An alternative to indexation may be the use of a different currency to compute the profits in. A current translation into another, operational currency of amounts in local currency by use of the exchange rate of the day of transaction, will basically pose the same problem as indexation. Whether the fluctuations of the foreign exchange rate are rational or distorted by speculative movements, and whether the economy of the country, whose currency is chosen as functional currency, develops soundly, is, of course, not guaranteed.

It is fair to say that the complication of the global adjustment systems is such that they are easy to argue against, politically, and difficult to make popular among taxpayers. Add to this the fact that the partial or *ad hoc* reliefs, mentioned earlier, in most cases are directed towards relief to taxpayers, leaving to global adjustment the unpleasant task of taking care of the compensating items, mainly on the debt side, and we understand why tax systems around the world show much more of partial and *ad hoc* adjustments than global adjustment systems.

Conclusion

In most industrial countries, inflation nowadays is not the rampant problem it used to be. Accordingly, the interest in adjusting tax systems for inflation has receded, and there is not the pressure of former years. If we want to gain experience on how to make a global adjustment for inflation work, we have to study the experience of those relatively few countries, particularly in Latin America, that have mastered the complicated trick, and whose inflationary experience has made their exercise of this fine art a regrettable necessity.

With respect to the other adjustments to inflation – speeding up tax payments, using withholding as much as possible, applying *ad valorem* rates, adjusting allowances and bracket limits, etc., the solutions are simpler and the experience correspondingly more general.

References and Further Reading

von Bahr, N. *et al.* 'Inflationskorrigerad inkomstbeskattning' (Inflation-Corrected Income Tax), *SOU 1989:36*, Stockholm 1989.

Casanegra de Jantscher, M., I. Coelho and A. Fernandez, 'Tax Administration and Inflation' in *Improving Tax Administration in Developing Countries*, eds. R. Bird and M. Casanegra de Jantscher, p.251, IMF, 1992.

Hirao, T. and C. Aguirre, 'Maintaining the Level of Income Tax Collections Under Inflationary Conditions', *IMF Staff Papers*, Vol. XVII, p.277, 1970.

Lapidoth, A., 'The Israeli Experience of an Inflation Adjusted Tax Base', *Bulletin for International Fiscal Documentation*, Vol. XL p.125, 1986.

Lindencrona, G., 'Real beskattning' (Real Taxation), *SOU 1982:1-3*, Stockolm 1982.

Pick, J. F., 'Introduction of an Inflation-Adjusted Tax Base in Israel', *Bulletin for International Fiscal Documentation*, Vol. XXXVII, p.259, 1983.

Piedrabuena R. *et al*, 'Sistema tributario chileno, analisis, evaluacion, alternativas de reforma', *Informe de la oficina de estudios tributarios*, Santiago, 1960.

Tanzi, V. 'Inflation, Lags in Collection, and the Real Value of Tax Revenue', *IMF Staff Papers*, Vol. XXIV p.154, 1977.

Thuronyi, V. 'Adjusting Taxes for Inflation' in ed. V. Thuronyi, *Tax Law Design and Drafting*, pp.434-476, IMF, 1996.

Västhagen, N., 'De fria avskrivningarna 1938-51' (The Free Depreciation 1938-51). *Första delen, Industrin, Företagsekonomiska Forskningsinstitutet vid Handelshögskolan i Stockholm*, Meddelande No. 49, Lund, 1953.

CHAPTER 10

ADMINISTRATIVE CONSTRAINTS ON TAX POLICY

Richard M Bird*

Introduction

The importance of good tax administration has long been as obvious to those concerned with tax policy as has its absence in most developing and transitional countries. Stanley Surrey (1958, pp.158-9) noted that 'the concentration on tax policy – on the choice of taxes – may lead to insufficient consideration of the aspect of tax administration. In short, there may well be too much preoccupation with *what to do* and too little attention to *how to do it*'. Unfortunately, there is surprisingly little evidence in the copious writing on tax reform since, that this warning has been taken sufficiently seriously. More characteristic is the view epitomised by Kaldor (1980) that administrative deficiencies can and must be rectified to permit desirable policy changes. In reality, such problems will persist for a long time in many developing countries as well as in the transitional countries of east and central Europe. Indeed, even in developed countries the life of tax administrators has become more difficult in recent years as a result of the increased globalisation of financial markets and the looming 'dematerialisation' of other tax bases as a result of growing electronic commerce. Not all these problems can be discussed in this short paper, however, so I shall concentrate here on the linkage between tax administration and tax policy in developing countries.[1]

---

* Professor of Economics and Director of the International Centre for Tax Studies, University of Toronto.
[1] For the most part, this paper follows parts of Bird (1992). Aspects of these arguments are developed further in Bird (1989, 1991). The related, but separate, subject of the reform of tax administration in developing countries is discussed in Bird and Casanegra (1992), Vazquez-Caro, Reid and Bird (1992), and Bagchi, Bird and Das Gupta (1995). The links between tax administration and tax policy in transitional countries are explored in several of the papers in Tanzi (1992, 1993), and the implications of globalization and electronic commerce for tax administration and tax policy in developed countries are discussed in e.g. Bird and McLure (1990) and Bird and Mintz (1994).

The Problem

The administrative dimension should be placed at the centre rather than the periphery of tax reform efforts in developing countries. As Casanegra (1990, p.179) put it: '...tax administration *is* tax policy.' Limited administrative capacity is a binding constraint on tax reform in many developing countries. It is not uncommon for half or more of potential income tax to be uncollected, and matters are not much better with respect to most other taxes. Even when there is not outright evasion, the tax structure in these countries is often designed, administered, and judicially interpreted in such a way as to ensure the emergence of a huge gap between the potential and the actual tax base. The result in most developing countries is that there is a great discrepancy between what the tax system appears to be on the surface and how it actually works in practice.

The effects of this discrepancy are pervasive. Not only is revenue lost but the elasticity of the tax system is also reduced – particularly, of course, in inflation when administrative lags alone will usually suffice to yield this result. Additional revenue must continually be secured through a series of discretionary *ad hoc* rate increases and new taxes. The patchwork character of the tax system of many developing countries arises in large part from their inability to administer the taxes they legislate, resulting in the continual need to legislate new tax changes.

The incidence and effects of the tax system are as sensitive to how it is administered as is its yield. Tax evasion inevitably undermines the horizontal equity of the tax system. No matter what the law says, the 'real' income tax in most developing countries is a schedular tax, with the effective tax rate depending largely upon the source of the income and almost always being heavier on wage than on self-employment or capital income. Taxes on property are even more sensitive to administrative interpretation. Even in the case of sales and excise taxes, in practice the products of small firms are usually favoured.

Most divergences between law and reality undermine the vertical equity of the tax system. It is the well-to-do who can most readily arrange for the law to contain convenient loopholes in the first place, and to exploit them once they are there with the aid of the 'rent-seeking' skills of tax accountants and lawyers (and the consequent waste of scarce resources). The same group receive much of their income in the forms that are hardest to track down. They may also more readily hold their wealth, and even spend it, in ways hard to detect (e.g. off-shore). Finally, they can not only most readily bribe and subvert administrators, but they have the most to gain from doing so. Since the incidence of a tax results from the interaction of statute law, the opportunities different groups have to evade it, and the rigor with which it is enforced – and the rich come out ahead on all three counts – taxation in developing countries is, as a rule, unlikely to cause much disturbance to the inhabitants of the upper ranges of the income distribution.

For similar reasons, the incentive effects of the tax system may be quite different from those that may be surmised from the law. The global progressive personal income tax established by law is in practice likely to amount to little more than at most a mildly progressive tax on wage-earners in the modern sector. The equally formidable looking modern corporate income tax may turn out to be a crude gross receipts tax in practice. Many so-called 'general' sales taxes in developing countries amount to little more than a levy on imports and a few excisables. In these circumstances, comparisons of the merits of general income or consumption taxes and lamentations about the heavy burden imposed on capital by nominally progressive income and corporate taxes often represent more obeisance to current trends in the academic literature than serious analysis of tax reform.

Tax administration in any country inevitably reflects to a large extent the nature of the country itself. If the country is a sea of corruption, as some are, the tax administration will not be an island of incorruptibles, and it is foolish to pretend it is. If most traders in the country are illiterate and keep no written records, no accounts-based tax (such an income or general sales tax) can effectively be levied on them, and it is futile to pretend to do so. If land titles are in chaos or non-existent, no effective land tax can be levied. If officials are judged solely by the tax revenue they produce and little else as in some developing countries, they are likely to get that revenue from the politically weaker sectors of the population (such as ethnic minorities), regardless of what the law says. If the only way for an honest official to make a living wage is to claim travel allowances, then he is forced to travel even if it is a complete waste of his time. If only the incompetent and the untrained are left to deal directly with taxpayers, as is the case in many administrative systems where advancement comes only in the form of being promoted to a desk job, then taxpayers will meet only the incompetent and the untrained. This catalogue of woes is not easily remediable even in principle, let alone in practice.

In some developing countries, the honesty of both taxpayers and tax officials is suspect. Governments have little control over officials, little information as to what is going on, and no easy way to get it. Even if the information were available, the administrative problem is inherently complex: market structures (and hence adjustment cost) vary widely, as do risk and time preferences, so that the costs, probabilities, and benefits of detecting evasion and corruption vary widely. Administrative cost functions are discontinuous and hard to interpret (Bird, 1982). Tax schedules, the interpretation of the law, the penalty schedule, and the appeals process all vary over time, as do enforcement efforts – and the reaction of taxpayers to such efforts.

Nonetheless, many tax analysts simply ignore the problem of tax administration – a problem that is epitomised in many countries by the phrase 'All taxes are negotiable' (Gray, 1987) – perhaps in the hope it will go away on its own. Even those most aware of these problems have sometimes done this. In a perceptive piece on tax administration in Nigeria 30 years ago, for example, Taylor (1967) began his analysis by saying these were only short-run problems which would undoubtedly be resolved in 20 or 25 years. An official report in Papua New Guinea (1971) similarly said of the income tax in that country that doubtless, by the end of the decade, its reach will have extended throughout the population. Both these predictions, like many similar ones made in other countries, turned out to be wildly optimistic. Most proposals for tax reform in developing countries have not paid even this passing obeisance to the problem of tax administration. Indeed, many reform proposals would make the life of administrators even more difficult. It is no wonder that tax administrators seem often to view would-be tax reformers as residents of an ivory tower who descend after the battle is over to shoot the wounded.

One reason for this apparent disinterest in administration is that it is hard to go beyond platitudes on this subject. A more basic reason, however, has less to do with platitudes than with attitudes. As Witt (1987, p. 140), puts it: 'Efficient and inefficient tax systems are not the result of some kind of "happy" coincidence but of social and political power constellations.' Whether administrative inertia shows that a society gets the tax administration it wants (or deserves) – perhaps because taxation reflects the reality of political power – or whether it shows that no administration can differ much from the society of which it is a part, is less important than the fact of its existence. Neither quick fixes nor head-on confrontations seem likely to change matters much in the foreseeable future in most countries. Tax administration thus seems likely to remain a binding constraint on tax policy in many developing countries for years to come. In these circumstances, what can be done?

Approaches to a Solution

Possible solutions to the administrative problems of tax reform may be rather arbitrarily divided into three groups: those that would change the environment, those that would change the administration, and those that would change the law.

Changing the Environment

Academic economists discussing policy issues often, in effect, advocate that the way the world works should be changed to fit the conditions assumed in their models. Tax reformers asserting the need to change the institutional context within which a tax system functions often sound equally futile. It is common to hear, for example, that modern direct taxes depend upon what is usually called 'voluntary compliance'. Such compliance is generally motivated less by civic conscience than by the fear of being caught. It is exceedingly difficult, perhaps impossible, to administer a tax if every hand is raised against it. One cannot put the entire population into jail. Equally, however, one cannot will into being a spirit of compliance that is not there. If the willingness of taxpayers to comply with their obligations depends upon their perception that the funds thus taken from them are put to good use and that they are treated fairly when compared to other taxpayers, the fiscs of many developing countries are in deep trouble indeed.

Make Government a 'Better Buy'. Several ways of attempting to remedy this serious 'environmental' defect have been mooted. One is simply to undertake a campaign of 'taxpayer education', to convince taxpayers that – in a famous phrase – taxes are the price they pay for a civilised society, and that they live in such a society. Such campaigns are unlikely to do much good, however, if reality is too obviously different. As Adam Smith put it: 'In those corrupted governments where there is at least a general suspicion of much unnecessary expense, and great misapplication of the public revenue, the laws which guard it are little respected' (quoted in Skinner and Slemrod, 1985, p. 353). Words alone are unlikely to change such basic attitudes. Deeds may do so, however, so one approach to loosening the administrative constraint is obviously to turn government into something which people see as adding to their lives rather than a burden.

Thorough-going expenditure reform, increased use of devices such as earmarking and benefit taxes that link taxes and expenditures in some believable way, the devolvement of functional and financial responsibilities on local communities – such fundamental changes in the way government is conducted may lead to a change in the attitude to taxation over time, and hence make the work of the tax collector, if never pleasurable, at least acceptable. At the very least, governments should not, as some now do, burden even willing taxpayers with such unnecessary discomforts as the need to stand in long queues to file returns or pay taxes, needless requirements to submit numerous copies of returns, and even charges for supplying returns in the first place.

Make the Tax System Fairer. The perceived fairness of the tax system may also be a factor in shaping attitudes. Fundamental changes in such matters, however desirable, cannot be made easily or quickly, however, so there is little immediate hope for relief from this source. On the other hand, one should not overdo the importance of securing any particular concept of equity in the context of the tax system. Most developing countries are at best limited democracies or constrained autocracies. Even in the most democratic countries, only limited groups are both tax-sensitive and politically significant. Most governments seem more concerned with the few who matter than with the burden on the many: 'horizontal equity' seems often to be viewed solely from the perspective of those sufficiently well-off to be subject to direct taxes. The treatment of the population as a whole sometimes seems to be considered primarily in terms of how to secure the necessary revenues with the least fuss. The 'ability to pay' doctrine as it applies in some countries seems concerned more with the ability of the government to make people pay than with abstract notions of equity.

Changing the Administration

Hire Better Administrators. An obvious approach to relieving the constraints imposed on tax reform by administrative limitations is to tackle those limitations directly. Some proposals for administrative reform, however, seem to amount to little more than looking reality squarely in the eye and passing on. An example is the common suggestion that an elite corps of tax administrators should be created. This hoary chestnut deserves to be put aside for once and all. Tax administration is part of the public service. It is a fantasy to think that it can for long be pulled out of the ruck of political favouritism, employment-generation, and the myriad other factors that account for the masses of low-paid, poorly-trained, poorly-motivated public servants found in most developing countries (Goode, 1981). Even if such an elite could be created, they cannot do the job properly without both good soldiers (the front-line clerks, tellers, and so on) and adequate tools (computers, communication system, etc.) neither of which is likely to prove easy to procure in developing countries, particularly for usually low-status revenue agencies.

A more promising approach may be to establish what is in effect a new tax administration, for example, by contracting collection of export taxes to the central bank or some other 'reliable' organisation, or by creating a new quasi-independent revenue authority (such as the Revenue Board in Jamaica). Such measures may be effective for a period, but over time the bad old ways are likely to creep in again – unless, of course, the underlying factors creating the problems in the first place have been corrected.

Saved by Computers? A popular way of ignoring the administrative problem is to pretend it can all be handled by a small staff equipped with appropriately up-to-date computers. In many areas of tax administration, good use can obviously be made of computers. Indeed, proper computerisation may in some instances obviate the need to acquire the skills of some highly-trained specialists (Hutabarat and Lane, 1990). On the other hand, the computerisation of tax administration is itself a complex task. Computers must be programmed and operated by people; they must rely on information obtained and inputted by other people; and their output must be acted upon by still other people. Since the motivations and incentives of all these people are unlikely to be altered by the introduction of new equipment alone, it is by no means obvious that the dawning of the computer age has significantly reduced the importance of the administrative constraint on tax reform in developing countries. Indeed, it is not hard to find instances in which the inappropriate introduction and use of computer systems has even made matters worse. On the whole, computerisation is clearly most useful where the tax administration is already well-organised (Corfmat, 1985) – and hence halfway to a solution in any case.

Clean up the Administrative Structure. Too often, tax administration in developing countries is neglected and archaic, characterised by poor training, low status, poor salaries, and poor equipment. An obvious remedy is to tackle these and other organisational and procedural problems head on: to see that the law is properly drafted and codified; that the administration is properly organised, staffed, and trained; that taxpayers are located, placed on the rolls, and their returns adequately examined and audited; that relevant information is obtained from other government departments and elsewhere and properly utilised; that controversies between taxpayers and the administration are satisfactorily resolved; that taxes due are collected; and that penalties are properly applied. This is the approach taken by Surrey (1958) in the seminal paper cited earlier. Unfortunately, necessary as such measures are, not only do they take much time and effort to carry through; they also are politically unpopular and seldom attract sufficient support to be successful.

Privatisation and Tax Farming. Perhaps surprisingly, the oldest means of dealing with the pervasive administrative problem is to 'privatise' tax collection. 'Tax farming', as this practice was known, has a bad name in view of the gross injustices to which it led in countries such as pre-revolutionary France. Nonetheless, tax farming also had real virtues in many countries during the centuries when it was the dominant form of tax collection. In particular, it ensured a reliable and steady stream of revenue into state coffers (Webber and Wildavsky, 1986). The practice went out of favour in Europe when modern public administrative structures began to emerge in the 17th and 18th centuries.

No one would recommend the revival of tax farming today. Some important features of tax administration in many developing countries, however, are not dissimilar to tax farming in both their good and their bad aspects. Moreover, the recent adoption of what is in effect the private administration of important customs functions in countries such as Indonesia may signify a new legitimacy for this practice. Of course not many developing countries have opted to hire foreigners, let alone local private firms, to collect their taxes – even on a commission basis as opposed to the fixed fees characteristic of traditional tax farming. This change in the fee basis obviously obviates some of the worst problems with tax farming. The basic problem with privatising monopolies like revenue collection, however, is to specify the terms of the contract. Indeed, if the contract is adequately specified, and compliance with it sufficiently monitored, it might be as efficient for the government to do the job itself. Nonetheless, as Ramirez Acuna (1992) discusses, many aspects of the tax administrative process could usefully be privatised in many countries, for example, the reception and processing of tax forms.

In fact, some aspects of how tax administration works in many countries are not unlike a distorted form of privatisation. In some countries (e.g. Senegal), tax inspectors are rewarded in accordance with the amount of additional tax and fines they collect. The earmarked taxes common in Latin America are sometimes shared between the collecting agency and the state. The 'third party' collection systems that are the backbone of most effective taxes in all countries also have a commission aspect since the collecting agent (the withholding employer, the sales tax payer) has the use of the funds for a legally or customarily agreed period before remitting them to the government. Finally, in all too many countries, tax collectors are more or less expected to make up for their poor salaries by supplementary collections from taxpayers – collections which are not accompanied by a corresponding remittance to the government. In many such corrupt situations, there is a conventionally-accepted level of private reward to the fortunate possessors of official positions which is regarded as no more criminal than the equivalent rake-off by a cook from the household budget.

Set Performance Targets. Yet another interesting variant of 'official tax farming' which exists in some countries is to establish revenue targets for each auditor, tax official, or district tax office. If such targets are used as the sole basis for evaluating performance, and if compliance with such targets is considered essential to ensure an adequate flow of revenue to the central authorities, such a system has both the virtue (stable revenue) and the vice (a licence for extortion) of traditional tax farming. Moreover, unless the targeting system is altered, tax policy changes intended to alter allocative and distributive outcomes will not have much effect in reality, however refined their design, since the basic incentive of officials will still be to meet their targets by collecting the most from those least able to resist.

In other instances 'targeting' may be simply a relatively innocuous device used as one part of an array of measures intended to keep administrators up to the mark. Indeed, one of the main purposes of such a system – and perhaps even its effect if there are adequate controls to restrain excessive zeal – may be to provide a higher degree of certainty to both the state and taxpayers. With respect to public as to private tax farming, full understanding of the possible merits and demerits of the practice in any particular country requires a detailed examination of its context and effects. Targeting may be condemned as arbitrary, inequitable, and discouraging administrative effort. Alternatively, it may be accepted as conforming to local standards of fairness and administrative probity while providing a modicum of oversight and not affecting administrative effort adversely (as may occur if the effort establishes the targets, rather than *vice versa*).

Monitor Tax Officials. As Webber and Wildavsky (1986, p. 39) note '...a tax collector's very function tempts him to cheat'. Much of their lengthy history of fiscal administration is devoted to detailing ways over the centuries that sovereigns have tried to restrain this natural impulse of their fiscal servants. Rewards for good performance and penalties for poor performance; overlapping, duplicative, and redundant administrative structures; the division of functions among different officers, both to use each as a check on the other and to make it more difficult and costly to bribe them; the use of internal and external 'spies' to check on the honesty of tax officials – such devices and others have long been employed for this purpose in different countries.

The most basic way to ensure that tax officials do what they are supposed to do, and no more, however, is to reduce to a minimum the amount of discretion they have in dealing with taxpayers. The more room there is for negotiation between official and potential taxpayer, the more scope there is for bribery by the one, arbitrary exaction by the other, and collusion by both. The more the tax to be paid is based on some readily measurable, observable, and verifiable base, the less scope there is for such maneouvres. If tax administration is to be effective and seen to be fair in the context of many developing countries it is thus necessary to apply clear, known, objective standards – however rough the ensuing justice – rather than leaving the application of a fine-sounding general statute to negotiations between taxpayers and officials.

Changing the Law

In the end, the best way to cope with the administrative constraint on tax policy is to design tax policy in the first place in full recognition of the severe limitations imposed by administrative realities. The administrative dimension is central, not peripheral, to tax reform in developing countries. Without significant administrative changes, the alleged benefits of many proposed tax reforms will simply not be achieved. Too many tax reform efforts have regarded tax policy and tax administration as quite separate matters. The world is not like that. No policy exists until it is implemented, and it is the manner of its implementation which really determines its impact. Those who would alter the outcomes of a tax system must therefore understand in detail how it is administered, and adjust their recommendations accordingly if they want to do good rather than ill.

Broadly, there are three ways to approach the question of modifying the legal structure to accord with the administrative realities of developing countries: the first, to develop some gadgetry to bypass the problem, is a false lead; the second, to provide an adequate legal structure for administration, is obviously important but in itself inadequate; while the third, to design the basic tax law properly in the first place is, in the end, the only sensible procedure.

Give Out Prizes. Many types of tax 'gadget' have been suggested to get around the administrative problem. The 'lottery' approach, for instance, uses the cupidity (or gullibility) of taxpayers to make their interests congruent with those of the administration. An example of this approach is a scheme suggested by Hart (1967) to encourage customers to collect their sales receipts, so that they could enter them for lottery prizes. Such schemes have been employed to various extents in some Latin American countries, Turkey, and Taiwan. The idea is to obtain more reliable information on both the gross receipts of business and the expenditures of taxpayers.

One problem with such schemes is that it is unlikely the probability of a prize is great enough to make it worthwhile for people to comply. Even if it is, the seller could easily offset this incentive by offering two prices, with and without receipt. Another problem is that there is no conceivable way most tax administrations in developing countries could use the information thus provided, since they are already swamped with usable but unused information. An example is the provision found in some countries permitting the deduction of professional fees only on the submission of appropriate receipts. The idea is to aggregate such receipts and match them with the declaration (or nondeclaration) of the professional in question. Unfortunately, this never seems to happen.

A 'Self-Enforcing' Tax System. For much the same reasons, the much-touted 'self-checking' feature of the value added tax has in fact amounted to as little in most countries as the more elaborate schemes along these lines proposed by Kaldor (1980). This is one area where computerisation in principle could be the answer, although it does not as yet seem to have amounted to much in the case of other 'information return' reporting systems (such as bank interest in Canada and the United States). Korea, for instance, at first matched all value added returns on the computer, although it seems unlikely that this elaborate exercise was more productive than a properly designed audit system would be (Han, 1990).

Nonetheless, tax administration is essentially about the gathering and utilisation of information, and in principle, the information governments can use to trace unreported amounts of income or revenues has become much easier to follow in the computer age. Not all signs are good for tax collectors, however. On one hand, legitimate concerns have been raised about individual rights to privacy: such concerns are likely to grow, not shrink, as time goes on, at least in democracies. On the other hand, government's right to follow the flow of information stops at the national border, and borders are increasingly porous (Bird and McLure, 1990). When millions of dollars move from one country to another as a result of an electronic impulse received by a satellite high above the globe, what price national fiscal sovereignty? Reliance on increased international co-operation seems a thin reed with which to cope with the implications of these trends, and the long-run prognosis for the ability of governments to track down cross-border manipulations seems dim. It is becoming ever harder to tax the rich and slippery.

Tax Amnesties. Another tax 'gadget' is the tax amnesty. Amnesties are of little use, however, unless the tax in question will henceforth be fiercely and strictly administered. History suggests that such tightening seldom follows and that those who miss out on one amnesty can likely count on another one in the future. Indeed, to the extent an amnesty successfully increases revenues, it often tends to *reduce* administrative efforts. For these reasons, tax amnesties will doubtless continue to be more popular with politicians than with tax analysts.

Tax Penalties. In contrast to the false hopes of gadgetry, there is clearly much to be gained by ensuring that the basic legal structure of tax administration is set out properly both substantively (Yudkin, 1973) and procedurally (Vazquez-Caro, Reid, and Bird, 1992). Even this path will not lead to Nirvana, however. In particular, while it is obviously important to have a correct, and enforceable, set of sanctions, the notion that some seem to have derived from the theoretical tax evasion literature that all that is needed to deter evasion is a correct penalty structure is simply fantasy.

As Mansfield (1987) notes, for the most part this literature ignores the constraints that permit the system to function at all. The one-off game between a rational tax evader and a two instrument administration postulated in this literature is too far removed from the real world to provide much useful guidance to tax designers or officials. So long as the probability of being caught is close to zero, as is the probability of being subjected to a severe penalty if one is caught, then even within the framework of this model, there would seem to be little penalty design can do to alleviate real world problems. Why would anyone who can costlessly evade a 50 per cent tax rate hesitate to dodge one of 30 or even 10 per cent?

Adapting the Tax Structure. In the end, the key to successful taxation in developing countries is to recognise administrative realities in designing tax policy in the first place. This does not mean that there is no place for an income (or other general direct) tax in any developing country. The moral is rather that those who would design a better direct tax system for such countries must realise that economic and administrative realities are usually such that what is really being done is to design a schedular tax. The tax analyst who approaches his task in this way is unlikely to design the same tax system as one who does not take into account the way the world works.

Schedular taxation, for example, has long had a bad press, much of which has been well deserved. As with tax farming and earmarking, however, wholesale condemnation of the schedular approach is by no means justified. Not only is the income tax in every developing country schedular in practice, but this outcome is inevitable, no matter what the law may say. It is simply not possible to apply a strictly 'global' income (or expenditure) tax in the circumstances of most developing countries.

Taxes should be withheld wherever possible, that is, when income is paid out as wages or in other ways by large organisations (Soos, 1990). Scarce administrative resources should be concentrated on ensuring that the larger taxpayers, who are generally already on the rolls, comply fully with their fiscal obligation. The scarce administrative skills available in most tax administrations – the 'detective' skills needed to uncover accounting fraud, for example – should be concentrated on those firms, seldom more than a few hundred in number, from which most taxes are collected, whether in the form of corporate income taxes, withheld personal income taxes, or sales, excise and payroll taxes, rather than dissipating them uselessly across a vast sea of noncompliant small and medium traders (Mutén, 1981). This may not be fair, but it is reality.

Moroever, the administrative case for a properly designed set of presumptive taxes is strong in most developing countries (Tanzi and Casanegra, 1987). Obviously, such crude methods should not be applied in the more organised sector, from which most taxes are likely to be collected in any event. But in the case of the well-off (and notoriously elusive) 'professional' class, whose noncompliance brings direct taxation into disrepute in so many countries, the best approach, as with small traders and farmers, is to impose as stiff a presumptive system as can be implemented, with the best officials being used to devise and adapt the standards rather than to deal directly with individual taxpayers.

These approaches – like the simple forms of land tax advocated elsewhere (Bird, 1974) – may not be glamorous or conducive to eliciting the kudos of tax policy aficionados around the world. But experience suggests strongly that tax policy that works in the administrative conditions of most developing countries is likely to be simple to understand, simple to explain, and simple to administer. Such policy may sometimes seem on the surface to be highly deficient in terms of the equity and efficiency goals generally stressed by public finance economists. In practice, however, with reasonable care in design the results can be not only about as good as can be achieved in these terms but also, and this is the main point, they may actually be achievable with the resources at hand, unlike the more complex proposals so often made in the tax reform literature, let alone the overly elaborate tax structures all too often found in the laws of many developing countries. Simplicity in tax design is of course not the whole answer to the administrative problem, and it may sometimes prove far from simple to achieve. But without close attention to this problem, in the context of most developing countries not much is likely to be achieved in terms of financing public sector activity in an adequate and sustainable way.

References and Further Reading

Bagchi, A., R. M. Bird, and A. Das Gupta, *An Economic Approach to Tax Administration Reform*, International Centre for Tax Studies, University of Toronto, Toronto, 1995.

Bird, R. M., *The Taxation of Agricultural Land*, Harvard University Press, Cambridge MA, 1974.

Bird, R. M., 'The Costs of Collecting Taxes: Preliminary Reflections on the Uses and Limits of Cost Studies', *Canadian Tax Journal*, Vol. 30, pp.860-65, 1982.

Bird, R. M., 'The Administrative Dimension of Tax Reform in Developing Countries', in ed. M. Gillis, *Lessons from Tax Reform in Developing Countries*, Duke University Press, Durham, NC, 1989.

Bird, R. M., 'Tax Administration and Tax Reform: Reflections on Experience', in eds. J. Khalilzadeh-Shirazi and A. Shah, *Tax Policy in Developing Countries*, World Bank, Washington, 1991.

Bird, R. M., *Tax Policy and Economic Development*, Johns Hopkins University Press, Baltimore, 1992.

Bird, R. M. and C. E. McLure, 'The Personal Income Tax in an Interdependent World', in eds. S. Cnossen and R. M. Bird, *The Personal Income Tax*, Elsevier, Amsterdam, 1990.

Bird, R. M. and M. Casanegra de Jantscher, eds., *Improving Tax Administration in Developing Countries*, International Monetary Fund, Washington, 1992.

Bird, R .M. and J. M. Mintz, 'Future Developments in Tax Policy', *Federal Law Review*, Vol. 22, pp.402-13, 1994.

Casanegra de Jantscher, M., 'Administering the VAT,' in eds. M. Gillis, C.S. Shoup and G. Sicat, *Value Added Taxation in Developing Countries*, World Bank, Washington, 1990.

Corfmat, F., 'Computerizing Revenue Administrations in LDCs', *Finance and Development*, Vol. 22,, No. 3, pp.45-47, 1985.

Goode, R., 'Some Economic Aspects of Tax Administration', *International Monetary Fund Staff Papers*, vol. 28, pp.249-74, 1981.

Gray, C., 'The Importance of Legal Process to Economic Development: The Case of Tax Reform in Indonesia', World Bank, Washington, 1987.

Han, S. S., 'The VAT in the Republic of Korea', in eds. M. Gillis, C. S. Shoup and G. Sicat, *Value Added Taxation in Developing Countries*, World Bank, Washington, 1990.

Hart, A. G., *An Integrated System of Tax Information*, Columbia University School of International Affairs, New York, 1967.
Hutabarat, H. and M. Lane, 'Computerization and the VAT in Indonesia', in eds. M. Gillis, C. S. Shoup and G. Sicat, *Value Added Taxation in Developing Countries*, World Bank, Washington, 1990.
Kaldor, N., *Reports on Taxation II. Reports to Foreign Governments*, Duckworth, London, 1980.
Mansfield, C., 'Tax Administration in Developing Countries: An Economic Perspective', *International Monetary Fund Staff Papers*, Vol. 35, pp.181-97, 1988.
Mutén, L., 'Leading Issues of Tax Policy in Developing Countries', in eds. A. Peacock and F. Forte, *The Political Economy of Taxation*, Basil Blackwell, Oxford, 1981.
Papua New Guinea, *Committee of Inquiry on Taxation*, Government Printer, Port Moresby, 1971.
Ramirez Acuna, L. F., 'Privatization of Tax Administration,' in eds. R. M. Bird and M. Casanegra de Jantscher, *Improving Tax Administration in Developing Countries*, International Monetary Fund, Washington, 1992.
Skinner, J. and J. Slemrod, 'An Economic Perspective on Tax Evasion', *National Tax Journal*, Vol. 38, pp.345-53, 1985.
Soos, P., 'Self-Employed Evasion and Tax Withholding: A Comparative Study and Analysis of the Issues', *U.C. Davis Law Review*, Vol. 24, pp.107-93, 1990.
Surrey, S. S., 'Tax Administration in Underdeveloped Countries', *University of Miami Law Review*, Vol. 12,, pp.158-88, 1958.
Tanzi, V., ed. *Fiscal Policies for Economies in Transition*, International Monetary Fund, Washington, 1992.
Tanzi, V., ed. *The Transition to Market: Studies in Fiscal Reform*, International Monetary Fund, Washington, 1993.
Tanzi, V. and M. Casanegra de Jantscher, *Presumptive Income Taxation: Administrative, Efficiency and Equity Aspects*, International Monetary Fund, Washington, 1987.
Taylor, M., 'The Relationship between Income Tax Administration and Income Tax Policy in Nigeria', *Nigerian Journal of Economic and Social Studies*, Vol. 9, pp.203-15, 1967.
Vazquez-Caro, J., G. Reid and R. M. Bird, *Tax Administration Assessment in Latin America*, World Bank, Washington, 1992.
Webber, C. and A. Wildavsky, *A History of Taxation and Expenditure in the Western World*, Simon and Schuster, New York, 1986.

Witt, P. C., *Wealth and Taxation in Central Europe*, Berg, Leamington Spa, 1987.

Yudkin, L., *A Legal Structure for an Effective Income Tax Administration*, Harvard Law School International Tax Program, Cambridge MA, 1973.

CHAPTER 11

TAX REFORM OF THE 'EIGHTIES IN RETROSPECT: WHAT CAN WE LEARN?

Cedric Sandford*

What is 'Tax Reform'?

'Reform' is an ambiguous term. One meaning is the removal of imperfections, a change for the better. Another meaning is literally 're-form' – to form over again or differently.

When ministers of finance talk about their own tax reforms, they use the term in both senses – a restructuring of the tax system which is also an improvement. But whether a tax restructuring is an improvement is a matter of value judgment. This should be clear from some examples from the United Kingdom since the mid 1960s. (Doubtless they could be replicated from other countries.) Labour Chancellors of the Exchequer introduced a classical system of corporation tax, a Selective Employment Tax, a Capital Transfer Tax, and increased income tax rates in the interests of equality, claiming in all these actions to be tax reformers. Conservative Chancellors replaced the classical system of corporation tax by a partial imputation system; abolished the Selective Employment Tax; dismantled Capital Transfer Tax; and reduced income tax rates in the interests of efficiency and claimed the mantle of the tax reformer in doing so. Nor do such reversals of policy necessarily depend on a change of political party in government. Mrs Thatcher's Conservative Government introduced the Community Charge as a reform of local government taxation; the succeeding Conservative Government abolished it. Whether re-form of the tax system is good or bad is very much in the mind of the beholder.

In what follows we use 'tax reform' in the second sense only – a restructuring of taxation, without implying any judgment on whether the change represents an improvement.

*Emeritus Professor of Political Economy, University of Bath, United Kingdom.

But does any change to the tax system constitute a reform? Clearly, to justify the term reform, the change must be significant, non-trivial. There is no hard and fast rule which enables one to say that this change is significant enough to constitute a reform whilst that change is not. But to justify the designation the change concerned must be underpinned by some fairly explicit purpose or philosophy – not just a move to get a bit more tax revenue, or effect some minor change in administrative methods.

That said, the possible range of measures which could justifiably come within the tax reform label is very wide, encompassing new taxes for old; changes in tax rates, thresholds, brackets and base; changes in tax mix; changes in the tax unit; radical changes in administrative methods; and measures such as indexing a tax system against inflation.

The Tax Reform of the 'Eighties

By the 'Tax Reform of the 'Eighties' we mean the worldwide tax reform with common characteristics, causes and philosophy, centred on the decade of the 1980s. For some countries, notably the United Kingdom, it began earlier, with Sir Geoffrey Howe's Budget of 1979. For many countries it continued into the 1990s, for example, in Canada, with the introduction, on 1 January 1991, of a federal VAT and in Sweden, where the 'tax reform of the century' began in 1990. But the philosophy and the motive power came essentially from the 1980s and hence the justification for the designation.

Worldwide Reform

The tax reform of the 'eighties was remarkable for its worldwide nature. Every continent was affected and, although differing in important respects, tax reform touched both advanced and less developed countries. In what follows, although drawing on a wide range of countries, the detailed analysis concentrates on six English-speaking countries which were amongst the leaders in tax reform: Australia, Canada, Ireland, New Zealand, the United Kingdom and the United States.[1] These countries

---

[1] The author wishes to acknowledge his debt to the University of Melbourne where the award of the Downing Fellowship enabled him to improve his knowledge of Australian and New Zealand tax reform and to the Leverhulme Trust for an Emeritus Fellowship which financed visits and interviews in the United Kingdom, the United States, Canada and Ireland. He is also indebted to Andrew Marsland, Ian Wallschutzky, Chris Evans, Donal de Buitleir, Adrian Sawyer and John Hasseldine for enabling him to up-date his knowledge of these six countries.

cover three continents, three are unitary and three federal states and within each of these groups differences of constitution and political practice are marked; moreover their geographical positions leave them open to differing influences. Taken together they provide a rich seam to mine and from which to draw lessons on tax reform.

Characteristics of Reform

Perhaps even more remarkable than the geographical extent of the tax reform of the 'eighties was its common characteristics. The universal feature of tax reform in advanced countries was a reduction of personal income tax rates; whilst lower rates were cut, the dominant feature was the slashing of top rates, which, for many countries, were cut dramatically, no more so than in the United Kingdom, where the top rate came down in two stages from 83 per cent to 40 per cent and an investment income surcharge, which, above a threshold, could add another 15 percentage points to the top rate, was also abolished.

Table 11.1 shows the extent of reduction of top income tax rates for central government personal income taxes for a range of OECD countries. The dates are chosen to illustrate a pre-reform situation, one part way through, and one more or less at the end of the process. The table should be treated with care for several reasons. It makes no allowance for differing thresholds at which the top rate comes into operation; nor for any other income-related taxes, like social security contributions, which may effectively add to income tax; nor for the existence in some countries of state or/and local income taxes. Nonetheless the overall message is clear. Top income tax rates were massively reduced.

Alongside this reduction in rates came a reduction in the number of steps in the income tax scale which were typically reduced to two or three, perhaps reflecting a recognition that almost any desired progression could be obtained with a variable threshold and just one or two rates (Dilnot, 1993).

The loss of revenue from the income tax reduction was at least partly paid for by a broadening of the income tax base. Tax expenditures (exemptions, reliefs, concessions) were eliminated or reduced.

The taxation of expenses was tightened up and payments in kind either taxed more heavily in the hands of the employee or, in Australia and New Zealand, made the subject of a fringe benefit tax on the employer. Capital gains, a form of income, were also taxed more heavily or, as in Australia, taxed for the first time, to bring them into line, or more nearly into line, with the taxation of other forms of income.

Table 11.1 Top Rates of Central Government Personal Income Tax for 1976, 1986 and January 1992 for Selected OECD Countries

Country	Top rates per cent			Percentage points reduction
	1976	1986	1992	1992 *minus* 1976
Australia	65	57	48	17
Austria	62	62	50	12
Canada[1]	43	34	29	14
Finland[1]	51	51	39	12
France	60	65	57	3
Germany	56	56	53	3
Ireland	77	58	52[4]	25
Italy	72	62	50	22
Japan[1]	75	70	50	25
Netherlands[2]	72	72	60	12
New Zealand	60	57	33	27
Norway[1]	48	40	13	35
Sweden[1]	57	50	20	37
United Kingdom[3]	83	60	40	43
United States	70	50	31	39
Unweighted Average	63.4	56.3	41.7	21.7

[1]Countries with income tax at lower levels of government, typical rates for 1992 being flat: Canada 17, Finland 16, Norway 28, Sweden 31; progressive: Japan 5 to 14, United States 2 to 14.
[2]1976 and 1986 figures refer to personal income tax only; 1992 includes social security contributions now levied on same base as income tax.
[3]In 1976 only, an additional 15 percentage points for investment income above a threshold.
[4]Reduced to 48 per cent in the 1992 Budget.
Source: OECD various.

Another feature of the tax reform was a reduction in the rates of corporate income tax, (typically falling from around 45 or 50 per cent to the middle 30s) allied also to base broadening – concessions being reduced and capital allowances brought more into line with economic depreciation. Indeed, such was the extent of base broadening that in the United States and Canada, despite the cut in rates, there was a net increase in revenue to help make good the fall from the personal income tax. In some countries, such as New Zealand and Australia, a notable feature of the reform of corporate income tax was a move to an imputation system to reduce or eliminate the double taxation of dividends.

Another general if not universal feature of the tax reform movement was a new emphasis on general consumption taxes as a means of reducing income tax. Generally this took the form of an increase in VAT, or its introduction, as in New Zealand and Canada. Where VAT was not introduced, as in Australia, the attempt was made to raise more revenue from existing sales taxes.

Other features, common but not universal, were the general tightening up of tax administration, the introduction of new measures to restrict evasion in the most vulnerable industries, actions to limit tax avoidance and, in a few countries, the introduction or extension of indexation of tax allowances and thresholds against the effects of inflation.

Causes of Reform

The geographical extent and common features of tax reform were without precedent in tax history save for periods of world war, when the belligerents were seeking additional ways of enhancing revenue. The obvious questions are, what were the causes of this reform movement? Why did it come when it did?

Taxes are never popular, but in many countries in the 1970s and early '80s there was a large and growing discontent with the tax system. Tax avoidance was rife to the extent that, in some countries, it was felt to be in danger of undermining tax morality and voluntary compliance. In the United States 'horror stories about millionaires and large corporations that managed to pay no income tax at all were commonplace' (Birnbaum and Murray, 1988, p.9). In Australia, in the 1970s, tax avoidance, merging into tax evasion, had become a national scandal and, as late as 1985, Paul Keating, The Treasurer, could refer to 'An avalanche of avoidance, evasion and minimisation' (September Statement, 1985). In Canada, concern with the extent of 'tax sheltering' was indicated by the introduction of a minimum personal income tax in 1986. In Ireland a tax commission was set up in 1980, in part as a response to an unprecedented march through Dublin and other cities of wage and salary earners protesting at the disproportionate burden falling on them compared with the farmers and the self-employed – a complaint which was echoed in many other countries.

In Australia and New Zealand, there was a particular cause of resentment of income tax. Although, in the 1970s income tax rates were significantly lower than, say, the United Kingdom or the United States, they impinged on only modest earnings. In Australia the top marginal rate of 60 per cent was levied on workers receiving only 1.5 times average earnings (Commonwealth Government, 1985). In New Zealand the top rate of 66 per cent cut in at under 2.5 times average earnings (Douglas, 1985, p.2).

Another cause of reform and part of the discontent with the tax system, was the belief that taxes were failing to achieve their intended social and economic objectives. The widespread tax avoidance meant that high marginal tax rates were failing to reduce inequalities of income and wealth. On the economic side, tax incentives were having unintended consequences, often generated tax avoidance and, in so far as they did promote the intended objective, often did so at a disproportionate cost in revenue.

Not only were the tax systems failing to achieve their social and economic purposes, the high marginal tax rates were creating costly distortions. A number of econometric studies (e.g. Browning, 1978; Stuart, 1984; Ballard, Shoven and Whalley, 1985) suggested that the economic and welfare losses from tax distortions were much bigger than had previously been thought.

Of course, one reason for the high tax rates, which fuelled and underlay much of the discontent with the tax systems, was the growth of government expenditure. Between 1965 and 1985 every OECD country registered an increase in government expenditure as a percentage of GDP, with the overall (unweighted) average increase being 10.5 percentage points or almost 40 per cent on the earlier year. Nor was it simply the increase that caused concern. The high inflation of the 1970s, acting on generally unindexed tax systems, caused particular inequities: those dependent on tax allowances which failed to keep pace with prices were hard hit, taxpayers were pushed into higher tax brackets even when their real income had not risen, whilst many savers found themselves, in effect, paying tax out of capital.

Whilst these factors help to explain the causes of tax reform, international influences assisted its geographical spread. Smaller countries with big neighbours, such as Ireland and the United Kingdom, and Canada and the United States, where there were common frontiers and high mobility of capital and labour, felt obliged, at least partly, to follow the example of big brother. More broadly, the growing internationalisation of the world economy was beginning to exercise its influence and, to maintain international competitiveness, some countries felt it necessary to follow suit, at least with a reform of corporate income tax. International organisations played a part in the spread of reform. The IMF and World Bank encouraged countries on the path of tax reform; the expanding EEC required new members to adopt a VAT; the OECD provided a forum for discussion.

Above all, however, the tax reform of the 'eighties reflected a fundamental change in economic philosophy. The tax reform movement can only be understood in a wider context. In the leading countries, tax reform was part of a programme of pushing back the boundaries of the state, deregulating, freeing exchange rates, privatising, promoting competition and, in the remaining public sector, increasing managerial efficiency. This was as true of Labour New Zealand and Australia as of Republican United States and Thatcherite Britain.

The 'sixties and 'seventies had seen increasing government expenditure and also, in many countries, increasing government intervention in the economy, based on optimistic assumptions about the ability of governments to influence for good the economy and society. In the 'eighties, disillusionment with the results led to a decline in belief in the efficacy of the state and a revival of belief in the efficacy of markets. It was a change which affected not only governments in the capitalist world, but also undermined the socialist planned economies.

Objectives of Tax Reform

This change in philosophy accounts for the characteristic features of tax reform in the 'eighties. The overriding objective was efficiency in the sense of the efficient allocation of the factors of production in the economy, with the ultimate purpose of promoting economic growth. Tax reform was primarily aimed at securing 'tax neutrality', at minimising the distortions caused by taxes, at reducing or removing hindrances to the free working of markets, both markets for products and markets for the factors of production. The phrase which became current was 'the level playing field'. High taxes and tax reliefs created bumps in the playing field. The object of tax reform was to remove or reduce these bumps.

Of course tax reform had other objectives and simplicity and equity are usually mentioned by the tax reformers. But, unlike reform in the 'sixties and 'seventies, where the dominant motive had often been to improve vertical equity (interpreted as proportionately heavier taxation on the better off to reduce inequalities) the equity sought by the reform of the 'eighties was horizontal equity (the equal treatment of those in similar positions) which fitted well with the idea of tax neutrality. With hardly an exception, vertical equity, if mentioned at all, was seen as a constraint rather than an objective; rarely was there an attempt to reduce inequalities; at most reformers sought to ensure that tax reform did not increase them, that it was distributionally neutral.

How Far Was Tax Reform Successful?

The question 'How far was tax reform successful?' can be usefully sub-divided into three questions: 'How far did tax reformers achieve their objectives at the time?' 'How have the reforms stood the test of time?' 'Were there any by-products of reform, good or bad, which affect our evaluation of its outcome?' Inevitably, whilst there are common threads, the extent of success varied as between countries and, whilst making some generalisations, we shall need to analyse in more depth than hitherto, the experience of individual countries.

How Successful Was Tax Reform at the Time?

On the basis of the criteria reformers set themselves, of which the principal one was efficiency in the sense of minimum distortion or tax neutrality, all six countries on which we shall concentrate achieved progress in cutting tax rates, especially top marginal rates, eliminating or reducing tax expenditures and taxing fringe benefits more heavily. Moreover the removal of tax reliefs helped what was for many countries a secondary object of reform, promoting horizontal equity. However, the progress in all countries was limited, though in different degrees and there were some differences in reform objectives.

In the United Kingdom the emphasis was almost exclusively to improve the performance of the economy (Lawson, 1988, p.4). This meant lowering taxes to improve incentives and removing distortions. Income tax and corporation tax rates were cut very heavily and a marked switch effected from income tax to VAT. Some tax expenditures were reduced or abolished, but the desire of Nigel (now Lord) Lawson as Chancellor of the Exchequer to reduce the tax reliefs on pensions and mortgage interest for owner-occupied homes and to reduce the distortions of VAT by extending the base, were largely, if not wholly, thwarted by the Prime Minister, Margaret (now Lady) Thatcher. In relation to his 1985 Budget, Lawson writes: 'The majority of the tax reforms I had hoped to introduce were controversial changes that I had to abandon, for the most part because

Margaret was not prepared to swallow them. They included extending the coverage of VAT to newspapers and children's clothes, confining mortgage interest relief to the basic rate, introducing a tax on consumer credit and taxing pension lump sums' (Lawson, 1992, p. 362). Moreover there was a potential contradiction in the United Kingdom approach. Whilst in general advocating tax neutrality, both the reforming British Chancellors, Sir Geoffrey (now Lord) Howe and Nigel Lawson, were prepared to promote new tax reliefs if it would 'help make the economy work better' (Lawson, 1988, p.4). Whilst they were eliminating old reliefs they were introducing new ones, such as the Business Start Up Scheme, developed into the Business Expansion Scheme (BES), which gave income tax relief for new investment in risk-bearing enterprises; measures to encourage employee shareholding and profit-related pay (PRP); and personal equity plans (PEPs), by which a limited sum could be annually invested in United Kingdom equities, through registered schemes, with freedom from income tax and capital gains tax. If these measures could be justified on the grounds of promoting the enterprise economy, or, with PEPs, putting equity saving more on a par with other forms of investment, like home ownership, the argument was even more dubious when applied to the tax reliefs they introduced on Inheritance Tax, expecially those to agricultural landlords.

In the United States the 'tax reform of the 'eighties' was essentially that of the Reagan years from 1981 to 1989. It centred round the Tax Reform Act of 1986 (TRA 86) but included earlier legislation, especially the Economic Recovery Tax Act of 1981, which had reduced income tax rates and provided for the indexation of the brackets, personal exemption and standard deduction in the personal income tax, as from 1985. The TRA 86 reduced income tax rates to two, 15 and 28 per cent (but marginal rates increased to 33 per cent in the upper middle band as the benefits of the personal exemptions and the 15 per cent rate were phased out). A particular feature of reform was the equalisation of the rates of tax on capital gains with that of other income. Whilst the cuts in the United States federal income tax were more dramatic than anything elsewhere, the reform was limited in its scope. There was no change in the form of corporation tax, though the first of the Treasury tax reform proposals (usually referred to as Treasury I) had contained measures to reduce the discrimination against dividends; nor was there any switch from taxes on income to taxes on spending, which characterised reform in most of the six countries. The core of the United States reform in both personal and corporate income tax was the abolition or reduction of tax expenditures, making possible lower rates for both taxes. Therefore a measure both of the success and limitations of tax reform is the tax expenditures abolished or reduced compared with those that remained. Neubig and Joulfain of the Treasury staff estimated that, at 1988 levels of activity, tax reform reduced $77 billion of tax expenditures directly by base broadening and another $116 billion indirectly because of their reduced value as a result of lower rates; but $315 billion of tax expenditures remained (quoted in Steuerle, 1991, pp.139-41).

Just as the removal of tax expenditures promoted the primary objective of tax reform – economic efficiency – with long-term effects on economic growth, so, together with the equal tax treatment of capital gains and other income, they also promoted horizontal equity – with similar limited success. The third objective of Reagan's tax reforms was 'simplicity'. Here, there is widespread agreement that, apart from those taken off the income tax rolls and those with very simple tax affairs, the effect of the reform was to complicate rather than simplify. A leading tax lawyer concluded: 'the 1986 tax reform fails as a simplification measure' (Graetz, 1988).

In Canada the reform agenda had a somewhat different emphasis from the other countries. 'Fairness' headed the official list of objectives, followed by 'competitiveness, simplicity, consistency and reliability' (White Paper, 1987). The elaboration of these objectives makes it clear that the first two are the most important. 'Fairness' covers both horizontal and vertical equity and 'competitiveness' embraces efficiency, tax neutrality and economic growth, with more concern than elsewhere about the international effects, primarily because of Canada's proximity and economic links with the United States. Reductions in the federal personal income tax and especially in corporation tax, together with the reductions in tax expenditures, improved efficiency and competitiveness, but were partly offset by increases by the provinces. The preferential treatment of capital gains was reduced, but substantial preference over other income remained. The most significant improvement in economic efficiency lay in the replacement of the manufacturers' sales tax (MST) by the goods and services tax (GST) – a value added tax. The MST was a particularly distorting form of sales tax – generating different effective tax rates at the point of consumption, having a narrow base, taxing capital inputs and making it virtually impossible to attain tax neutrality in relation to exports and imports. However, the improvement was less than it might have been, because of the zero rating of 'basic groceries' and other base-narrowing provisions that limited the gain in neutrality, whilst a retreat, in face of opposition, from a 9 per cent to a 7 per cent rate, minimised the value of the change as a means of reducing income tax or cutting the federal budget deficit.

There seems little doubt that the Canadian tax reform improved horizontal equity. Canada was the only one of the six countries which specified an improvement in vertical equity as an objective and it seems likely that replacement of the MST by the GST, with its inclusion of services in the tax base, and accompanied by a refundable sales tax credit in income tax and the zero rating of 'basic groceries', increased progressiveness at the lower end of the income scale. The net effect of the other changes – such as the removal or reduction in tax shelters, the new minimum personal income tax, the increased proportion of capital gains subject to income tax – may well have been to raise the overall progressiveness of the Canadian tax system despite the reduction in corporate tax rates and in top income tax rates (which was in any case more modest than in the other five countries); but, because of the difficulties of assessing effective incidence, we cannot be sure.

Whilst some of the changes promoted the object of simplicity, the net effect of the tax reform was the opposite. The GST brought many more traders into the federal tax net than the MST; the zero rating added borderline problems; worst of all, the failure to agree with the provinces on a national sales tax meant that, in most provinces, retailers had to administer both GST and a provincial sales tax.

The Irish tax reform was unusual. The Irish Commission on Taxation produced five reports between 1982 and 1985, characterised as 'the most comprehensive and thoroughgoing analysis of the taxation system in the history of the state' (National Economic and Social Council of Ireland, 1986, p.228). Yet the Fine Gael and Labour Coalition, in power during the whole period in which the Commission was publishing its reports, showed no interest in tax reform and made no formal response to the Commission (perhaps partly explained by the fact that the Commission had been set up by the previous government). The first substantive moves in tax reform came with Ray MacSharry as Finance Minister, from March 1987 to November 1988. In his Budget of March 1987, he recognised that 'There must be reform in order to remove barriers to economic activity and to make the system fairer'. MacSharry was responsible for corporation tax reforms, presided over the administrative changes which were a marked feature of Irish tax reform, widened the income tax bands and extended the VAT base. The tax reform movement quickened in 1989 when the small Progressive Democrat Party, which strongly espoused tax reform, joined in coalition with Fianna Fail – income tax rates were reduced, fringe benefits attacked, corporation tax further reduced and accelerated depreciation phased out, the VAT base widened and the number and level of rates reduced.

The objectives of tax reform as set out in the Coalition document of the Fianna Fail-Progressive Democrat Coalition of 1989-92, are typical of the reformers' objectives in general and can be summarised as efficiency, equity and simplicity.

Efficiency was the core element in the Fianna Fail-Progressive Democrat programme. Whilst, as already implied, considerable progress was made, there were distinct limitations. The failure to index the income tax, together with insufficient discretionary changes, meant that many less well paid workers received no lasting benefit from lower marginal rates. The measures to widen the personal income tax base had not gone very far; in 1991 allowances, reliefs and exemptions still represented 68 per cent of the base (OECD, 1991, p.71); and the position was not dissimilar with corporation tax.

Equity, as generally elsewhere, appeared to mean horizontal equity; there was no suggestion that the reforms should be redistributive in effect. The administrative measures undoubtedly helped towards this objective, but the limited success with removing tax expenditures was a constraining factor.

On simplification progress was very limited; the most important gains were administrative.

In Australia the Labour Government with Bob Hawke as Prime Minister and Paul Keating as Treasurer sought consensus on tax reform through a unique 'Tax Summit' of representatives of business, trade unions, welfare organisations, the professions and academics. As with the reforms elsewhere, the Government's Draft White Paper identified equity, efficiency and simplicity as the major criteria of tax reform (AGPS, 1985, p.3), but other considerations included the need to minimise evasion and avoidance and to recognise the impact of inflation on the tax system.

In advance of the Tax Summit, the Government put forward a series of options. The one it preferred included a broad-based consumption tax, but this component was dropped by Hawke because of opposition from trade unions and welfare organisations at the Tax Summit.

This omission represented the biggest deficiency of the Australian package. Income tax marginal rates were reduced and the income tax base broadened by a reduction in tax expenditures; a new tax on capital gains and a new fringe benefit tax (FBT) levied on employers were introduced and a tougher line taken on business expenses, along with administrative measures to curb evasion. All this, followed by a reform of company tax in 1988, increased efficiency; but the scope for reducing dependence on income tax was limited in the absence of a broad-based consumption tax. Australia was left with a distorting wholesale sales tax. Moreover, in the absence of indexation, the income tax reductions were soon shown as nominal rather than real for many income tax payers.

Undoubtedly there was improvement in horizontal equity as a result of the new taxes on capital gains and fringe benefits, but on simplicity no progress was achieved, rather the reverse. Inevitably the CGT and FBT added complications; but apart from them, the Australian income tax remained excessively complicated. Roughly 70 per cent of Australians currently pay tax agents to complete and submit their tax returns – though this is encouraged by generous deductibility provisions.

Another deficiency of the Australian tax reform, bearing on complexity, might be mentioned. Like the United States and Canada, tax reform in Australia addressed only the federal tax scene. Whilst it is understandable that the White Paper should not take up the contentious issue of state taxing powers, it is less excusable that it failed to address those areas of state taxation which overlapped with Commonwealth (federal) taxes.

New Zealand's tax reform of the 'eighties is the reform of the Labour Governments, 1984-1990 and, in particular, the period when Roger (now Sir Roger) Douglas was Finance Minister, July 1984-December 1988. The reform consisted of two major packages with some complementary measures in between.

The objectives were, as usual, equity (primarily interpreted as horizontal equity) efficiency (reducing distortions) and making the tax system more certain and simple.

Roger Douglas' first package, presented as a whole programme in the Budget of November 1984 and implemented over a period to October 1986, was probably the most successful tax reform ever, taking New Zealand a long way towards implementing the efficiency objective. The keynote was the introduction of a VAT, called a goods and services tax (GST) on a very wide base, to replace a wholesale sales tax. The GST, together with a widening of the income tax base by reducing tax expenditures and introducing a fringe benefit tax, enabled income tax rates to be reduced by nearly 20 per cent overall (top rates down from 66 to 48 per cent). At the same time a new family assistance package was introduced to offset the effect of the GST on the budgets of the poor.

The second main package, December 1987 to October 1989, was much less successful and was partly aborted; but the net result was to reduce income tax rates still further, to raise the rate of GST and to introduce a new imputation system of company tax with a maximum rate of 33 per cent (equal to the top rate of income tax).

The effect of these changes was very substantial gains in efficiency and, at the same time, by means of the fringe benefit tax and the removal of many tax expenditures, improved horizontal equity. The most obvious deficiency for both objectives was the failure to introduce a CGT, or, more generally, improve the taxation of income from capital. The Government announced this objective in the July 1988 Budget, but shelved it before the 1990 General Election; it lapsed with Labour's defeat. Roger Douglas himself would have seen as a deficiency his failure to implement a single flat rate of personal income tax, a measure torpedoed by David Lange as Prime Minister. Another limitation was the lack of any indexation.

As elsewhere, the tax reform failed to deliver the objective of simplification: rather the reverse.

How Successful was Tax Reform in Retrospect?

One vital criterion in judging the success of any tax reform is how well it has stood the test of time. Has it been sustained? Has it been built upon? A tax reform, however brilliant, is of little use if it is overthrown shortly afterwards. Then any short term benefit is likely to have been outweighed by the high costs of major change.

In fact, one of the remarkable features of the tax scene in the six countries we have examined is how far, a decade or so later, the characteristic features of reform remain in place – despite changes of party government in all the countries. As of 1997 there has been little change in the structure of personal income tax and corporate tax rates in all six countries. In four, the top rate of personal income tax remains as established by reform; in Canada it is a fraction higher by virtue of a surcharge. Only in the United States is there a significant change, with the top rate having risen from 28 to 39.6 per cent.

As for corporate income tax, in New Zealand the top rate has remained at 33 per cent; in Ireland, Australia and the United Kingdom it is a percentage point or two lower than at the end of the 'eighties, after reform; in Canada it has increased marginally because of a surcharge and in the United States it is also marginally higher.

The lesson seems to have been fully learned that high rates of personal income tax, such as rates in the range of 70 and 80 per cent, common in the 'sixties and 'seventies, are self-defeating. They encourage avoidance and evasion, distort the economy and may even have negative effects on yield. It is also clear that, with a global economy, corporate taxation must be kept low. Indeed, in at least one country, there has been an over-reaction. There is nothing sacrosanct about a particular set of tax rates, yet in the United Kingdom, both the Conservatives and the Labour parties have become obsessed with the view that to raise income tax rates would be electorally disastrous – and hence they have both sought other ways of raising finance, including changes in allowances, which, effectively, if not nominally, put up rates.

However, apart from those at the top of the income tree, the policy of keeping marginal rates down has not been quite as successful as at first appears. In countries without indexation, (or with limited indexation, as with Canada) there is a danger that discretionary changes of allowances and thresholds fail to keep pace with prices; then many taxpayers in the middle and lower levels are pushed into higher marginal tax brackets even if their real income is unchanged. Australia is the outstanding case. Between September 1985 and 1990 income tax rates were adjusted downwards on four occasions. Between 1985-86 fiscal year and 1989-90 fiscal year, the consumer price index rose approximately 36 per cent. Over the same period the tax free threshold increased by only 3 per cent, whilst the threshold for the top rate – of 47 per cent – did not increase at all. On 1 January, 1991 the tax free threshold was raised to a figure 9 per cent higher than in 1985-86; the top threshold was raised by 42 per cent, but a new rate (of 46 per cent) was inserted below the top rate, the threshold for which was only 3 per cent above the threshold for the top rate in 1985-86. In 1996-97, the threshold for the lowest rate is 6 per cent higher and that for the top rates is the same as in 1990-91. Meanwhile the CPI has risen by approximately 13 per cent. Whilst intermediate rates have again fallen marginally, many income tax payers on the same real income are paying more and paying at higher marginal rates than in 1985-86.

However, an indexation provision is no guarantee that taxpayers will not find themselves on higher marginal rates even though their real income has not risen. Indexation provisions can always be over-ridden by a needy finance minister. Thus, in the United Kingdom, in a desperate search for revenue to restrict the budget deficit, for three successive years 1991-92 to 1993-94 the threshold for the top rate of income tax was frozen; meanwhile the number of income tax payers paying at the top marginal rate of 40 per cent increased by nearly one-quarter. At least, with an indexation provision, the finance minister who overturns it in a particular year has to do so explicitly and openly.

One important element in relation to both the efficiency and the horizontal equity objectives was the broadening of the tax system – both by removing or reducing tax expenditures and by taxing forms of income such as fringe benefits and capital gains more nearly on a par with other income. Since tax reform, in all countries there have been measures of this kind which have increased tax neutrality but others which have reduced it; but, on balance, overall, the direction of change has probably been to promote the objectives of reform. To mention some of the most notable: in the United Kingdom the tax concession to home owners has been much reduced and the Business Expansion Scheme ended, whilst the Profit-Related Pay scheme has been put under notice. In Australia, the concessions to R and D have been reduced whilst the FBT rate has been grossed up at the top rate of income tax and made tax deductible; there is now no tax advantage in offering fringe benefits. In Canada the CGT lifetime exemption ($Can 100,000) is no longer available for gains after 22 February, 1994.

The biggest exception, not surprisingly, is the United States, with its division of powers, loose party system, strong lobbies and hence its vulnerability to special interests. John Witte has written of 'the inability of the system to resist change' (Witte, 1985). The most notable reversal of reform relates to the CGT. TRA 86 had equalised the rates of CGT and other income. When the top income tax rate was revised to 31 per cent and then 39.6 per cent the CGT rate was left unchanged at 28 per cent. Then the August 1997 Budget cut the CGT rate to 20 per cent for assets held for 18 months and to 18 per cent for assets purchased after the year 2000 and held for 5 years. Thus the link with income tax has been well and truly cut, generating horizontal inequity and opening the way to tax avoidance.

In relation to one of the lesser objectives of tax reform, simplification, where little or nothing had been achieved in the 'eighties, some notable progress has since been made. As we have mentioned above, the failure of the Conservative Government in Canada to obtain the agreement of the provinces to a national sales tax left business in most provinces grappling with both a retail sales tax (RST) and the GST. The GST had come under heavy fire and the incoming Liberal Government had promised a review. The outcome from an extensive Select Committee review, which considered a range of alternatives, was the recommendation for the retention of the GST in the form of a Harmonised Sales Tax (HST). In

1997 the Government was able to announce the agreement for an HST with the provinces of Nova Scotia, New Brunswick and Newfoundland and Labrador, by which, effectively, the RST was replaced by a higher GST with revenue shared between federal government and provinces. However, the most populous provinces have yet to come into line.

Another simplification measure has been major projects for simplifying the tax law, now well under way in the United Kingdom, Australia and New Zealand (see Chapter 5). One of the objectives of the tax law re-write is to reduce compliance costs and this objective has been prominent in five of the six countries. Governments in the United Kingdom, Australia, New Zealand, Canada and the United States have sponsored research into tax compliance costs and undertaken measures to reduce them; in the United Kingdom, Australia and New Zealand new tax legislation has to be accompanied by a compliance cost assessment (or 'tax impact statement' as it is called in Australia).

One indication of the limitations of the tax reform of the 'eighties is the continued cry in some countries for 'tax reform'. Despite the eulogy which greeted TRA 86 in the United States, demands for reform have continued there. In Australia, there has recently been a crescendo of complaints against the existing tax system. Despite the undisputed fact that the proposal to introduce a GST (VAT) as part of a tax reform package was one of the reasons for the electoral failure of the Liberal-Country parties in 1992 (Lewis and Wallschutzky, 1995), the present Liberal-Country Coalition under John Howard as Prime Minister, is raising the issue as a possibility for the next parliament.

By-products of Tax Reform

The major question to be considered under this heading is: 'Did tax reform accentuate inequalities of income?' There is no simple answer. The data are poor. Different definitions give somewhat different answers. There may even by perverse effects, for example, that where a country taxes capital gains as income for the first time, inequality may seem to increase because gains now appear in the income statistics instead of being omitted altogether. Big cuts in the upper rates of income tax when accompanied by the removal of tax expenditures do not necessarily increase inequality if their effect is to reduce widespread tax avoidance and evasion. Moreover disentangling the effects of market changes from discretionary tax measures is difficult, as is the effect on income distribution of different stages of the trade cycle.

The general picture[1] would appear to be that, in the 'eighties and 'nineties, market changes were accentuating inequalities in most advanced countries. On the basis of an unchanged pre-reformed tax system, much of this market inequality would have been cancelled out automatically by the progression in the tax system. In Canada, the one of our six countries which included vertical equity as an objective of tax reform, the combination of automatic and discretionary changes in taxes and transfers cancelled out the rise in market income inequality; much the same was true of Australia. In the United Kingdom tax reform offset the automatic changes and failed to check the rise in inequality and the same was probably true of New Zealand. In the United States there has been controversy on whether TRA 86 made the tax system more or less progressive, but, taking the Reagan tax changes as a whole, there is no doubt of the result. To quote a recent report, 'In the USA, taxes and transfers accelerated the effects of a widening distribution of market incomes; disretionary policy changes more than offset the automatic reaction to rising market inequalities.' (Hills, 1995)

In the United Kingdom during the 'nineties, as a result of the freezing of the threshold for higher rate tax and the series of reductions in the value of mortgage interest relief for owner-occupiers, there may have been some slight reversal of the trend to inequality.

Another feature of tax changes in the 'eighties and after, whilst peripheral to the declared purposes of reform, served to accentuate inequalities – i.e. policy on gift taxes and taxes at death. In the United Kingdom the Labour Government in the 'seventies had replaced estate duty by Capital Transfer Tax, under which gifts were taxed and there was cumulation of gifts with gifts and with the estate at death in determining the rate of tax. Under successive Conservative Chancellors of the Exchequer the features of cumulation and the taxation of gifts were whittled away, a progressive structure of rates rising to 70 per cent replaced by a single 40 per cent rate (now inappropriately named Inheritance Tax) and reliefs for business and agriculture greatly extended. In the United States in 1981, gifts and legacies between spouses were exempted from the estate and gift tax, the exempt credit increased and the rate scales substantially reduced. In Ireland the top rate of Capital Acquisition Tax was reduced from 50 to 40 per cent whilst in New Zealand in December 1992 the estate duty was effectively abolished,

[1]This account is based largely on the research summarised in Hills, 1985.

leaving in place only a modest gift tax. Death duties as such in Canada and Australia had already disappeared before the era of reforms.

This reduction or abolition of taxation on intergenerational transfers of wealth can be expected to have a continuing and increasing effect on income inequalities.

Where, as in most of these six countries, the effect of tax reform was to accentuate growing inequalities of income and wealth, it is a matter of individual value judgement whether the efficiency gains from reform outweigh the distributional consequences.

Tax Reform of the 'Eighties – What Can We Learn?

There are obvious dangers in trying to draw lessons about tax reform in general from a sample of six engaged in a particular tax reform with a particular dominating motive. It would certainly be wrong to expect such a sample to answer all the questions we might wish to ask. But the six were all, in their way, leaders in tax reform; they offer variety in their geographical situations, their constitutional practices, their tax policy procedures, the weight they assigned to different objectives and their degree of success. There is much that we can learn from them about the success and failure of tax reform.

Political Will and Doughty Champions

Crucial to the success of any major tax reform is a strong political will. This means, in effect, a doughty champion or champions. In the 'Westminster system' (where the government is drawn from the legislature) as in five of the six countries, the champion almost inevitably has to be the finance minister. In the United States system several champions are needed; with TRA 86 they included Secretary Regan, Dan Rostenkowski (Chairman of the House Ways and Means Committee), Senator Packwood (Chairman of the Senate Finance Committee) and Senator Bradley. Champions need to be energetic, committed and tough to withstand the lobbies. The commitment will normally rest on a conviction of the importance of the objectives sought by tax reform, but, as with some United States reformers, it may rest on narrower motives such as the belief that reputation or career depend on the success of the policy. Doughty champions in the Westminster systems were Nigel Lawson (United Kingdom), Paul Keating (Australia), Roger Douglas (New Zealand), Michael Wilson (Canada).

Also essential to the success of tax reform is the support of the Chief Executive, be he or she president or prime minister. President Reagan's support and vital interventions at crucial points, was probably the most important single factor which secured the passage of TRA 86. In the United Kingdom, Mrs Thatcher generally gave support to Geoffrey Howe and Nigel Lawson, but was not convinced about the objectives and hamstrung their efforts to expand the base of income tax and VAT. In Canada Prime Minister Mulroney stood by Finance Minister Michael Wilson ensuring the passage of the GST despite intense opposition. In Australia whilst Prime Minister Hawke, like Treasurer Keating, sought tax reform, when the strength of the opposition at the Tax Summit to the broad-based consumption tax became apparent, Hawke ditched it in a deal with the trade unions behind the back of his Treasurer. In New Zealand as long as Prime Minister Lange was prepared to support Finance Minister Roger Douglas, tax reform was eminently successful. When Douglas' plan for a single rate of income tax was more than Lange could swallow, he repudiated it whilst Douglas was abroad. Thereafter tax reform lost much of its momentum and the breach between the two heralded the subsequent defeat of the Labour Government at the polls.

This is not to argue that Hawke or Lange was necessarily wrong to jettison a cherished objective of their finance ministers, though the manner of doing so left much to be desired; (indeed, from the standpoint of his party's fortunes, Mulroney might have done better to abandon the GST). The point is, simply, that tax reform requires at least the tacit support of prime minister or president if it is to be successful.

The Method – Incrementalism or Package

Whether tax reform is best secured by a series of incremental changes or the 'big bang' approach is a matter of controversy. The terms themselves are not without ambiguity. The incremental approach is here taken to imply that, whilst there is some pre-determined goal, or at least a guiding philosophy, the changes are announced and implemented in a series of relatively small steps over a fairly substantial time period. With the 'big bang' or package approach, the main components of tax reform are announced at the same time and are clearly seen to be inter-related; implementation of all the components may not be simultaneous, but the time span for full implementation is short. In the six countries we are examining the United Kingdom and Irish tax reforms were incremental. The United States, Australian and New Zealand reforms fall into the 'big bang' or major package variety. Canada started on the incremental approach, but the White Paper of 1987 presented a more comprehensive package.

The incremental approach commends itself to the more cautious politician and tends to be favoured by revenue departments. Because there has been no commitment to a major package, if things turn sour the process can be stopped without loss of face. For departments whose prime purpose is to keep the revenue flowing in, there is no big leap in the dark. It has also been argued that gradualism is more acceptable to a conservative populace (Brooks, 1988, p.18).

But incrementalism carries disadvantages. Reform takes longer – the defects of the system are not as quickly remedied. Because it lacks an initial comprehensive statement of intent reform may drift and lose its purpose and continuity. Pressure groups have to be fought one by one and have time to anticipate the next moves and prepare against them. Moreover it is hard to create a constituency for reform; if tax expenditures are being removed, the losers oppose strongly whilst the gains of the beneficiaries are so diffuse as not be be appreciated. Where compensation may be required to make reform acceptable, incremental reform may not generate sufficient revenue for it – or be disproportionately costly. Such a situation arose in the United Kingdom with the removal of zero rating from domestic fuel and power, announced in 1993. There was a politically irresistible demand to compensate the old and poor; it would have been much more economical and effective to have removed all or most zero rating, except for exports. This would have generated the means for a substantial compensation package, which could, if desired, have over-compensated the poor, because, in absolute terms, it is the richest who gain most from zero rating and who lose most by its removal.

The big package approach avoids these disadvantages, but it is more of a political risk and it requires special administrative measures to counter over-loading of the tax departments.

There is no doubt that the most successful reform of the 'eighties was the first big package of the New Zealand Government, which consisted of the replacement of a wholesale sales tax by a VAT or GST (on a very wide base), abolition of a range of tax reliefs, and a fringe benefit tax on employers, all of which helped to finance big cuts in income tax and a new family assistance benefit to offset the effects of the GST. The package was outlined in Roger Douglas' first Budget, in November 1984, and implemented over a period to October 1986.

Roger Douglas himself set forth the lessons he had learnt from other people's earlier attempts at tax reform:

'(1) Reforms which are politically successful have to be undertaken on a much larger scale so that the pluses are real and substantial enough for ordinary people to see past the minuses...
(2) Successful reform takes courage and boldness on the part of the government. There is simply no way vested-interest groups can ever be persuaded to a detailed package of comprehensive tax and benefit reforms before a government introduces it. Their interests are too diverse. The government has to take a leading role and work from a set of principles which can be widely accepted and endorsed by the community...
(3) The new system has to keep closely to the established values, otherwise it can unravel very quickly. If you leave privileged tax treatment for one group it becomes very difficult to remove it from someone else.'

(Douglas, 1987, pp. 195-6)

The Power of the Lobbies

The previous section gives some idea of the significance of the lobbies in relation to tax reform – Roger Douglas adopted the 'big bang' approach partly to deal with them. He was not alone amongst the reformers to run into problems caused by the pressure groups. It can be argued that it was the pressure groups, particularly the Australian Council of Trade Unions, which led to the abandonment of the Australian Government's preferred option of the broad-based consumption tax. It was because the lobbies in the United States were so powerful that the TRA 86, which represented their, at least partial, defeat was greeted with near euphoria by the reform-minded (and the struggle immortalised in *Showdown at Gucci Gulch, Lawmakers, Lobbyists and the Unlikely Triumph of Tax Reform*, Birnbaum and Murray, 1988). In Canada a rather different kind of lobby came into play to hamper and derange tax reform – the provinces. Reform was delayed in Canada because the government first considered a form of VAT, known as a Business Transfer Tax (BTT), which would not impinge on the retail sales taxes of the provinces. When the BTT proved impracticable and federal government plans focussed on the common type of VAT, implementation was again delayed because the Progressive Conservative Government sought to obtain agreement with the provinces to a national sales tax which would incorporate the retail sales taxes. No such agreement was forthcoming. In the meantime reform lost momentum and the link between income tax reduction and the GST was severed. In fact the lower tiers of a federal state are amongst the most powerful of interest groups. They have extensive resources, many opportunities for putting their case, are able to withhold cooperation on other unrelated matters and, where the political complexion of the state or provincial government is different from that of the federal government, they may see political advantage in discrediting federal policy.

United Kingdom Chancellors also had troubles with the lobbies; as Nigel Lawson has written: 'The campaigns against VAT extension were as nothing compared to the barrage that emanated from the beneficiaries of occupational pensions and the industry that catered for them.'

A particularly difficult issue arises where the lobbying group is one which is a significant financial supporter of the party in office, whether the pressure group is a business or a trade union. What can be done about it? In a witty and perceptive lecture[1] Peter Cropper, one-time head of the Conservative Research Department and a special adviser both to Sir Geoffrey Howe and to Nigel Lawson, maintains that a prerequisite for a comprehensive tax reform along tax neutral lines is a fundamental reform of the system of financing political parties. In his view 'The central functions of the political parties should ... be largely financed by allocations of public money. This would include policy research, political education and campaigning.' Such an insider's view must carry great weight. And if that is a necessary remedy in the United Kingdom, how much more must it be true of the United States, where the expense of elections is so much bigger. The loose party system makes congressmen heavily dependent on local support and their susceptibility to special interests has been much increased by the mushrooming of business Political Action Committees on which they are increasingly dependent for their fundraising.

Constitutional Law and Practice – Constraints and Possibilities

It is clear from an analysis of tax reform in the 'eighties that the constitutional law and practice of a country exercises a considerable influence on the methods and indeed the success of tax reform. To mention a few examples: in Australia and New Zealand the maximum length of a parliament is three years; this had an inhibiting effect on tax reform in Australia: because a VAT would take longer to introduce than a retail sales

[1] *An Extra Pair of Ears*, lecture to the Addington Society, 22 May 1996.

tax, the Hawke Government, in 1985, chose the latter as its broad-based consumption tax option (Hawke, 1995, p.300); this choice may have affected the outcome of the Tax Summit, where the tax was dropped because of widespread opposition. In Ireland a judicial interpretation of the constitution (which contains a pledge to guard with special care the institution of marriage) led to an income tax regime exceptionally favourable to married couples as against single persons. The problems which can arise in a federal state have already been discussed in relation to Canada, where the provinces were uncooperative over a federal VAT. The outstanding example of the constitution and constitutional practice inhibiting tax reform is the United States with its division of powers, two chambers which have to agree and a relatively loose party system. Whilst the President usually proposes reform measures, it is Congress that disposes and presidential proposals, invariably, are substantially changed by Congress.

The government most free from restrictions is that of the United Kingdom. With a 'first past the post' electoral system a government is usually drawn from one party with a parliamentary majority; party discipline is tight and almost any measure the government proposes can be enacted. However, it does not follow that the United Kingdom had the most successful tax reform. Indeed, it suffered the biggest failure – the Community Charge or poll tax. This tax has not so far been mentioned in our review of tax reform in the United Kingdom as it was a local tax, outside the mainstream of tax reform and not the responsibility of the Chancellor of the Exchequer and the revenue departments. But it illustrates the lack of checks and balances in the system. The Community Charge was very much the creature of Prime Minister Margaret Thatcher. Although many of her party, including Cabinet Ministers, were very unhappy about it, her dominance enabled her to push it through into law. The Community Charge was deemed to be grossly unfair and was highly unpopular and, having got rid of Mrs Thatcher, the Conservative Party lost little time in replacing the Community Charge.

The United States and the United Kingdom situation represent two opposite ends of a spectrum. In the United States there is an excess of checks and balances which inhibits consistent action. In the United Kingdom there are no checks and balances to prevent a tax folly.

Like the constraints arising from the existence of powerful economic neighbours or those resulting from the globalisation of the economy, generally tax reforming politicians have to work within the confines determined by the constitution. But in the case of the United Kingdom some checks could usefully be introduced. Thus, for example, the requirement that a new tax had to be the subject of a Select Committee inquiry, which would scrutinise proposals and take evidence from the public, might prevent such costly debacles[1].

Consultation and Discussion

This reference to a Select Committee of Parliament raises the question of discussion and consultation. How much of a proposed tax reform should be open to discussion? What should be the forum of discussion? How long should the discussion be allowed to continue?

The extent and form of discussion and consultation in the six countries we have been considering varied markedly. In the United Kingdom and the Republic of Ireland public discussion and consultation was minimal. In the United Kingdom the Government published some green (discussion) papers on corporation tax and the taxation of husband and wife, but the outcome on these topics was not closely related to the content of the green paper. In the United States discussion focused on Congress, where the drama of TRA 86 was conducted largely in public with much media comment. Australia had the most remarkable form of consultation with the National Tax Summit. In Canada extensive use was made of Select Committees of both Houses of Parliament. In New Zealand the need for tax reform was aired at an Economic Summit and the first and major package was the subject of Labour Party conferences; a 'Budget Task Force' which went round the country receiving representations; and draft legislation on which the public was invited to make submissions on the details to a private sector panel; in addition the GST Bill was referred to a Select Committee of the House of Representatives which took further evidence both written and oral.

What can we learn from these varied procedures? As in other ways, New Zealand provides the best model. The extent of discussion and consultation helped to legitimise the reforms and defuse antagonism. On the question of how much should be open to discussion, it is vital that the government should give a clear lead. The Australian proposals came unstuck partly because the Government lead was weak with its 'preferred

---

[1] Select Committees of Parliament have been used in the past, most recently when Antony (now Lord) Barber and Denis (now Lord) Healey were Chancellors of the Exchequer. But there was no legal requirement for them; whether they were appointed rested on the whim of the Chancellor.

option'. Conversely, Roger Douglas, in New Zealand, set out a clearly defined and determined structure of changes, but left the details open to discussion and modification.

As to the forum of discussion, it is important that it includes the possibility for contributions to be probed. Again, the Australian Tax Summit did not provide this, with contributions taking the form of set speeches in which the various lobbies entrenched their positions. The Select Committee procedure gives opportunity for views to be scrutinised and challenged.

Speed in implementing reform is regarded as essential by both Nigel Lawson and Roger Douglas – at opposite ends of the spectrum in regard to discussion and consultation. After his experience with the lobbies, Lawson took the view that 'reform would be more likely to be achieved by a well-directed side offensive with no prior warning' (Lawson, 1992, pp. 367-69). Secrecy, subtlety and speed might be regarded as his watchwords. Douglas, whilst providing full opportunities for discussion and consultation, nonetheless proceeded to implement the whole package with remarkable speed. In short, in answer to the third of our questions, the discussion and consultation period should not be unduly prolonged.

This point was stressed by Douglas Hartle, who headed the research team of the Carter Commission in Canada; he is a strong proponent of openness and consultation, but from his post-Carter experience evolved 'The following general rule: the longer the period of time between announcement by the party in power that a particular tax structure proposal is under consideration and the final decision on its disposition, the greater the influence of entrenched interests'. (Hartle, 1988, p.413). Such interests have much more resources to maintain a protracted struggle than public interest groups. The Mulroney Government in Canada, for very understandable reasons, was unable to implement its package speedily and accordingly found it partly derailed.

The lessons would seem to be that whilst openness, discussion and consultation are desirable, probably essential, to give reform legitimacy, defuse opposition and prevent tax follies like the Community Charge, for successful tax reform the government must give a firm lead; the forum for discussion must be one which gives the opportunity for views to be probed; and the process must go forward with as much speed as is compatible with full consultation.[1]

---

[1] For a fuller discussion of these issues and the relationship between tax reform proposals and electoral success, see Sandford, 1993, pp.205-11.

Economic Rationality Versus Political Rationality

There are other minor lessons that can be learnt from a detailed examination of the tax reforming procedures of the six countries studied. Tax policy-making in the United Kingdom and Ireland might benefit from the procedure of the other countries which assembled a concentration of experts – economists, lawyers, accountants – in the finance ministry or tax department prior to major reform. New Zealand provides an example of the extensive use of private sector expertise in tax reform. Professor Brian Arnold has stressed the importance of closely integrating policy-making and legal drafting (Arnold, 1990) and held up Canada as a model which might usefully be followed by most of the other countries, where drafting is quite separate from policy-making. New Zealand's innovative programme of education and guidance to taxpayers on the implementation of the GST is an example which might usefully be studied by countries introducing new taxes. Also it may be important to know where to stop with tax reform – or at least to offer a major pause. Whilst we have stressed the value of a comprehensive package and the need to keep up the momentum in implementing it there is a limit to the amount of change which taxpayers and tax practitioners can digest within a short period of time; Roger Douglas, in New Zealand, after that first very successful package, perhaps attempted to go too far too fast.

One final important lesson emerges from the study of tax reform in the 'eighties and of its aftermath. Tax reform of the 'eighties had economic rationality as its driving force – the prime objective was tax neutrality, the minimisation of tax distortions in order to promote economic growth. But policy is made by people who are primarily political animals. It may often be true, as Kenneth Clarke, the United Kingdom Chancellor of the Exchequer, 1993-97, was fond of saying, that 'Good economics is good politics', but this is not invariably seen to be so. The process of tax reform in the 'eighties offers examples of political rationality winning out over economic rationality. To take just the example of Australia, the National Tax Summit was not the best forum for considering tax reform; but it was proposed by Hawke to keep all tax options open whilst silencing the Opposition's claims that a Labor government would mean new capital taxes. Again, Hawke ditched the broad-based consumption tax because he deemed it so unpopular as to prejudice the re-election of his Government. Similarly, since tax reform, governments have introduced new tax expenditures perhaps for no better reason than that they feel they ought to be seen to be doing something in that particular area. We have to accept that, in the last resort, pragmatism will prevail over economic principle, political rationality will take precedence over economic rationality. Perhaps the art of statesmanship in tax policy-making is to convince the population, or at least a majority, of the rightness of the tax reform proposals so that good economics becomes good politics, as Roger Douglas succeeded in doing with the New Zealand tax reform, 1984-86, or as Ronald Reagan and his reforming allies in Congress, managed against all the odds, to achieve with TRA 86.

References and Further Reading

Ballard, C. L., J. B. Shoven and J. Whalley, 'General Equilibrium Computation of the Marginal Welfare Costs of Taxes in the United States', *American Economic Review*, Vol. 75, No. 1, pp.128-38, 1985.

Birnbaum, J. H. and A. S. Murray, *Showdown at Gucci Gulch: Lawmakers, Lobbyists and the Unlikely Triumph of Tax Reform*, Vintage Books, Random House, New York, 1988.

Brooks, W. N., 'The Royal Commission on Taxation: An Overview' in ed. W. N. Brooks, *The Quest for Tax Reform: The Royal Commission on Taxation Twenty Years Later*, Carswell, Toronto, 1988.

Browning, E. K., 'The Burden of Taxation', *Journal of Political Economy*, Vol. 86, No.4, pp.649-71, 1978.

Commission on Taxation, Five Reports 1982-85, Stationery Office, Dublin.

Dilnot, A., 'The Income Tax Rate Structure' in ed. C. T. Sandford, *Key Issues in Tax Reform*, Fiscal Publications, Bath, 1993.

Douglas, R. and L. Callon, *Toward Prosperity*, David Bateman, Auckland, 1987.

Graetz, M. J., 'The Truth About Tax Reform', *University of Florida Law Review*, Vol. 40, No.4, Fall, 1988.

Hawke, B., *The Hawke Memoirs*, Heinemann, London, 1994.

Hills, J., *Joseph Rowntree Foundation Inquiry into Income and Wealth*, Vol. 2, Joseph Rowntree Foundation, York, 1995.

Lawson, N., *Tax Reform. The Government's Record*, Conservative Political Centre, London, 1988.

Lawson, N., *The View from No 11, Memoirs of a Tory Radical*, Bantam Press, London, 1992.

Lewis, A. and I. Wallschutzky, 'Tax Perceptions and Tax Reform' in ed. C. T. Sandford, *More Key Issues in Tax Reform*, Fiscal Publications, Bath, 1995.

National Economic and Social Council, *A Strategy for Development*, Report No. 83, Dublin, 1986.

Reform of the Australian Tax System, Draft White Paper, AGPS, Canberra, 1985.

Reform of the Australian Tax System, Statement by the Treasurer, the Hon Paul Keating, AGPS, Canberra, Sept. 1985.

Sandford, C. T., *Successful Tax Reform – Lessons from an Analysis of Tax Reform in Six Countries*, Fiscal Publications, Bath, 1993.

Steinmo, S., *Taxation and Democracy: Swedish, British and American Approaches to Financing the Modern State*, Yale University Press, Newhaven, 1993.

Steuerle, C. E., *The Tax Decade*, Urban Institute Press, Washington, 1991.

Stuart, C. 'Welfare Costs per Dollar of Additional Tax Revenue in the United States', *American Economic Review*, Vol. 74, No. 3, pp.352-62, 1984.

Witte, J. F., *The Politics and Development of the Federal Income Tax*, The University of Wisconsin Press, Madison, 1985.